D1348575

A SKETCH-MAP ECONOMIC HISTORY OF BRITAIN

BY

J. L. GAYLER LL.B. B.Com.

BARRISTER-AT-LAW
FORMERLY PRINCIPAL NEWCASTLE-UPON-TYNE COLLEGE OF COMMERCE

IRENE RICHARDS B.A.

AND

J. A. MORRIS B.Sc.(Econ.)

LATYMER'S SCHOOL EDMONTON LONDON

THIRD EDITION REVISED

GEORGE G. HARRAP & CO. LTD
LONDON TORONTO WELLINGTON SYDNEY

The Sketch-Map Histories

General Editor : GEORGE TAYLOR, M.A.

Crown 4to

First published in Great Britain 1957
by GEORGE G. HARRAP & CO. LTD
182 High Holborn, London, W.C.1

Reprinted : 1958 ; 1959 ; 1961 ; 1962

Second edition, revised and enlarged, 1964

Third edition, revised, 1965

*Composed in Baskerville type and printed by Morrison & Gibb, Ltd
London and Edinburgh*
Made in Great Britain

PREFACE

SOME teachers who have used the *Sketch-Map Histories* already published have regretted that the subject matter has concerned political history almost exclusively. This book has been written to satisfy the need they felt for a well-mapped text in economic history which would cover the needs of candidates in the G.C.E. Ordinary Level, R.S.A., and similar examinations. It has been designed not only to form a study-guide for such pupils, but also to serve as a revision course for more advanced students in all types of secondary and technical school, technical institutes, and W.E.A. classes. The book, for instance, should be of great help to A Level G.C.E. students. Principals who are interested in liberalizing technological studies may also find the work of some use.

Many students, especially those who are still at school, have no knowledge of public finance or commercial life, and their lack of practical business experience ill fits them to understand modern social and economic problems in all their complexity. The authors have tried to give the facts in the simplest language consistent with accuracy. Beyond the method of presentation, they claim little original work in the book. For their material and ideas they have drawn on many sources—far too many to acknowledge separately—for it was their wish to avoid presenting the views of any one school of thought.

Modern research has challenged opinions and ideas which have long been cherished. To quote one example: the prevalence of universal distress among the working-classes, and their exploitation during the early years of the nineteenth century, has been questioned. Yet the work of Mr Maurice Beresford, producing archæological evidence which supports the views expressed by contemporary writers, clearly counsels caution in accepting uncritically some of this ' historical revision ' which would discredit the older views.

In previous *Sketch-Map Histories* a note has been included offering the reader advice on the best way to use the book. The value derived from copying the maps cannot be too often stressed, and though in the present volume the text is not merely a series of expanded headings, the authors feel that the student who builds up his sketch-map or diagram as he masters the text will derive the greatest value from the book.

Suggestions for the improvement of the book will be gratefully received.

J. L. G., I. R., J. A. M.

NOTE TO SECOND EDITION

Some twenty years after the end of the War it has seemed appropriate to revise the book to include, not only more detailed study of the early twentieth century, but also an outline of the changes resulting from two great upheavals. A few alterations have also been made in the earlier part of the book to bring the text in line with the views of modern scholarship.

NOTE TO THIRD EDITION

Minor alterations have been made in the post-War history and the section on Trade Unions has been completely revised.

CONTENTS

PART VI : THE FIRST WORLD WAR (1914–18)

PART VII : 1919–39 : BETWEEN TWO GREAT WARS

MAP 1

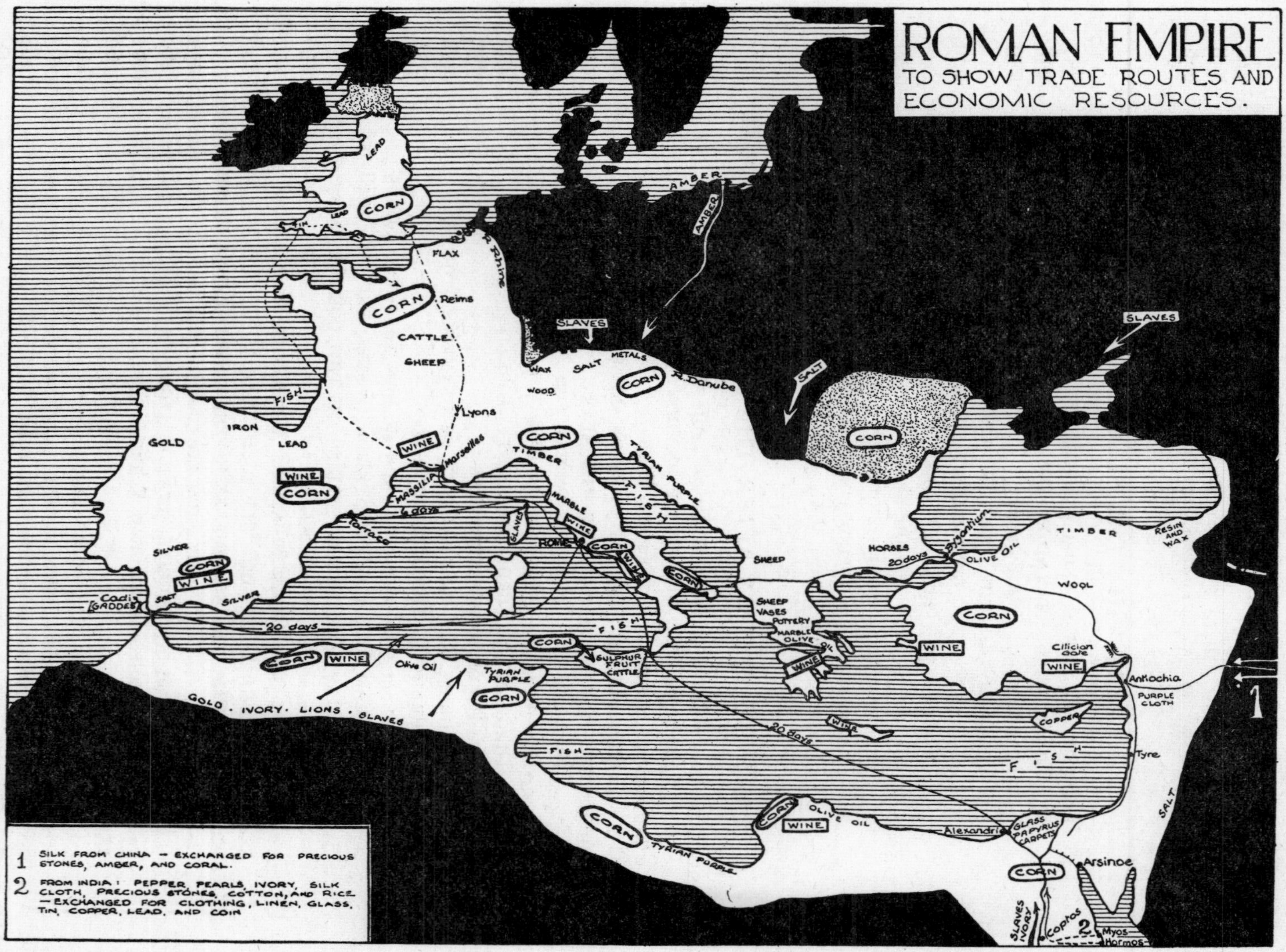
ROMAN EMPIRE
TO SHOW TRADE ROUTES AND ECONOMIC RESOURCES.
LEAD
CORN
TIN
LEAD
FLAX
R. Rhine
CORN
Reims
CATTLE
SHEEP
AMBER
AMBER
SLAVES
WAX
SALT
METALS
CORN
R. Danube
WOOD
Lyons
SALT
CORN
SLAVES
FISH
GOLD
IRON
LEAD
WINE
CORN
WINE
Marseilles
MASSILIA
CORN
TIMBER
TYRIAN PURPLE
FISH
6 days
Tarraco
MARBLE
WINE
SLAVES
ROME
CORN
WINE
CORN
SILVER
CORN
WINE
SALT
SILVER
Cadiz
GADDES
20 days
SHEEP
HORSES
20 days
Byzantium
OLIVE OIL
TIMBER
RESIN AND WAX
WOOL
SHEEP
VASES
POTTERY
MARBLE
OLIVE
OIL
CORN
FISH
CORN
WINE
Olive Oil
TYRIAN PURPLE
CORN
SULPHUR
FRUIT
CATTLE
WINE
CORN
WINE
Cilician Gate
WINE
Antiochia
PURPLE CLOTH
GOLD . IVORY . LIONS . SLAVES
20 days
WINE
COPPER
FISH
FISH
Tyre
SALT
CORN
CORN
WINE
OLIVE OIL
TYRIAN PURPLE
Alexandria
GLASS
PAPYRUS
CARPETS
Arsinoe
CORN
SLAVES
IVORY
Coptos
Myos Hormos
1
2
1 SILK FROM CHINA – EXCHANGED FOR PRECIOUS STONES, AMBER, AND CORAL.
2 FROM INDIA: PEPPER, PEARLS, IVORY, SILK CLOTH, PRECIOUS STONES, COTTON, AND RICE – EXCHANGED FOR CLOTHING, LINEN, GLASS, TIN, COPPER, LEAD, AND COIN

PART I: ROMAN AND MEDIEVAL BRITAIN

1. THE ROMAN OCCUPATION OF BRITAIN

A. *The Roman Empire*

For a period of five hundred years the area shown in Map 1 was ruled as one vast empire, centred round the Mediterranean Sea. Within its frontiers the Romans maintained peace and held back the barbarian tribes which threatened the unity and civilization of their Empire. Not only did they preserve the culture of the ancient world but they developed a system of law and justice. They set up town communities held together by a vast network of roads. The Roman colonists opened up the wealth of the lands they occupied, and luxury goods moved from outlying provinces to Rome and other important cities. The mineral resources and products of the conquered were sent as tribute to Rome. A good coinage, and fair dealing, peace, and security, ensured by the presence of the Roman soldiers, enabled trade to expand, and the great military roads provided the necessary communications for traders.

B. *Roman Britain*

For nearly four hundred years Britain was politically and economically part of the Roman Empire. Britain was a Roman province, but the authority of the Romans was never seriously established beyond Hadrian's Wall, which was built across the north of England from the Tyne to the Solway.

Map 2 shows clearly that the Roman settlement was affected by the geological structure of the country. In the mountainous area of the north and west the conquest of the inhabitants was much more difficult, and the Romans were content to establish a military occupation. In the more fertile lands of the south-east the conquest was rapid, and the inhabitants were more easily influenced. Even so, probably only the wealthy Britons adopted the customs and speech of the Romans. It is in the south-east that most of the Roman remains are found.

C. *Economic Effects of the Roman Occupation*

Agriculture. The Romans cleared swamps and forests and improved the soil, and so enlarged the area of cultivation. They valued the corn which was grown and exported it in sufficient quantities for Britain to be called the 'Granary of the North.' Most of this corn was grown on large estates known as the 'Villa settlements,' cultivated by either Roman or Romanized British landowners. The *villa*, the dwelling of the landowner, was surrounded by outbuildings for the workers, stables, granaries, and all the buildings needed by a community which was self-sufficient. Some of the workers were slaves, and others *coloni*. These *coloni* were at first free tenants paying dues and services, but later they also lost their liberty.

The British villages whose inhabitants cultivated small and rectangular-shaped fields surrounding their huts remained almost untouched by Roman civilization, though as time went on some villagers became *coloni* on the villa settlements.

Mining. Britain's mineral wealth—lead, silver, gold, copper, iron, tin, and coal—was known to the Romans, and it has been suggested that this was one of the motives for their conquest of the island (see Map 3).

MAP 2

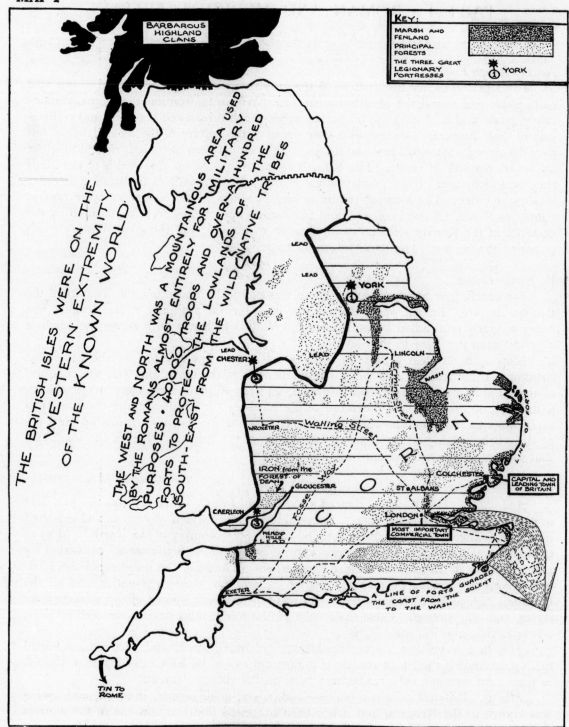

BARBAROUS HIGHLAND CLANS

KEY:
MARSH AND FENLAND
PRINCIPAL FORESTS
THE THREE GREAT LEGIONARY FORTRESSES
YORK

THE BRITISH ISLES WERE ON THE WESTERN EXTREMITY OF THE KNOWN WORLD.

THE WEST AND NORTH WAS A MOUNTAINOUS AREA USED BY THE ROMANS ALMOST ENTIRELY FOR MILITARY PURPOSES. 40,000 TROOPS AND OVER A HUNDRED FORTS TO PROTECT THE LOWLANDS OF THE SOUTH-EAST FROM THE WILD NATIVE TRIBES

LEAD

LEAD

YORK

LEAD

LINCOLN

Ermine Street

WASH

CHESTER

WROXETER

Watling Street

LINE OF FORTS

IRON from the FOREST OF DEAN

Fosse Way

GLOUCESTER

ST ALBANS

COLCHESTER

CAPITAL AND LEADING TOWN OF BRITAIN

CAERLEON

LONDON

MENDIP HILLS LEAD

MOST IMPORTANT COMMERCIAL TOWN

EXETER

A LINE OF FORTS GUARDED THE COAST FROM THE SOLENT TO THE WASH

TIN TO ROME

ROMAN BRITAIN

Industry. Even before the Roman Conquest British chieftains had secured Roman goods from Gaul, and these imports were increased after the occupation. Later, British artisans profited by the skill of craftsmen from over the seas, copied Roman designs, improved their standards, and greatly increased their output of manufactured goods, mainly pottery, glass, bronze and iron ware. The Romans introduced the making of bricks and tiles.

Trade. Britain was more closely connected with the Continent, and both imports and exports increased. Wine and oil were imported from Italy and Spain, and pottery from Gaul and the Rhineland. Exports from Britain included corn, cattle, oysters, minerals, and slaves. Internal trade was stimulated by the building of towns and the construction of roads.

Towns. Roman civilization and colonization were founded on town life. In addition to *coloniæ* (towns set aside for retired soldiers settled on the land—such as Verulamium, Colchester, York, Gloucester, and Lincoln) the Romans constructed towns in Britain as part of their system of administration and government. (Examples of these were Winchester, Silchester, Exeter, Chichester, Canterbury, Caister, Dorchester, Leicester, Wroxeter, Caerwent-on-Wye, Aldeburgh, Cirencester.) They became centres where artisans made goods to supply the increasing demands especially from the Romanized Britons. Bath was a fashionable watering-place.

London was larger than any other town, and became in later Roman times the seat of government in Britain. It was the centre of the country's communications, and depended for its importance on the flow of goods into and out of the port. It was of economic importance even in Roman times.

Roads. The Romans constructed a network of roads in these islands with good levelling and alignment, together with deep foundations and good drainage. They were built for the conquest and government of the country and not primarily for the purpose of furthering trade and commerce. They connected one town or fort with the next by the most direct route. The roads radiated from a number of centres, thus assisting the dispatch of troops, and enabling rebellions to be suppressed without delay. London, Cirencester, and Silchester were main road centres; Winchester, Canterbury, and Bath are examples of minor centres.

The construction of roads led to the building of bridges over rivers. Important bridges to carry roads were made over the Tyne at Newcastle and Corbridge, and over the Medway at Rochester. Most important of all was the bridge built over the Thames at London. It is probable that all the bridges of any size that existed in England before the Norman Conquest were of Roman construction.

Communication by Water. The Romans developed the Channel ports Reculver, Dover, Lympne, and Richborough.

Population. It is probable that the population of these islands increased under Roman administration, especially in the south-east. The bulk of the people lived in the country and were engaged in some form of agriculture.

MAP 3

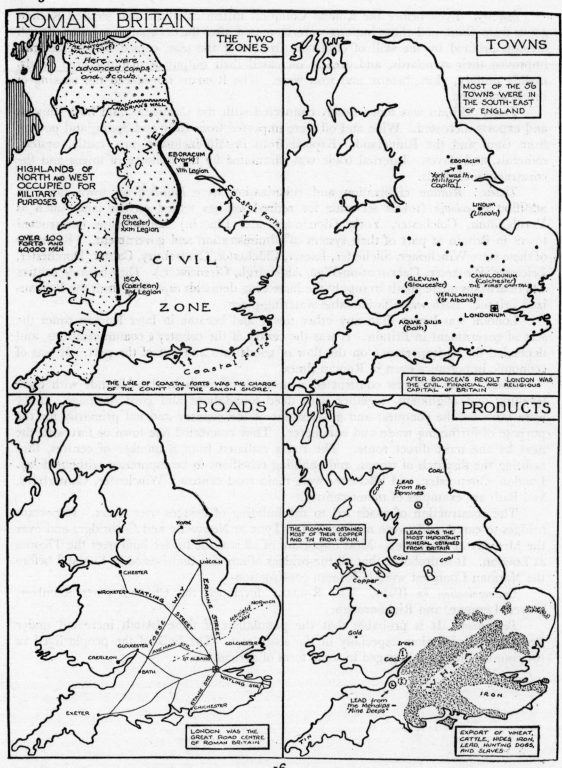

ROMAN BRITAIN

THE TWO ZONES

THE ANTONINE WALL (TURF)

Here were advanced camps and scouts.

HADRIAN'S WALL

EBORACUM (York) VIIth Legion

HIGHLANDS of NORTH and WEST OCCUPIED FOR MILITARY PURPOSES

Coastal Forts

OVER 100 FORTS and 40,000 MEN

DEVA (Chester) XXth Legion

CIVIL

ISCA (Caerleon) IInd Legion

ZONE

Coastal Forts

THE LINE OF COASTAL FORTS WAS THE CHARGE OF THE COUNT OF THE SAXON SHORE.

TOWNS

MOST OF THE 56 TOWNS WERE IN THE SOUTH-EAST OF ENGLAND

EBORACUM
York was the Military Capital.

LINDUM (Lincoln)

GLEVUM (Sloucester)

CAMULODUNUM (Colchester) THE FIRST CAPITAL

VERULAMIUM (St Albans)

LONDONIUM

AQUAE SULIS (Bath)

AFTER BOADICEA'S REVOLT LONDON WAS THE CIVIL, FINANCIAL, AND RELIGIOUS CAPITAL OF BRITAIN

ROADS

YORK

CHESTER

WROXETER WATLING WAY

ERMINE STREET

LINCOLN

NORWICH

Icknield Way

FOSSE WAY

GLOUCESTER AKEMAN STR.

COLCHESTER

CAERLEON

ST ALBANS

BATH

STANE STR.

WATLING STR.

CHICHESTER

EXETER

LONDON WAS THE GREAT ROAD CENTRE OF ROMAN BRITAIN

PRODUCTS

COAL

COAL

LEAD from the Pennines

THE ROMANS OBTAINED MOST OF THEIR COPPER AND TIN FROM SPAIN.

LEAD WAS THE MOST IMPORTANT MINERAL OBTAINED FROM BRITAIN

Coal

Copper

Coal

Gold

Iron

Coal

WHEAT

IRON

LEAD from the Mendips "Mine Deeps"

TIN

EXPORT OF WHEAT, CATTLE, HIDES, IRON, LEAD, HUNTING DOGS, AND SLAVES

2. THE DEPARTURE OF THE ROMANS AND THE ENGLISH CONQUEST

THE coming of the Angles, Saxons, and Jutes is one of the most important events in the history of these islands, but we have only a vague idea of what happened during the two hundred years which followed the withdrawal of the Romans.

Few traces of Roman civilization survived the pressure of the conquerors, though it must be remembered that, a century before the departure of the Roman legions, town life was already decaying and some Roman cities, such as Verulamium, Silchester, and Wroxeter, were depopulated. Most of the villas survived, but many of these even were deserted.

The English did not set out to destroy Roman civilization. There was a long struggle between the Britons and the invaders, during the course of which Roman cities fell into disuse and the influence of Roman ideas steadily diminished.

Some Britons were enslaved, some exterminated, some were driven westward, but for the most part the English (large numbers being freemen) settled on land side by side with Britons. They introduced their own methods of agriculture which were practised side by side with those already established. Gradually the two races intermingled under the control of the English lords. New farming methods developed. By the end of the tenth century many people had lost their independence and lived in villages under the protection of powerful lords. They cultivated their land in large open fields.

Much of the heavy clay land of the Midlands which the Romans and Britons had avoided was tilled, and here, and in the south, wheat, barley, oats, and rye crops were grown under a system of rotation.

In East Anglia and some northern areas there were differences due to the Danish invasions. The villages were larger, and there were greater numbers of freemen. In Kent the villages show some connexion with the Roman villa system. In the west there were scattered hamlets in which British ways predominated.

Town Life. The English disliked living in towns. They settled in villages at some distance from the Roman roads. For nearly two hundred years, while English kings were warring together, town life in England practically came to an end. By the eighth century, however, peace and order had been sufficiently restored by strong kings like Offa of Mercia and Ini and Egbert of Wessex to enable trade to develop, and this gave an active stimulus to the growth of towns. It is believed that south-east England and Merovingian Gaul had trade connexions, and we know that King Offa of Mercia made a treaty with Charlemagne in 796 by which Charlemagne guaranteed protection to English traders and merchants visiting his dominions.

The laws of Alfred show that traders were sufficiently important to be mentioned.

MAP 4

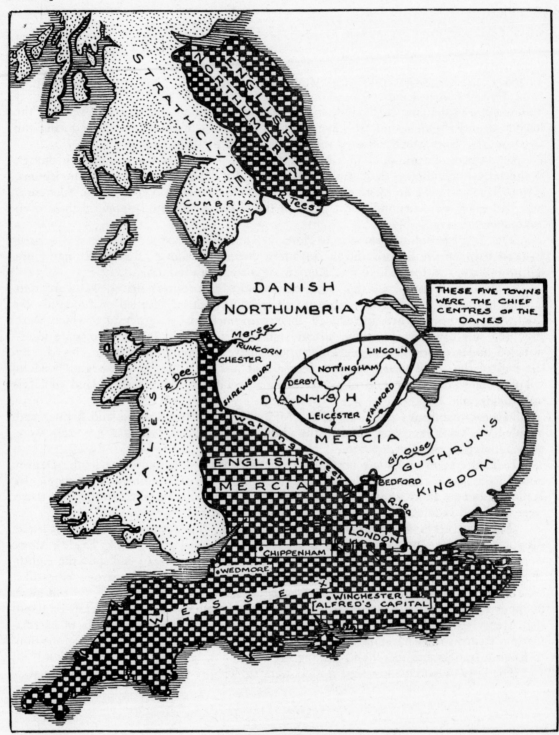

THE DANELAW

3. THE DANISH INVASIONS

THE orderly and peaceful progress of the English towards civilization was disturbed in the ninth century by the attacks of new invaders—the Northmen. The northern kingdoms of England were overwhelmed, and it was not until Wessex met the full force of these attacks that they were repelled. The area known as the Danelaw was left in the hands of the Danes, who built fortified towns ('boroughs'), such as Derby, Lincoln, Leicester, and Stamford, to defend themselves from the attacks of the men of Wessex. These fortresses became centres of trade, for they were places of safety, and merchants were attracted to them. Alfred and his successors reconquered the Danelaw, and they adopted the same method of building fortified towns to defend the neighbouring countryside. Examples of these were Hertford, on the river Lea; Tamworth, to protect the Mercian border against the Danish army based on Lincoln; Stafford, to bar the entry of Danes from the Trent valley. Sites fortified by Edward the Elder (901–25), son of Alfred the Great, became centres of local trade within fifteen years of his death.

At the end of the tenth century the Danes renewed their attacks on England, and under Canute established control over the whole country.

The Vikings were the great sailors and traders of their time. They travelled to far-distant places (the Mediterranean Sea, the Black Sea, and into Russia), and wherever they went they established trading centres. Danish rule gave encouragement to trade between Scandinavia and this country. The Baltic trade route of that time was of considerable importance, and England was at a point where two important trade routes met—one from Italy to the ports of the Low Countries, and the other from Russia along the coast of the Baltic to the North Sea.

Proof that the English traders shared in the commerce of the Continent is that King Canute secured trading concessions for English and Danish merchants from the Holy Roman Emperor and the King of Burgundy to ease their journeys to Rome. Many towns (York, Lincoln, Thetford, Norwich, Ipswich, Colchester) had populations too large to be supported on internal trade alone.

London rose to supreme importance among the boroughs. It was the largest city, with the greatest volume of trade. Foreign merchants from France, Normandy, Flanders, Scandinavia, brought their products to London, and many Danish merchants settled there. The overseas trade was carried on mainly by foreigners, not native merchants.

Although the importance of trade in the towns must be emphasized, the inhabitants were as much concerned with agriculture as with commerce. Most of the early towns had arable land in large fields outside their walls.

MAP 5

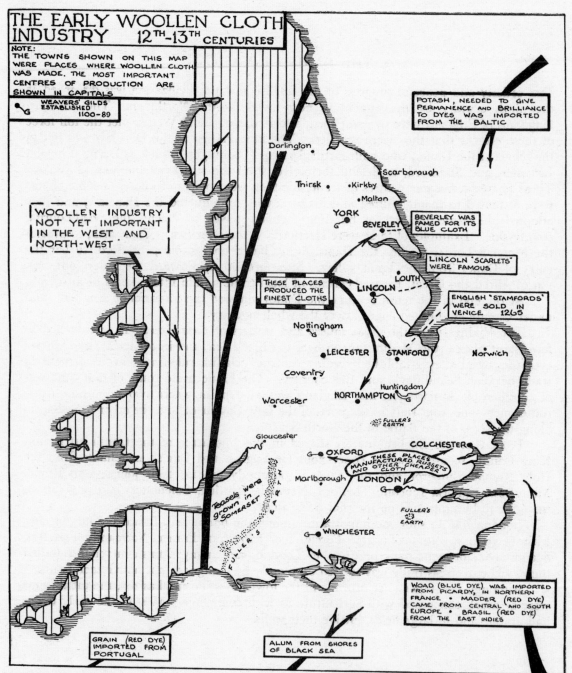

THE EARLY WOOLLEN CLOTH INDUSTRY 12TH-13TH CENTURIES

NOTE:
THE TOWNS SHOWN ON THIS MAP WERE PLACES WHERE WOOLLEN CLOTH WAS MADE. THE MOST IMPORTANT CENTRES OF PRODUCTION ARE SHOWN IN CAPITALS

WEAVERS' GILDS ESTABLISHED 1100-89

POTASH, NEEDED TO GIVE PERMANENCE AND BRILLIANCE TO DYES WAS IMPORTED FROM THE BALTIC

WOOLLEN INDUSTRY NOT YET IMPORTANT IN THE WEST AND NORTH-WEST

BEVERLEY WAS FAMED FOR ITS BLUE CLOTH

LINCOLN "SCARLETS" WERE FAMOUS

THESE PLACES PRODUCED THE FINEST CLOTHS

ENGLISH "STAMFORDS" WERE SOLD IN VENICE 1265

Darlington
Scarborough
Thirsk · Kirkby
· Malton
YORK
BEVERLEY
LOUTH
LINCOLN
Nottingham
LEICESTER
STAMFORD
Norwich
Coventry
Huntingdon
NORTHAMPTON
Worcester
FULLER'S EARTH

Gloucester
COLCHESTER
OXFORD
THESE PLACES MANUFACTURED RUSSETS AND OTHER CHEAPER CLOTH
Marlborough
LONDON
Teasels were grown in Somerset
FULLER'S EARTH
FULLER'S EARTH
WINCHESTER

WOAD (BLUE DYE) WAS IMPORTED FROM PICARDY, IN NORTHERN FRANCE · MADDER (RED DYE) CAME FROM CENTRAL AND SOUTH EUROPE · BRASIL (RED DYE) FROM THE EAST INDIES

GRAIN (RED DYE) IMPORTED FROM PORTUGAL

ALUM FROM SHORES OF BLACK SEA

SHEEP-FARMING AND THE WOOLLEN INDUSTRY : THE TWELFTH AND THIRTEENTH CENTURIES.

4. MEDIEVAL AGRICULTURE

FEUDAL SOCIETY

By the eleventh century, and particularly in the southern and eastern parts of England, society could well be described as feudal—that is, as a society in which every portion of property in land involved its occupier in certain duties of keeping order and performing military service. Landowners were expected to be soldiers, and they were required to keep order on their estates.

CHARACTERISTICS OF FEUDAL SOCIETY

(i) There was a bond between the lord and his man. A man 'commended himself to a lord,' who was his superior, and to whom he paid homage.

(ii) Services were rendered in return for the holding of land. The rich gave military service ; the poor, labour on the land.

(iii) Important landowners were expected to defend the country in time of war and to find soldiers for the King.

(iv) The lord helped to govern and keep order among the tenants on his estate. He held a local law court ; this was also a source of profit to him.

This form of society grew up all over western Europe, and was a consequence of the constant disorder and bloodshed and uncertainty of the times. In England, especially during the Danish invasions, freemen with few resources sought protection from the richer nobles to whom they 'commended themselves' while the King granted estates to his followers in return for their military help. The great change which took place after the Norman Conquest in 1066 was that William the Conqueror introduced all the institutions which were familiar to him. He took possession of every acre of land, and granted estates or manors to tenants-in-chief (mainly Normans) in return for forty days' service each year by a number of armed knights varying with the amount of land held. Through these tenants-in-chief—who swore an oath of fealty to him, and from whom he received as a right certain dues such as aids, reliefs, wardship, marriage, and escheat— the King had complete control over his kingdom. The mass of the people—villeins— continued to live as they had done before the Conquest, except that they worked for a Norman instead of a Saxon lord.

TENURE AND STATUS

The person who farmed every plot of land in the kingdom held the land either immediately of the King or, alternatively, of a tenant or sub-tenant of the King. There might be numerous links in the chain between the actual cultivator and the King. The type of service rendered by a tenant to his overlord was determined by the *tenure* by which he held his land.

Tenures were either free or unfree (villein). Free tenants were protected by the King's (common law) courts, but if a person holding by villein tenure was ejected from his land the King's courts could give him no redress. His remedy was to ask assistance (to which he had no legal right) from his manorial court. The King's courts had difficulty in determining who was entitled to their protection, for all the peasants worked side by side in the fields, though some held their land by free and others by unfree tenure. The former, however, rendered services which were well-defined, whereas the tenants in villeinage ' did not know in the evening what they would be doing in the morning '— it might be hedging, ploughing, or some other task as their overlord required.

As well as free and unfree tenures of land there were free men and unfree men (bondsmen, villeins, serfs). Personal freedom had no necessary connexion with free and unfree tenure. A man might be personally free yet hold his land by villein tenure, or he might be personally a bondsman yet hold land by a free tenure, though such a man had few rights he could maintain against his lord. His chattels were his lord's, and if he threw up his holding and ran away his lord could bring him back.

The vast majority of the people held their land by villein tenure, and were also personally unfree. A man's economic position, however, did not depend on whether he held by free or unfree tenure or on whether he was personally free or not. Villeins, particularly in the Midlands, had holdings up to thirty acres, while many men in the Danelaw, personally free and holding their land by free tenure, had but five acres. Persons holding only a few acres were often called bordars or cottars.

DIAGRAM 1

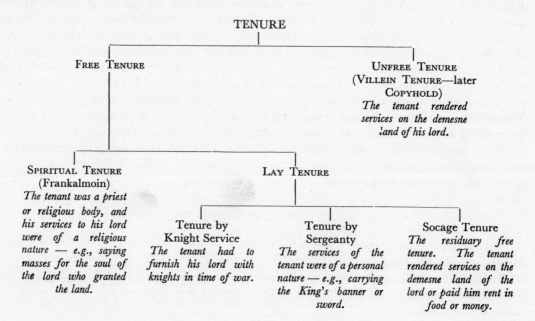

The Domesday Survey (1086)

We owe much of our knowledge of England in the eleventh century to the fact that William the Conqueror ordered a survey to be made of his kingdom to record the owners and value of the land at the time of the Survey, at his accession in 1066, and in Edward the Confessor's reign. This covered the extent of the estates, the number of men who ploughed the land—the ploughing teams—the number of cattle, sheep, pigs, etc. Parts of the country were only imperfectly surveyed, but the carefully noted details give a clear picture of the land and its inhabitants. One interesting fact is that the value of the land declined for a period after the coming of the Normans.

Methods of Farming

Geographical factors determined, as they do to-day, the type of farming which was carried on in different parts of the country. The lowland plains of the south and east were suited to arable farming and corn was grown, but the hilly districts of the north and west were fit only for the pasture of sheep. Sheep were important in the arable areas too, for they were folded on the fields, and their manure maintained the fertility of the land.

Map 8 shows areas in which two different types of sheep were kept—small sheep with short wool which could be used to make heavy woollens, and larger sheep with long wool which was made into lighter textiles, known as worsteds.[1]

All kinds of landowners kept sheep : bishops, abbots of monasteries, lords great and small. The powerful owned very large flocks, sometimes scattered up and down the country. Even before 1066 there was sheep farming providing wool for export. Domesday Book records that Ely Abbey had over thirteen thousand sheep on estates in six counties. The production of wool grew rapidly in the twelfth and thirteenth centuries, and was fostered by religious Orders that had recently come to England— the Cistercians and others. These Orders, for various reasons, tended to build their monasteries in remote parts of England suitable only for sheep-rearing.

The tenants of the great landowners also kept sheep on their own account. In the pastoral areas of England they often owned considerable numbers, the wool being sold for export ; in the arable areas, each peasant owned one or two sheep.

In the arable farming areas of England there was no fixed method of corn production. The methods typical of the Midlands were different from those of East Anglia, which in turn differed from those of Kent. Some villages had two main fields, one of which lay fallow when the other was under corn. Some had four fields, but most had three. In the poorer highland areas of the west and north, where pastoral farming was the rule, there were also two fields, of which the smaller infield was continuously cropped. The second, or outfield, was used for the common pasture of the cattle (the infield-outfield or run-rig system).

[1] A modern writer has suggested that in medieval times the distinction between long and short wools was insignificant.

MAP 6

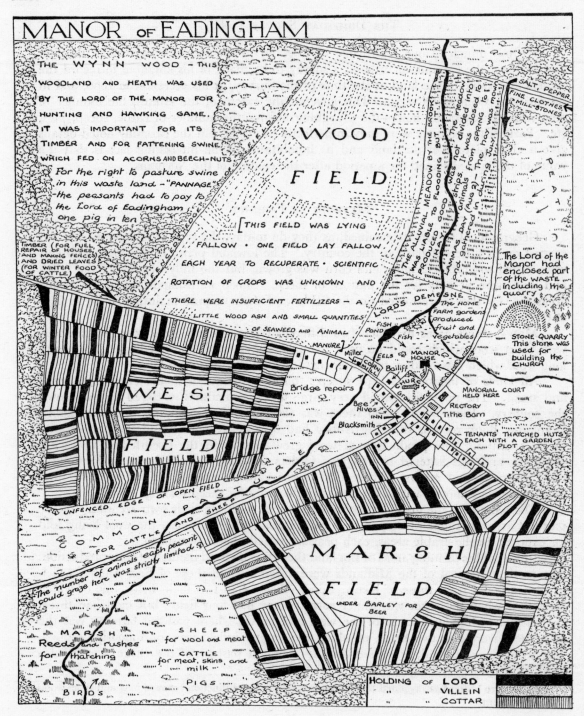

MANOR of EADINGHAM

THE WYNN WOOD - THIS WOODLAND AND HEATH WAS USED BY THE LORD OF THE MANOR FOR HUNTING AND HAWKING GAME. IT WAS IMPORTANT FOR ITS TIMBER AND FOR FATTENING SWINE WHICH FED ON ACORNS AND BEECH-NUTS

For the right to pasture swine in this waste land - "PANNAGE" - the peasants had to pay to the Lord of Eadingham one pig in ten

TIMBER (FOR FUEL, REPAIR OF HOUSES, AND MAKING FENCES) AND DRIED LEAVES (FOR WINTER FOOD OF CATTLE).

WOOD FIELD

[THIS FIELD WAS LYING FALLOW · ONE FIELD LAY FALLOW EACH YEAR TO RECUPERATE · SCIENTIFIC ROTATION OF CROPS WAS UNKNOWN AND THERE WERE INSUFFICIENT FERTILIZERS — A LITTLE WOOD ASH AND SMALL QUANTITIES OF SEAWEED AND ANIMAL MANURE]

THE ALLUVIAL MEADOW BY THE BROOK WAS LIABLE TO FLOODING BUT IT PRODUCED GOOD HAY. The meadow was not divided into strips. It was closed to animals and day from spring to LAMMAS DAY (Aug 2) - The hay was mown and gathered in during July.

SALT, PEPPER, FINE CLOTHES, MILL-STONES

PEAT

The Lord of the Manor had enclosed part of the WASTE including the quarry

STONE QUARRY This stone was used for building the CHURCH

LORDS DEMESNE The home FARM gardens produced fruit and vegetables

Fish Pond
EELS FISH
Miller CORN MILL
Bailiff
MANOR HOUSE
Bridge repairs
Bee Hives
Blacksmith
CHURCH graveyard
INN
MANORIAL COURT HELD HERE
RECTORY Tithe Barn
TENANTS' THATCHED HUTS EACH WITH A GARDEN PLOT

WEST FIELD

UNFENCED EDGE OF OPEN FIELD

COMMON PASTURE FOR CATTLE AND SHEEP

The number of animals each peasant could graze here was strictly limited

MARSH Reeds and rushes for thatching

SHEEP for wool and meat
CATTLE for meat, skins, and milk
PIGS
BIRDS

MARSH FIELD
UNDER BARLEY FOR BEER

HOLDING of LORD
" " VILLEIN
" " COTTAR

24

A Village of the Midlands of England

Eadingham (Map 6) was a village common in the English Midlands where the soil was well suited for growing corn. Its site had originally been a small clearing in a dense forest at a point where two paths crossed near a ford across a brook. As the village grew, more of the forest had been cut down, and the land ploughed for crops. The arable land had been greatly extended, though in Norman times, as the map shows, Eadingham was still surrounded by woodland.

You will notice that there were no homesteads scattered about the cornfields; all the houses were in the middle of the village grouped into a compact or nucleated settlement.

The land of the village comprised :

(i) the cultivated land around the village
(ii) the water meadows from which hay was obtained
(iii) the common pasture
(iv) the woodland

(i) *Arable Land.* The cultivated land was divided into three fields, each about six hundred acres in extent. These were open fields—that is, they were not divided by hedges, though wooden fences were erected around the fields in which corn was grown. These temporary fences were taken down after harvest, and then the village cattle were allowed to pasture there. Woodfield was lying fallow (without crops) for the year, and cattle were grazing the stubble of last year's barley crop. It was ploughed twice during the summer, and in autumn a crop of winter wheat was sown. Westfield was growing wheat and rye for cakes and bread, and Marshfield was growing barley for beer-brewing. The crops were stunted, for the standard of farming was low.

The plan shows that the fields were divided into strips, most of which were one or one-half acre in size. An acre strip would be one furlong ('furrow-long') in length and four rods (22 yards) in width. Between the strips were balks of untilled land. The strips of the villagers were scattered about, so that all had a share of the good, fertile land and of the badly drained or weedy land.

(ii) *Meadow Land.* Near Woodfield was a large water-meadow sown with hay grasses to provide the village with winter food for the animals. There was not enough hay to feed them all, and many cattle were slaughtered at Martinmas (November). The meadow was divided into temporary strips by fences, and distributed among the villagers.

(iii) *The Common Pasture.* There was a large area of pastureland not divided into strips, but left open all the year round to village cattle, sheep, and swine, though the number of animals each villager might keep was strictly limited.

(iv) *Woodland.* The woods surrounding the village were usually grouped with the common pasture and called 'waste.' From the forest the villagers drew brushwood for fuel, and timber for repairing their houses and ploughs; pigs fattened on acorns and beech-nuts. For the right to pasture the swine—'pannage'—the villagers had to pay one pig in every ten to the Lord of the Manor.

DIAGRAM 2

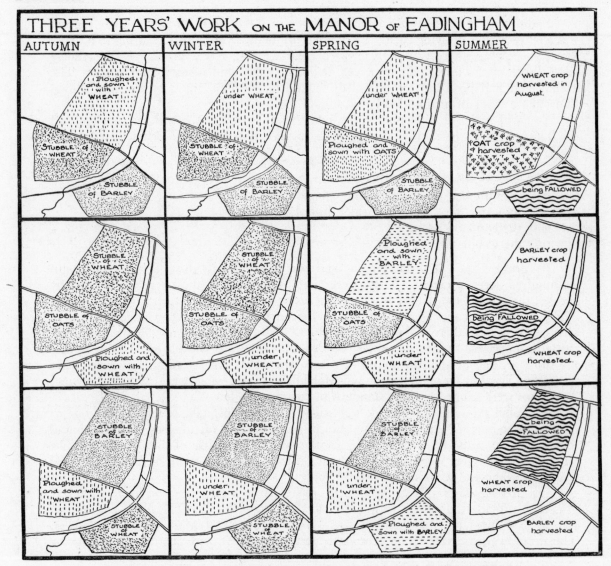

ROTATION OF CROPS ON THE MANOR OF EADINGHAM

The People of the Village [1]

(i) *The Lord of the Manor and the manorial Officials*

The only imposing house in Eadingham was the manor house—the home of the Lord of the Manor. He was a very important person, and all the people of the village were subjected to him. During the troubled times of the Danish invasions the villagers had sought protection from the enemy, and had agreed to work for the Lord of Eadingham if he would protect them. They were now his tenants, and the whole village was his estate or manor. As tenants of their lord the villagers owed various services to him : they ploughed his land, sheared his sheep, mowed his hay, reaped and carted his corn, and carried out any other necessary work.

The lord who owned several manors on some of which were several villages went round from one to another consuming the food which had been grown on the demesne (or estate). A steward or seneschal also travelled round from manor to manor acting as general manager of all the lord's manors. He heard complaints from the tenants and saw that the lord's interests were not suffering. At least once a year he arranged the manorial court. The lord's bailiff lived on the manor so that he could watch the tenants and see that they gave all the services which custom demanded. The man who allotted the various jobs to the villeins and cottars was called the reeve. He was one of the villagers who had been chosen for the unenviable task. Ploughs were drawn by eight oxen, and several peasants had to combine to make up the plough teams as very few owned so many animals.

(ii) *Priest, Miller, Smith*

The church stood in the centre of the village, and near by was the priest's house. It stood next to a huge thatched barn—the tithe barn—for nearly every one gave to the Church a portion, or tithe, of their crops. Near the village crossroads was the blacksmith's cottage. The smith was kept busy making and repairing the ploughs and tools of the villagers and mending the wheels of any carts which had been broken on the very rough roads. All the corn grown in the village had to be ground into flour at the lord's mill, which was built where the road crossed the local brook. The village was practically self-supporting. All the main necessities of life, food and clothing, were grown or made by the villagers, and only iron, fish, salt, millstones, and fine clothes for the lord were purchased from outside. (Diagram 2.)

(iii) *The Peasants*

A small number of the peasants were free men. They could sell their land, their oxen, and marry off their sons and daughters without the lord's consent. Free men were more numerous in areas which had been in the Danelaw, and it is possible they were descendants of Danes. Most of the people of the village were not free. There were villeins who held about thirty acres of arable land—that is, ten-acre strips in

[1] A village is a geographical area containing a small number of houses. A manor is an estate worked by a lord with the aid of his tenants. Some villages contained two or more manors, and sometimes a manor spread over more than one village.

each of the open fields. They lived in thatched cottages of three rooms, in one of which cattle were stalled. Round the cottage was a croft, a vegetable patch in which were cultivated peas and beans, leeks, and other small crops. They also kept beehives in the crofts, for honey was the usual method of sweetening. The villein had a strip of land in the meadow, and could pasture a number of his animals in the waste. Custom demanded that he worked two or three days each week (week-work) on his lord's land, and at seed-time and harvest extra help was demanded (boon-work). He had to provide two oxen for ploughing and carting when the lord's bailiff demanded them. A third of the people were cottars holding only five acres of arable land. They were not, however, required to give as many services to the lord as the villein was, and consequently had time to spare. The cottars became hired labourers working for both the more prosperous villeins and for the lord at the busy times of the year. Farming was co-operative in the sense that a villager could not grow what he liked, but had to conform to the crop system of the village.

The Kentish System

In Kent a tenant's holding was a single, compact whole and there was little of the co-operative village agriculture so common in the Midlands. Another difference between the two areas was that in Kent a lord's tenants were often spread out over many miles of territory, and not, as in the Midlands, very near together. In Kent, too, each tenant paid rent or rendered small labour services to his lord, but week-work was uncommon.

The East Anglian System

The villages of East Anglia were large and generally shared among several manors —that is, ' owned ' by several lords. The open fields were divided into strips, but the holdings of each tenant were not scattered but compacted together. The farmer could, therefore, decide what he wanted to grow on his land, for if a rotation of crops occurred, it was not a rotation on the open field but one within the farmer's own holding.

Holdings in East Anglia were small (usually only fifteen acres) compared with other parts of England. There were also a larger proportion of free tenures and free men. The payment of money rents was common.

How far was the Village Self-sufficient?

The village in the early Middle Ages was self-sufficient in the sense that it produced the bulk of its food. But this picture of self-sufficiency was broken in some instances :

(i) There was an exchange of salt, fish, and iron for cloths.

(ii) Where the lord did not move from one manor to another he often prescribed a fixed place to which his manors should send contributions of food (p. 27).

(iii) The ecclesiastical estates sent large quantities of corn to the market. Some peasants rendered services by cartage. Corn moved up and down the coast.

(iv) The free tenants, at least, sent some corn to the local market ; but the quantity before the thirteenth century was not great.

(v) From the earliest of times wool entered into international trade.

5. MEDIEVAL INDUSTRY

THE GILD SYSTEM IN THE MIDDLE AGES

By the twelfth century in England, owing to the growth of trade, many more towns had developed—though some were little more than large villages, whose inhabitants were still mainly concerned with agricultural pursuits. Like the people on the manor, the townsmen, as tenants of a feudal lord, had to perform the services required of them, and, in addition, tolls and dues were imposed on all those who engaged in trade. The interference of the King's Sheriff, who collected the King's share of these tolls, was a source of great irritation to the townsmen.

It is not surprising, therefore, that the main object of the town in the twelfth century was to free itself from the tyranny of both lord and sheriff. This they did by purchasing from the King a charter which conferred the right to collect their own taxes, to hold a court, and to elect magistrates : the charter gave the town the status of a borough.

Merchant Gilds. The demand for a charter generally came from leading merchants, the most influential of the townsfolk. In many towns—not in London, Norwich, Colchester, the Cinque Ports—they formed an association called a merchant gild to protect their trade interests. Towns which had a gild usually came under its control. Members had the exclusive right to buy and sell without the payment of a toll. Foreigners (inhabitants of other towns) had to pay tolls for the privilege of trading, and even then sometimes they could buy from or sell to gildsmen only. The merchant gild tried to obtain the maximum trading profit for members, to protect them in dealings with traders in other towns, to give assistance when they were in debt or without work, to give support to widows and orphans of their members. Merchant gilds reached the height of their influence about 1250.

Craft Gilds. The more familiar and lasting craft gilds arose in the late twelfth century : as their name implies, they were associations of all the members of a particular craft—for example bakers, weavers, skinners, etc.—and they developed spontaneously as trade became more specialized. In towns with a merchant gild the craft gilds were formed by groups of small craftsmen who were denied opportunities of trade by the richer merchants who dominated the merchant gild.

The master craftsman purchased his raw material, and made and sold goods in his own home. His work was supervised and the prices determined by officers of the gild ; in this way a high standard of workmanship was maintained, and a price fair to producer and consumer ensured. Apprenticeship was an important feature of this organization ; the duties of a master and apprentice were rigorously enforced. At the end of his apprenticeship the young worker was a journeyman until his ' masterpiece ' was accepted by the gild, when he became a master. Training, moral and technical, and skill, but not capital, were the essentials. The craft gilds were thus in their early days democratic institutions in which the humblest member could rise to the highest level.

Later Changes. By the fifteenth century changes had undermined the character of the gilds. The expansion of markets made it impossible for one man to produce and sell his own goods. Merchants who acted as middlemen became the link between the

MAP 7

TRADE AND INDUSTRIES OF MEDIEVAL ENGLAND

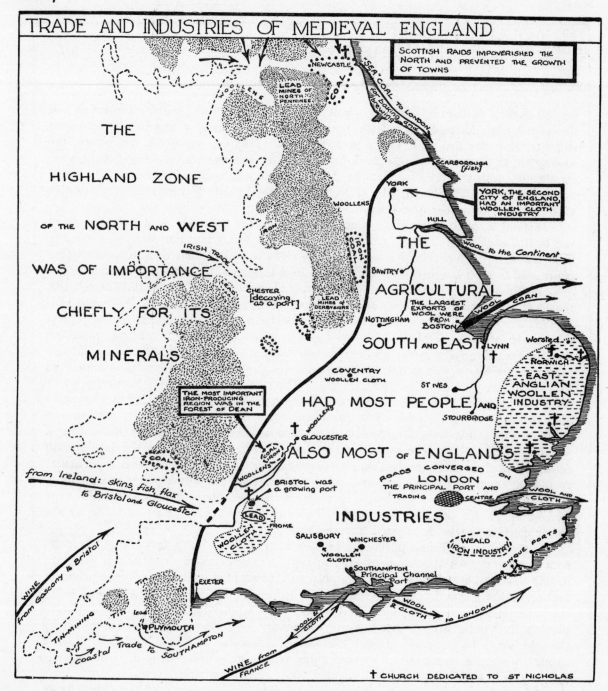

SCOTTISH RAIDS IMPOVERISHED THE NORTH AND PREVENTED THE GROWTH OF TOWNS

THE

HIGHLAND ZONE

OF THE NORTH AND WEST

WAS OF IMPORTANCE

CHIEFLY FOR ITS

MINERALS

LEAD MINES OF NORTH PENNINES

COAL

WOOLLENS

NEWCASTLE

"SEA" COAL to London for baking & brewing

SCARBOROUGH [fish]

YORK

HULL

YORK, THE SECOND CITY OF ENGLAND, HAD AN IMPORTANT WOOLLEN CLOTH INDUSTRY

WOOLLENS

IRON

IRON COAL

Wool to the Continent

IRISH TRADE

LEAD

CHESTER [decaying as a port]

LEAD MINES OF DERBYSHIRE

COAL

BAWTRY

NOTTINGHAM

THE

AGRICULTURAL

THE LARGEST EXPORTS OF WOOL WERE FROM BOSTON

WOOL CORN

SOUTH AND EAST

LYNN

Worsted

NORWICH

EAST ANGLIAN WOOLLEN INDUSTRY

COVENTRY WOOLLEN CLOTH

ST IVES

STOURBRIDGE

HAD MOST PEOPLE AND

THE MOST IMPORTANT IRON-PRODUCING REGION WAS IN THE FOREST OF DEAN

COAL IRON

WOOLLENS

GLOUCESTER

ALSO MOST OF ENGLANDS

ROADS CONVERGED ON

LONDON

THE PRINCIPAL PORT AND TRADING CENTRE

WOOL AND CLOTH

from Ireland: skins, fish, flax to Bristol and Gloucester

COAL IRON

WOOLLENS

LEAD

BRISTOL was a growing port

FROME

INDUSTRIES

WEALD IRON INDUSTRY

WOOLLEN CLOTH

SALISBURY

WINCHESTER

CINQUE PORTS

WOOLLEN CLOTH

WINE from Gascony to Bristol

TIN

TIN-MINING

Tin

lead

EXETER

PLYMOUTH

Coastal Trade to SOUTHAMPTON

SOUTHAMPTON Principal Channel Port

WOOL & CLOTH

WOOL & CLOTH to London

WINE from FRANCE

† CHURCH DEDICATED TO ST NICHOLAS

MAP 8

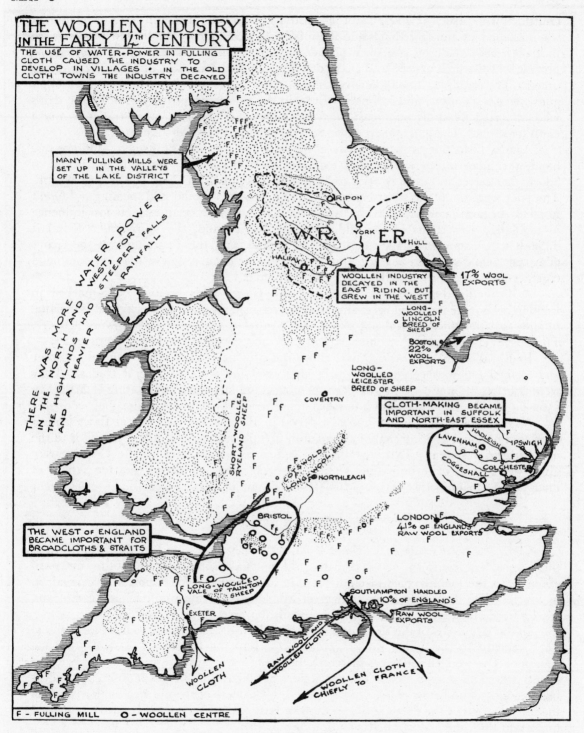

THE WOOLLEN INDUSTRY IN THE EARLY 14TH CENTURY

THE USE OF WATER-POWER IN FULLING CLOTH CAUSED THE INDUSTRY TO DEVELOP IN VILLAGES · IN THE OLD CLOTH TOWNS THE INDUSTRY DECAYED

MANY FULLING MILLS WERE SET UP IN THE VALLEYS OF THE LAKE DISTRICT

THERE WAS MORE WATER-POWER IN THE NORTH AND THE HIGHLANDS HAD WEST, FOR FALLS STEEPER AND A HEAVIER RAINFALL

RIPON

W.R.   YORK   E.R.   HULL

HALIFAX

WOOLLEN INDUSTRY DECAYED IN THE EAST RIDING, BUT GREW IN THE WEST

17% WOOL EXPORTS

LONG-WOOLLED LINCOLN BREED OF SHEEP

BOSTON 22% WOOL EXPORTS

LONG-WOOLLED LEICESTER BREED OF SHEEP

COVENTRY

CLOTH-MAKING BECAME IMPORTANT IN SUFFOLK AND NORTH-EAST ESSEX

LAVENHAM   HADLEIGH   IPSWICH
COGGESHALL   COLCHESTER

SHORT-WOOLLED RYELAND SHEEP

COTSWOLDS LONG-WOOL SHEEP   NORTHLEACH

BRISTOL

LONDON 41% OF ENGLAND'S RAW WOOL EXPORTS

THE WEST of ENGLAND BECAME IMPORTANT FOR BROADCLOTHS & STRAITS

LONG-WOOLLED VALE OF TAUNTON SHEEP

EXETER

SOUTHAMPTON HANDLED 10% OF ENGLAND'S RAW WOOL EXPORTS

WOOLLEN CLOTH

RAW WOOL AND WOOLLEN CLOTH

WOOLLEN CLOTH CHIEFLY TO FRANCE

F - FULLING MILL   O - WOOLLEN CENTRE

31

craftsmen who made the goods and the consumers who bought them. This development was hastened by the fact that some manufactures demanded complicated processes, so that they were made by craftsmen of several gilds. The craftsmen who completed the process sold the final article, and by so doing established some sort of authority over the others. For example, the saddlers became in effect the employers of men of three other gilds, joiners, painters, and lorimers. Even in the thirteenth century some of the dyers who imported dyestuffs employed weavers, fullers, and men of other trades to make cloth for them. The gild system never fully applied in the export industries.

Again, distinction grew up between the rich and the poor craftsmen. On the one hand, the more prosperous masters extended their business. The gildsmen began to adorn themselves in costly liveries or uniforms as symbols of their power and wealth. The poor were unable to meet expenses. They ceased to attend gild meetings. ' Great masters ' began to rule the gilds in their own interests ; the small masters lost influence in regulating the affairs of the gild. On the other hand, the journeymen found it difficult to become masters through lack of capital, and the obstruction of the richer gildsmen, who demanded heavy entrance fees. There came a time when they combined together in associations to strike against their masters.

A distinction between the richer and the poorer gilds became very marked in London, where the richer gilds became companies—e.g. the Merchant Taylors' (the name implies that the gildsmen did not make their own cloth) whose members wore a livery. The poorer gildsmen were Yeomanry, and sold their goods to the Livery Companies.

In Elizabethan and early Stuart times the provincial gilds often banded together and formed omnibus companies which supervised the work of several trades. They were able to stifle competition from non-members, and later used the Statute of Artificers, 1562–63 (p. 64) to enforce apprenticeship upon the different trades under their control.

As the market for English goods widened in Elizabethan and Stuart times from a local to a national and international one, an attempt was made to adapt the gilds to the new industrial system. Existing gilds, in return for a payment to the Crown, were given wider areas of jurisdiction. Companies were given by Royal Charter patents of monopoly to manufacture certain articles—for example, soap.

The Woollen Industry

Cloth has been made in England from very early times, and in the Middle Ages there were very few towns or villages that did not make some woollen cloth. But until about 1250 the manufacture of cloth for sale in London or for export was carried on in towns. The main towns are shown on Map 8. The raw wool, fuller's earth, and teazles were obtained at home. Most dye-stuffs, however, were imported.

In the latter part of the thirteenth century, following the introduction of mechanical improvements in the fulling process,[1] mills were built on the banks of swiftly flowing streams. The woollen industry, therefore, began to move away from the towns into the countryside, and thus to escape the restrictions of gilds which in this industry had never been complete, and now entirely disappeared. The new centres of production were in the hilly districts of the north and west, and in East Anglia, where the industry remained important until the Industrial Revolution (see p. 76).

[1] The fuller beat the cloth in water, and this caused it to shrink and the fibres to felt together, giving the material a smoother finish. The new invention was a series of wooden hammers attached to the spindle of a water-wheel. For a note on the processes involved in making woollen cloth, see p. 73.

6. MEDIEVAL TRADE : INTERNATIONAL TRADE IN THE MIDDLE AGES (I)

ONE of the most remarkable features of the twelfth and thirteenth centuries was the great expansion of international commerce due to :

(i) The establishment of strong feudal states which gave protection to traders and merchants. Many rulers, such as those in Flanders and the Champagne province of France, showed an enlightened policy towards trade and industry.

MAP 9

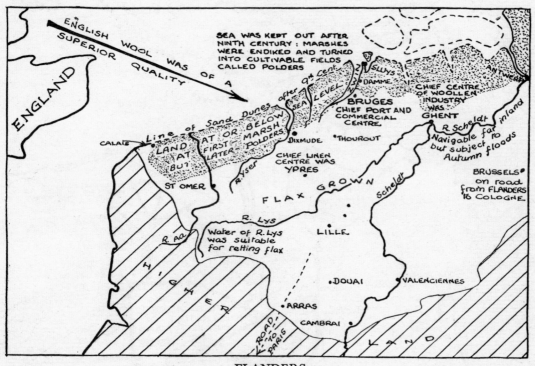

FLANDERS

(ii) The twelfth and thirteenth centuries were centuries of expanding population and cultivation in Western Europe. This expansion led to some industrialization and urbanization. There was a growth of towns and town life. Towns were founded upon industry and commerce. In Italy, Germany, and Flanders (see Map 9, Flanders), cities, sometimes city states, grew up, and both politically and economically they were forces to be reckoned with. As we shall see, the Hansa League of North German cities monopolized the Baltic trade for many centuries.

(iii) The Crusades indirectly gave a strong impetus to trade and to the growth of towns. The Eastern Mediterranean was opened to commerce with Europe. The Italian cities of Venice, Pisa, and Genoa were able to establish trading-posts in this area, and

MAP 10

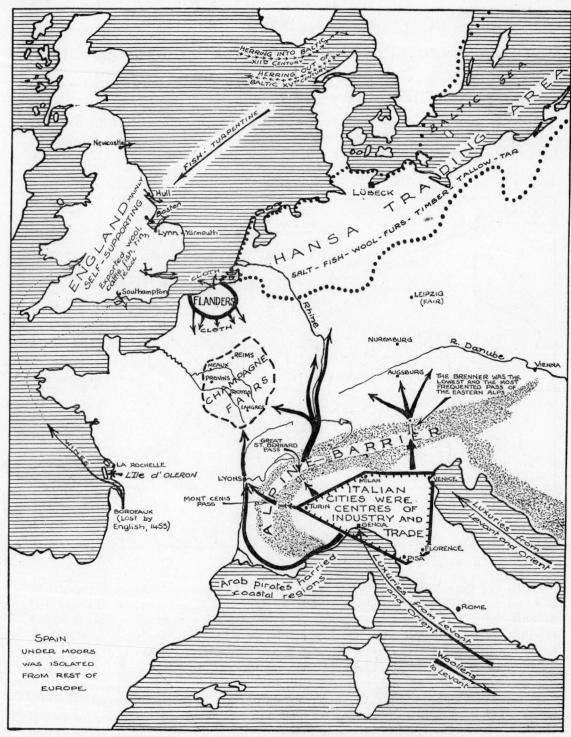

EUROPEAN TRADE IN THE EARLY MIDDLE AGES

MAP II

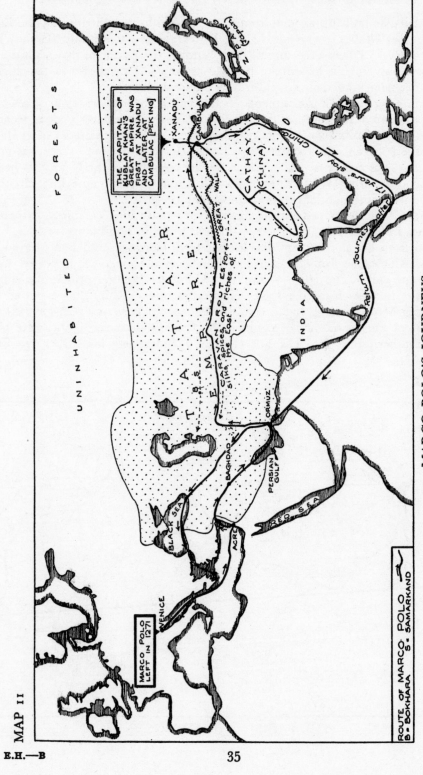

FORESTS

UNINHABITED

THE CAPITAL OF
KUBLAI KHAN'S
GREAT EMPIRE WAS
FIRST AT XANADU
AND LATER AT
CAMBULAC [PEKING]

XANADU

CAMBULAC

CATHAY
(CHINA)

T A R T A R

E M P I R E

17 years stay in China

CARAVAN ROUTES for
spices and riches of
silk, the East

GREAT WALL

BURMA

Return Journey partly

INDIA

ORMUZ

BAGHDAD

PERSIAN
GULF

BLACK SEA

ACRE

RED SEA

VENICE

MARCO POLO
LEFT IN 1271

E.H.—B

35

MARCO POLO'S JOURNEYS

ROUTE OF MARCO POLO
B= BOKHARA   S= SAMARKAND

Venice in particular built up an empire and grew wealthy by distributing the luxuries of the East. (See Map 11, showing Marco Polo's journey to Cathay (China) in the thirteenth century.) Towns grew up all over Europe, the power of manufacturers and merchants developing at the expense of the barons who sold privileges to the citizens of the towns to get money for their adventures in the Crusades.

(iv) Certain technical improvements, better ships, the construction of sea-charts, and the introduction of the compass from the Arabs gave the seafarer greater security.

(v) The early Muslim conquerors acquired most of Europe's stocks of gold. The trade of Europe between A.D. 400 and 1000 had perforce to decline—there was no gold to settle international accounts. After A.D. 1000 the countries of the Near East began to import commodities from Western Europe. Gold once again came into circulation, and the accounts of international traders could now be settled.

As a result there developed an extensive luxury trade in silks, spices, carpets, and precious stones from the East, and a considerable trade in non-luxury articles. Spain exported iron from her northern mines, leather from Cordova, and fine Merino wool. Olive oil and wine came from the south of France, while the north exported woollen cloth, linen, and salt. The cities of southern Germany became prosperous entrepôts distributing the luxuries from the East. The cities of the Rhineland exported wine, and those of northern Germany engaged in the exchange of corn and beer for the timber, wax, and furs of the Scandinavian countries. Herrings from the Baltic were sent to central and southern Europe. The fine cloth of Flanders was famed, as was English raw wool.

MAP 12

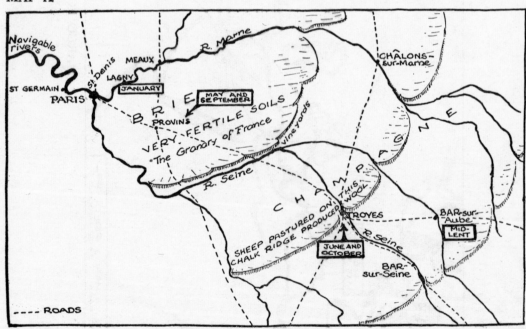

THE FAIRS OF CHAMPAGNE

THE FAIRS

Fairs were the main centres for international trade in the early Middle Ages; they were, indeed, a necessity, as exports were at first too insignificant for permanent trading settlements to flourish throughout the year. They were held at fixed times and places, two of the great centres being Flanders and the Champagne province of France (see Map 12). Others were held round Paris, at Saint-Denis and Saint-Germain-des-Prés, and at Lyons. Noted fairs were also held at Frankfurt-on-Main, in western Germany, at Frankfurt-on-Oder, in eastern Germany, at Nijni-Novgorod, on the Volga, in Russia, at Nuremberg and Leipzig, in central Germany, and at Seville, on the Guadalquivir river, in southern Spain (see Map 16).

The Champagne fairs owed their importance to their geographical position almost midway between the Mediterranean and the North Sea and close to Germany. There were six held at Lagny, Bar-sur-Aube, Provins (twice), and Troyes (twice). Each fair lasted from sixteen to sixty days and, with intervals for preparation and transport, they spread over the whole year. 'Troy' weight is still used as the measure in the gold and jewellery trades.

Flanders, on the sea-coast, with a good seaport (Antwerp) and fine inland waterways,

MAP 13

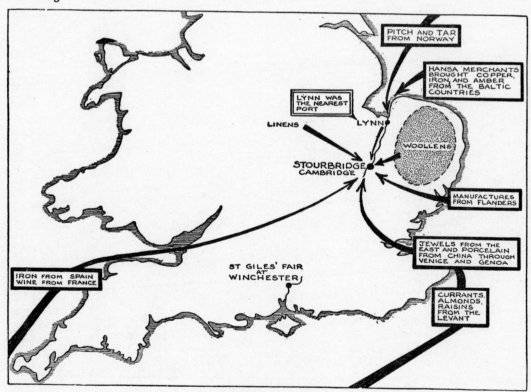

ENGLISH FAIRS

was admirably placed for international trade.   The oldest of the Flemish fairs was held at Thourout ; Bruges became the most important.

English Fairs.   In England there were many noteworthy fairs.   Their names are reminiscent of their origin as religious festivals.   They were held at Boston (St Botolphs), in Huntingdon (St Ives), at Winchester (St Giles), at Smithfield, in London (St Bartholomew).   The most famous of all was Stourbridge Fair, held near Cambridge, and this survived until the eighteenth century.

The king or feudal lord who owned the fair had complete control, and received from the merchants rents for their stalls and tolls for entry into the fair, as well as fines levied at the Fair Court (Court of Pie Powder) [1] which settled disputes between traders. Traders accepted these regulations willingly, because once admitted to the fair they were free to trade with anyone, unhampered by the restrictions of the gilds.   During the period of the fair, shops in the town were closed.   Disturbers of the peace were severely punished, and the protection thus afforded was of great value to foreign merchants, whose rivals were numerous and often violent.   To minimize disturbances merchants of one country were assigned quarters separate from those of another.

Fairs began to decline in importance after the fourteenth century, as traders could more readily go from town to town in all parts of the country and at all times of the year.

[1] " Court of the Dusty Feet " (*pieds poudrés*).   The wayfaring merchants went from fair to fair, and could not wait for the sitting of the regular courts.

7. INTERNATIONAL TRADE AT THE END OF THE MIDDLE AGES (II)

WE have seen (Chapter 6) that international trade in the Middle Ages was centred on the two seas—the Baltic and the Mediterranean. For centuries the Baltic trade was controlled by the Hansards and the Mediterranean trade by the Italians :

The Hansards and the Baltic Trade. The most powerful of all the groups were the Hansards, or the Easterlings, as they were called, who in the fourteenth century had formed an association of a large number of German cities, including Bremen, Hamburg, Danzig, and, most powerful of all, Lübeck, in defence of their trade interests. They established trading stations at Bergen, in Norway, Novgorod, in Russia, at Bruges, in Flanders, and in a large number of towns on the coasts of the North and Baltic Seas. (See Map 14.) Their main trading-centre in England was in London at the " Steelyard," the site of which is near the present Cannon Street railway station, but they had smaller settlements at Boston, in Lincolnshire, and King's Lynn, in Norfolk. At these centres they lived together as a community, but traded separately. Because of their great wealth and power they acquired great privileges in England, and paid lower customs duties than other merchants, not excluding the English themselves. The Baltic trade was a non-luxury trade, and the main commodities were timber, furs, fish, salt, naval stores (turpentine, tallow, pitch, and ropes). From England the Hansa merchants exported wool and, later, cloth.

The Italians and the Mediterranean Trade. The Italians monopolized the trade with the Mediterranean lands (Map 15). They brought luxury goods from the East, many of them from China. Chinese junks laden with silks and spices sailed to Java and Sumatra, and on to Ceylon. Here they were met by ships from India and ports around the Arabian Sea, laden with European goods. After the exchange the Arab ships returned to Basra, on the Persian Gulf, or went through the Red Sea to Suez. From Basra caravans brought the merchandise to Bagdad and on to Trebizond, on the Black Sea, or via Damascus to Aleppo and Antioch, on the Mediterranean coast, where Venetian galleys awaited them. There was also an overland route from China to Samarkand and Bokhara and thence, by a change of caravans, to the cities of Asia Minor (see Map 15).

The Italians transported their goods to western Europe in three different ways :

   (i) by the overland route across the Alpine passes to the fairs of the cities of southern Germany, such as Nuremberg and Augsburg (see Map 16) ;

  (ii) by sea to Marseilles, and thence up the Rhône valley and down the Seine to Paris and the fairs of Champagne ;

 (iii) by sea, through the Strait of Gibraltar, to Flanders. This route was not used to any great extent owing to fear of piracy, until the fourteenth century, when the Italian fleets became organized under Government protection. Bruges and Ghent then prospered, while the fairs of Champagne declined in importance. Some of the ' Flanders galleys ' sailed to Southampton and returned to the Mediterranean laden with wool and woollen cloth, England's main exports.

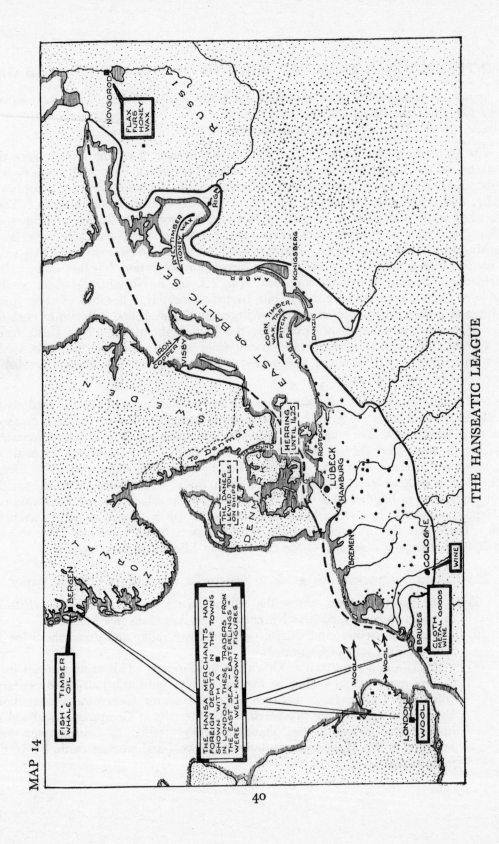

MAP 14

THE HANSEATIC LEAGUE

RUSSIA

NOVGOROD
FLAX
FURS
HONEY
WAX

RIGA

RYE · TIMBER
HONEY · WAX

EAST OR BALTIC SEA

AMBER

KONIGSBERG

CORN · TIMBER
WAX · TAR
PITCH

AMBER

DANZIG

IRON
COPPER

VISBY

SWEDEN

HERRING
UNTIL 1425

ROSTOCK

LÜBECK

HAMBURG

THE DANES
LEVIED TOLLS
ON SHIPS

To Denmark

DENMARK

BREMEN

COLOGNE

WINE

CLOTH
METAL GOODS
WINE

BRUGES

NORWAY

BERGEN

FISH · TIMBER
WHALE OIL

THE HANSA MERCHANTS HAD
FOREIGN DEPOTS IN THE TOWNS
SHOWN WITH A
IN LONDON THESE TRADERS FROM
THE EAST SEA — EASTERLINGS —
WERE WELL-KNOWN FIGURES.

WOOL

WOOL

LONDON

WOOL

MAP 15

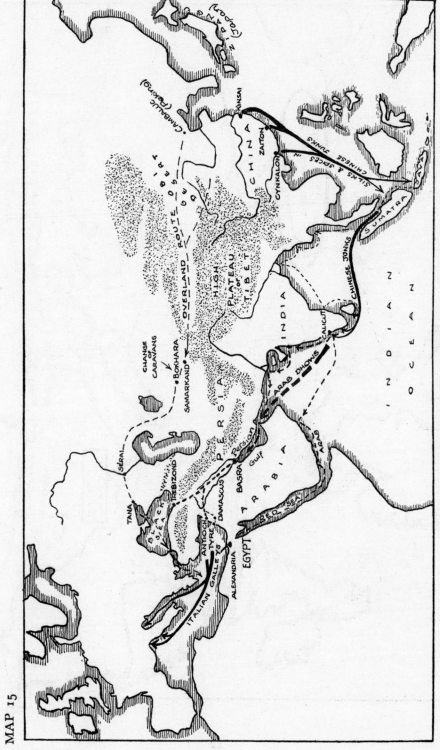

TRADE ROUTES TO THE FAR EAST

MAP 16

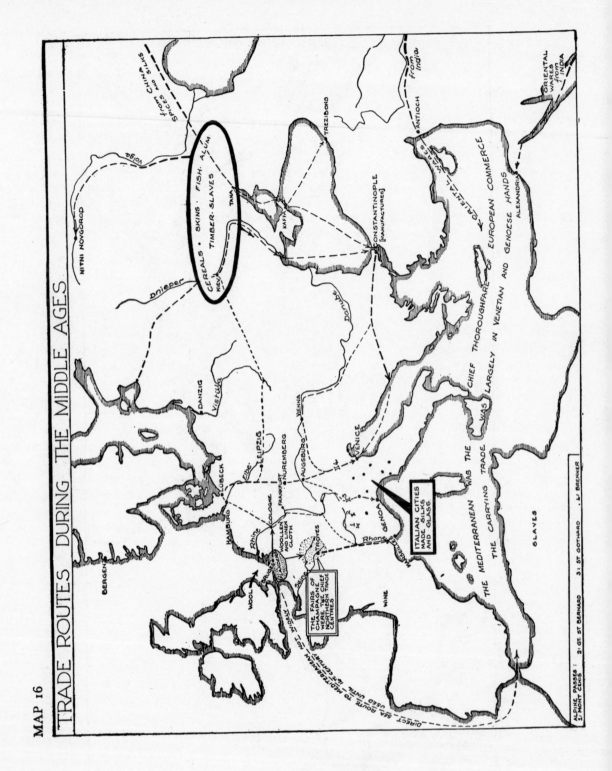

TRADE ROUTES DURING THE MIDDLE AGES

The Conflict between English Merchants and Foreign Merchants

In the early Middle Ages English merchants, in the main, left overseas trade to foreign merchants, the Flemings, Hansards, Jews, and Italians. Foreign merchants sold their goods at English fairs and markets. They were exceedingly unpopular with the gildsmen of the towns, who did all in their power to limit their privileges. Kings and barons protected the foreigners, however, because they helped them overcome their financial difficulties with loans and payments for licences to trade. By the middle of the sixteenth century English foreign trade was predominantly in English hands. The wool trade illustrates that this change took place through the granting of monopolies to traders by the State.

Export of Wool—the Merchants of the Staple

Method of collecting the Wool for Export. Sometimes the whole of a large crop of wool was bought by the exporters direct from the big landowners or from the monasteries. Sometimes, however, woolmen or broggers (middlemen) and the monasteries collected the wool from the small, scattered farmers and sold it to the export merchants. North-leach, in the Cotswolds, was the chief meeting-place of the broggers and the wool exporters (see Map 28). Other Cotswold towns, such as Chipping Campden and Cirencester, still show the wealth of those woolmen who beautified their towns with splendid houses and churches; so also do Lavenham and Sudbury, important towns in the woollen area of Suffolk.

To finance his wars Edward III levied heavy taxes (up to 33⅓ per cent.) on the export of raw wool, and also borrowed from Italian merchants on the security of the wool taxes. To ensure that the duties were properly collected certain towns, known as ' staples,' were chosen from which alone wool could be exported. The staple was finally fixed at Calais (1390). Calais was then in English hands, and the staple remained in the town for the most part until its conquest by the French in 1558.

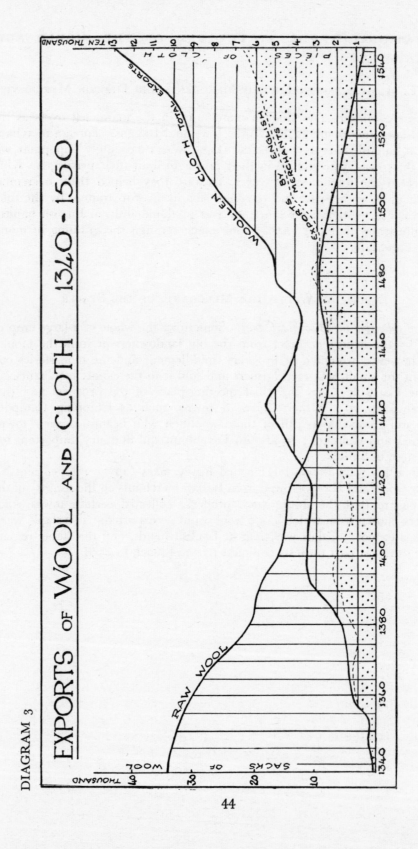

DIAGRAM 3

EXPORTS OF WOOL AND CLOTH 1340 - 1550

When Edward III defaulted and could obtain no further loans from Italian merchants he turned to an English company—the Merchants of the Staple, or Merchant Staplers—for help, and, in return for a loan, granted them a virtual monopoly of the export of wool from this country. The Merchants of the Staple at first prospered greatly, but the export taxes on wool became so high that foreign cloth-producers could not compete with English manufacturers, who purchased their wool at much lower prices. By the end of the fourteenth century exports of wool had begun to decline (Diagram 3) and the Staplers ceased to be important by the end of the sixteenth century.

EXPORT OF CLOTH—THE MERCHANT ADVENTURERS

From the early Middle Ages the export of woollen cloth had been largely in the hands of English merchants, prominent among whom were the Merchant Adventurers. Just as the Merchants of the Staple succeeded in ousting foreign competitors in the export trade in raw wool, so the Merchant Adventurers obtained the exclusive privilege of exporting woollen cloth. At first there was conflict with the Merchants of the Staple. Foreign competition was formidable, too, especially from merchants of the Hanseatic League. The Adventurers established trading-posts in Flanders, Germany, and Scandinavia, exchanging English cloth for Baltic products (see p. 39). They thus infringed the monopoly of the Hansards, who for a time were successful in excluding the English merchants from Baltic trade. The Adventurers endeavoured to restrict the privileges of the Hansa merchants in London, the chief market for the purchase and sale of woollen cloth. Clothiers brought their cloth to London, and from the end of the fourteenth century had to sell it at Blackwell (Bakewell) Hall ; here both Hansards and Adventurers purchased cloth.

After a long and bitter struggle the privileges of the Hanseatic League were revoked in 1552, and Elizabeth finally expelled them from England in 1580. The monopoly of the Merchant Adventurers remained until 1688. Other chartered corporations (largely controlled by Merchant Adventurers) were formed to trade with those parts of the Continent other than the Low Countries and Germany, where the Adventurers had established themselves.

In return for loans they made to the Government the Merchant Adventurers secured a monopoly of the export trade in woollen cloth. They were able to exclude not only foreigners but English merchants who were not members of the company. They also strove to restrict the production of cloth in order to secure higher prices. To this end they persuaded the Government to enact the Statute of Artificers (1562–63), forbidding anyone to be apprenticed to a weaver save he be the son of a £3 freeholder, and the Weavers Acts, of 1555 and 1558, restricting the number of looms a weaver could possess, as well as limiting the industry to the existing areas of production.

The trading companies described above are known as regulated companies, because all the merchants accepted the same trading rules, though they sold their goods individually. In the second half of the sixteenth century joint-stock companies were formed (see p. 57).

MAP 17

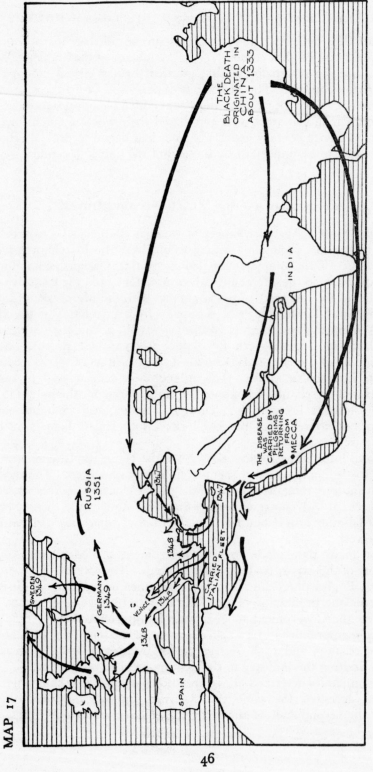

THE BLACK DEATH ORIGINATED IN CHINA ABOUT 1333

INDIA

THE DISEASE WAS CARRIED BY PILGRIMS RETURNING FROM
• MECCA

RUSSIA 1351

SWEDEN 1349

GERMANY 1349

VENICE

1347

1348

1348

1348

SPAIN

CARRIED BY ITALIAN FLEET

1347

HOW THE BLACK DEATH CAME TO ENGLAND

46

8. THE BREAKDOWN OF THE AGRICULTURAL SYSTEM

WE have noticed certain characteristics of the twelfth-century agriculture :

(i) Each village was largely self-sufficient, except for a few articles like salt, fish, and metals.

(ii) The inhabitants produced enough food for themselves, but seldom had a surplus to sell.

(iii) A man's rights and duties were defined by custom, and could not be changed except by permission of the lord.

During the thirteenth century this organization began to decay.

1. Enclosure of unused land took place. There was a growing population on the manor. Sons of villeins, unable to find land in the open fields, were forced to seek the lord's permission to cultivate land on the more fertile portions of the waste.[1] For this they paid a money rent. It was a satisfactory arrangement for the lord, as his estate was improved and his income raised. This extension of arable land, and the consequent increase in crops, led to a surplus of corn above the requirements of the manor. Excess food was usually sold to neighbouring towns. New holdings reclaimed from the waste were compact and not divided into strips : they were fenced from the straying cattle.

2. A peasant who grew rich from the sale of his surplus corn sought freedom from labour services he disliked by the payment of a money rent to the lord. Frequently, indeed, the lord himself was anxious to make the change, for he preferred to hire the more efficient workers from the ranks of the cottars and freed villeins. This practice of paying rent instead of doing work was known as the commutation of service, and developed gradually. In most cases week-work was commuted first and boon-work later : this was natural enough, for it must always have been a difficult problem to find enough labour on the lord's demesne at harvest-time.

(*Note :* Money was beginning to circulate more extensively owing to the growth of trade in towns and fairs ; otherwise the change-over could not have taken place.)

Particulars of the contract between the lord and the peasant were often made on the parchment rolls which recorded the transactions in the Manorial Court and the villein received a ' copy of the enrolment.' He was then said to hold his land ' by copy,' and known as a copyholder. Others remained villeins, but paid a money rent (molmen).

3. *The Black Death* (Maps 17 and 18). This terrible plague which spread westward from Asia, reaching its height in England between 1348 and 1349, carried off a third of the population ; a succession of cool, wet summers in Western Europe preceded the scourge, and the peasant population was weakened by lack of food. The consequences were serious—crops rotted in the fields, land lay idle, for there were few people left to cultivate it ; in some cases all the inhabitants of a village disappeared. Rich and poor alike suffered, though it appeared that the immediate result was beneficial to the lords, whose demesnes were greatly enlarged by the death of many tenants without heirs.

But the scarcity of labour proved to be an insuperable difficulty for the landlords,

---

[1] A process known as **assarting**.

MAP 18

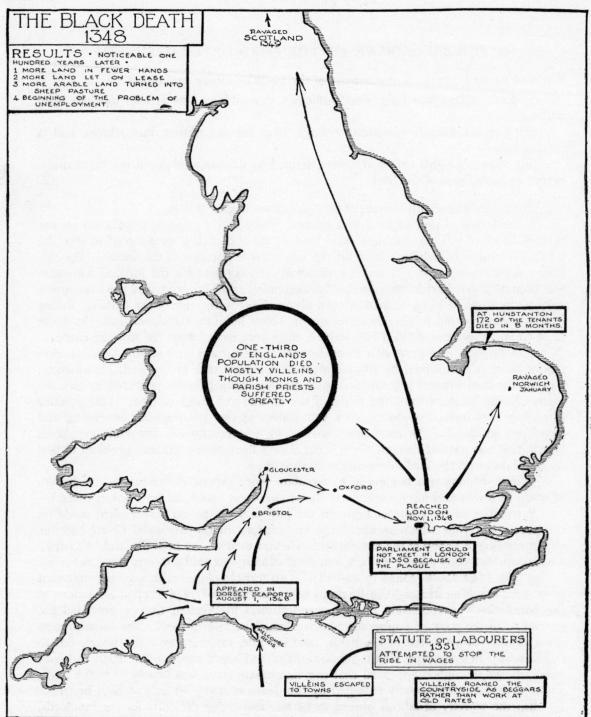

**THE BLACK DEATH
1348**

RESULTS · NOTICEABLE ONE
HUNDRED YEARS LATER ·
1 MORE LAND IN FEWER HANDS
2 MORE LAND LET ON LEASE
3 MORE ARABLE LAND TURNED INTO
  SHEEP PASTURE
4 BEGINNING OF THE PROBLEM OF
  UNEMPLOYMENT.

RAVAGED
SCOTLAND
1349

AT HUNSTANTON
172 OF THE TENANTS
DIED IN 8 MONTHS.

ONE-THIRD
OF ENGLAND'S
POPULATION DIED
MOSTLY VILLEINS
THOUGH MONKS AND
PARISH PRIESTS
SUFFERED
GREATLY

RAVAGED
NORWICH
JANUARY

GLOUCESTER

OXFORD

BRISTOL

REACHED
LONDON
NOV. 1, 1348

PARLIAMENT COULD
NOT MEET IN LONDON
IN 1350 BECAUSE OF
THE PLAGUE.

APPEARED IN
DORSET SEAPORTS
AUGUST 1, 1348

MELCOMBE
REGIS

STATUTE OF LABOURERS
1351
ATTEMPTED TO STOP THE
RISE IN WAGES

VILLEINS ESCAPED
TO TOWNS

VILLEINS ROAMED THE
COUNTRYSIDE AS BEGGARS
RATHER THAN WORK AT
OLD RATES.

THE BLACK DEATH IN ENGLAND

48

and, in the long run, it was the labourers who benefited most by demanding and securing higher wages. The lords met the problem in two ways.

(i) They sought the help of Parliament, which, by a royal ordinance of 1349 and a series of statutes between 1351 and 1368, generally known as the Statutes of Labourers, required every able-bodied man to hire himself out to a master at such wages as were paid before the Black Death.

This was the first attempt of the State to regulate wages in England. In spite of heavy penalties and serious attempts at enforcement, the statutes failed to prevent the continued rise of wages.

(ii) The lords not only refused further commutation of services but tried to restore the old system of labour services, though without success, for labour was so scarce that a villein found it possible to get work elsewhere. If the lord attempted to force the villein to work on his demesne, he fled and hoped to obtain his freedom by remaining uncaptured for a year and a day.

The general discontent of the times led to the widespread Peasants' Revolt of 1381. The determination of the villeins to be free was the chief cause, but heavy taxation to pay for war and hostility to the Church aroused by the preaching of the Lollards played their part in a rising in which every one with a grievance joined. The peasants gained none of their demands ; the rising was quelled, and the bitter struggle between lord and peasant continued (see Map 19).

The older organization rapidly decayed in the fourteenth century, for the Black Death helped to accelerate changes already at work :

Enclosures. Landlords consolidated their strips into compact holdings surrounded by hedges and fences, and the villeins found it convenient to do so as well. This practice was by no means uniform everywhere, but it was increasingly adopted.

Leasing of the Lord's Demesne. Landlords began to lease their demesne land to a tenant for a money rent. To the lord this was an advantage, since with the increase of towns and markets he could buy a regular supply of food and other commodities without the trouble of administering an estate.

In the first instance the tenant paid a rent not only for the land but for the implements and stock of animals as well. As the tenants grew richer land only was rented, as at the present time. A lord would often lease his manor including all the rights attached to the land and then go to live in a town on the income.

Enclosure for Sheep-farming. In the fifteenth century the sheep-farmers were interested in another form of enclosure, that of turning land which had previously been arable into pasture. (See Chapter 11.)

LANDHOLDING IN 1500

By 1500 land in England was held by three different types of person—the freeholder, the leaseholder, and the copyholder. The freeholders were about one-eighth of the total, and on the whole had small holdings of land. The leaseholders were about one-fifth of the total, and generally held their leases for short terms or at the will of the lord.

MAP 19

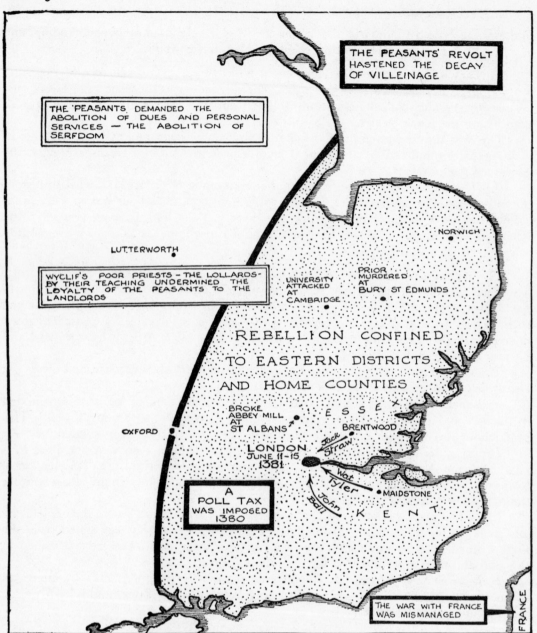

THE PEASANTS' REVOLT HASTENED THE DECAY OF VILLEINAGE

THE PEASANTS DEMANDED THE ABOLITION OF DUES AND PERSONAL SERVICES — THE ABOLITION OF SERFDOM

WYCLIF'S POOR PRIESTS — THE LOLLARDS — BY THEIR TEACHING UNDERMINED THE LOYALTY OF THE PEASANTS TO THE LANDLORDS

LUTTERWORTH

NORWICH

UNIVERSITY ATTACKED AT CAMBRIDGE

PRIOR MURDERED AT BURY ST EDMUNDS

REBELLION CONFINED TO EASTERN DISTRICTS AND HOME COUNTIES

BROKE ABBEY MILL AT ST ALBANS

ESSEX

OXFORD

BRENTWOOD

Jack Straw

LONDON JUNE 11-15 1381

Wat Tyler

John Ball

MAIDSTONE

A POLL TAX WAS IMPOSED 1380

KENT

THE WAR WITH FRANCE WAS MISMANAGED

FRANCE

THE PEASANTS' REVOLT

When the lease ran out they could be evicted. (Contrast this with the security of the freeholder.) The copyholders were very numerous, and to a certain extent had security of tenure as long as they paid their rent : but upon the death of a tenant the lord could demand a heavy fine from the incoming heir, who was forced to pay or see his land leased to another.

The most striking change in land-ownership in England during the period 1300–1500 was the increasing proportion of leaseholders.

MAP 20

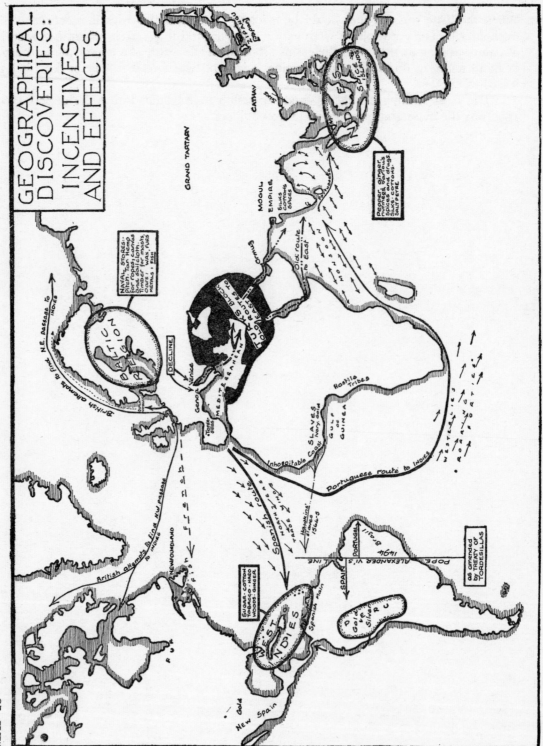

GEOGRAPHICAL
DISCOVERIES:
INCENTIVES
AND EFFECTS

52

PART II: TUDOR AND STUART PERIOD

9. THE WORLD AT THE END OF THE FIFTEENTH CENTURY

A Changing World

REMARKABLE changes occurred in Europe in the second half of the fifteenth and in the sixteenth century ; so far-reaching were they that they are considered to mark the beginning of modern history.

1. *The Enlargement of the Physical World*

For a thousand years Europe had few contacts with other continents, and little of the earth's surface was known. From the knowledge slowly acquired, however, geographical discovery became possible in the fifteenth century. This led to the spread of the civilization of Western Europe to the New World, and to the extension of its influence to parts of Africa and Asia.

2. *Enlarging the Intellectual World*

(i) *The Birth of Science.* In the Middle Ages men were more concerned with the purpose of nature than with its mechanism. Largely through Arabic influence in Spain, scholars had long been acquainted with the far-reaching thought of the great Greek thinkers : Moors, too, had introduced the science of mathematics into Europe. The earth and the stars were now studied in a new way, and astonishing discoveries in astronomy were made.

(ii) *Artistic Development—the Renaissance.* In the city states of Italy, the most cultured part of Europe, artists and writers had long discarded the restrictions imposed by ecclesiastical art. During the sixteenth century this attitude of mind (humanism) found its highest expression in the great scholar Erasmus, and in the supreme artists Raphael, Michelangelo, and Leonardo da Vinci. The introduction of the printing-press was a powerful factor in spreading the new learning.

(iii) *The Reformation.* The most far-reaching of these changes was the disruption of the Church which had given some unity to Europe for a thousand years.

3. *Social and Economic Changes*

Throughout the Middle Ages life on the manor was changing, and by the fourteenth century serfdom had begun to disappear in England, France, and Italy. The developments of trade and industry had led to the rise of a new middle-class of wealthy merchants.

4. *Change in Government—the Rise of National States*

In the fifteenth and sixteenth centuries there was a new type of king who attacked the power of the nobles and tried to unite his country. In England this process was

MAP 21

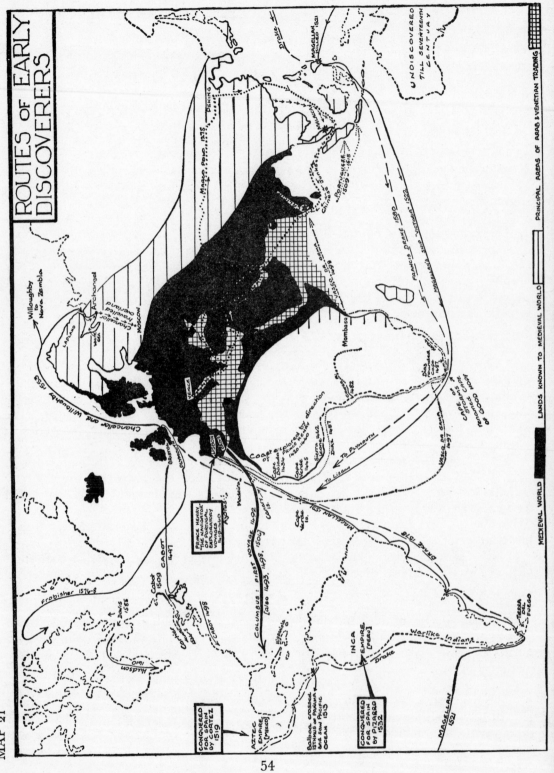

ROUTES of EARLY DISCOVERERS

facilitated by the Wars of the Roses ; on the Continent it was much slower. The middle class, hostile to the feudal nobles who interfered with trade, supported the King against the nobles.

THE GEOGRAPHICAL DISCOVERIES

There were many incentives to exploration in the fifteenth century.

1. *Need for a New Route to the East*

(i) The cost of carriage was extremely high, because goods had to be unloaded and transported by caravans (see p. 39).

(ii) The Turks obtained control of the trade routes early in the fifteenth century ; they did not wish to check trade but they imposed heavy tolls.

2. *Economic Stimulus*

Trade had greatly developed in the thirteenth and fourteenth centuries, and as Europe became more prosperous there was an increasing demand for the luxuries of the East. Surplus capital was available to finance a search for new markets. Trade with the East was draining Europe of silver, and merchants hoped to find new markets where they might exchange goods instead of silver.

3. *Religious Motives*

Prince Henry the Navigator of Portugal, the first man to organize voyages of explora-tion, was largely inspired by the desire to convert the African savages. Queen Isabella sent Columbus on a crusading mission. Later Jesuits played a large part in colonizing.

THE VOYAGES

1. *The Portuguese Route round Africa*

Prince Henry the Navigator prepared the way, until his death in 1460, by making maps of the west coast of Africa and by studying the science of navigation. In 1486 Diaz rounded the Cape, but returned after meeting heavy storms. In 1497 Vasco da Gama made the first sea-voyage to India. The Portuguese soon dominated the spice-trade in the Indian Ocean, and Venice lost its eastern trade.

2. *The Spanish Route—Westward*

In 1492 Columbus, a Genoese sailor, persuaded Ferdinand and Isabella of Spain to allow him three small ships to attempt the westward route to the east. After ten weeks he reached the Bahamas, but, having miscalculated the circumference of the earth, he assumed he had reached the East Indies. His subsequent voyages failed to reveal his mistake. A few years later Cortez and Pizarro revealed and obtained for Spain the wealth of the New World.

3. *The English and French attempts—north-west*

Cabot was dispatched by Henry VII in 1497 to the north-west. He reached the Canadian coast of Newfoundland, already known to Breton fishermen. In 1534 Cartier, a Frenchman, sailed up the St Lawrence. Many attempts were made, even until the end of the eighteenth century, to find a north-west passage. In 1553 Willoughby and Chancellor tried the less likely north-east route ; Willoughby was drowned in 1554. Chancellor, however, opened up trade with Muscovy, but was himself drowned in 1556.

RESULT OF THE DISCOVERIES

1. *New Significance of the Atlantic Seaboard*

The Portuguese sea-route to India increased the wealth and importance of countries on the Atlantic seaboard. Lisbon succeeded Venice as the headquarters of the Indian trade ; the Mediterranean lost its economic supremacy.

2. *Influx of Silver and its Widespread Effects*

From Mexico, Peru, and New Granada silver poured into Spain, and from hence to other states to pay Spanish debts. It provided a great stimulus to trade, which had suffered from a scarcity of bullion. The increase in the quantity of silver led to an increase in the price of goods, and prices trebled between 1550 and 1600 ; the poorer classes suffered intensely during the period of adjustment, and became discontented everywhere in Europe. The middle class, and especially the merchants, became richer and more powerful.

3. *Other Effects on Trade*

(i) The Portuguese discoveries brought an immediate increase of Indian trade (spices and silks), though other nations did not gain directly until the seventeenth century.

(ii) The Spanish discoveries brought new commodities—tobacco, sugar, and the potato. The English developed the iniquitous slave trade in the New World.

4. *Colonies and Imperialistic Wars*

The discoveries led to rivalry among the European states. Portugal and Spain were the first to establish colonies. The English and the Dutch attacked the Spaniards and the Portuguese in the sixteenth century, and then followed conflict between the English and Dutch in the seventeenth century, and between the English and French in the eighteenth century.

5. *A New Type of Ship*

The oared galley suitable for the inland Mediterranean Sea was displaced by the ocean-going sailing-ship. Lepanto (1571) was the last victory of the galley ; the defeat of the Armada (1588) the first victory of the new ship.

10. COMMERCIAL EXPANSION UNDER THE TUDORS: CHARTERED COMPANIES

IT was in Elizabeth's reign that a great expansion of overseas trade took place. She encouraged merchants to form trading companies, and gave them charters conferring a monopoly of trade in stated areas, with the right to defend their trade by force. Only a few of these were regulated companies (see p. 45), such as the Merchant Adventurers, which was active well into the seventeenth century, and the Eastland Company, formed in 1579, which took control of the Baltic trade.

The new type of trading organization, the joint-stock company, in which the

MAP 22

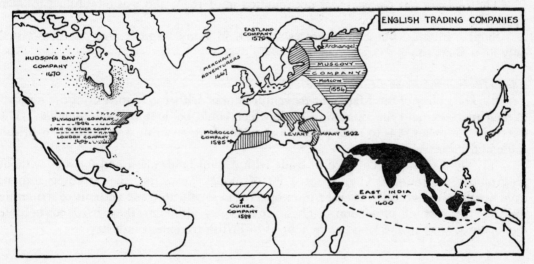

merchants put their capital into a common fund and shared the profits, was more suitable for trading in distant lands.

The *Russia Company*, formed in 1553, was the first. It financed Willoughby and Chancellor's explorations (see p. 54), and gained concessions for trading with Russia. For a short time trade was opened up with Persia. This Company declined in the seventeenth century.

The *Levant Company*, founded in 1592 by the amalgamation of two older companies, for trade with Turkey and the Mediterranean, also opened up trade with Persia, and soon outdistanced the Russia Company in trade with the East. Its trade was limited to the Mediterranean after the formation of the East India Company. Its monopoly survived until the beginning of the nineteenth century.

The Africa Companies, such as the *Morocco Company*, formed in 1585, and the *Guinea Company*, formed in 1588, developed the slave trade.

Greatest of all these chartered companies was the *East India Company*. The first voyages, begun in the year following Elizabeth's charter of 1600, were joint stock for separate voyages—that is to say, stock was sold and capital and profits redistributed after each voyage. In 1612 a system of joint stock for a fixed number of voyages was attempted ; transformed into a permanent joint-stock company in 1657, the company was able to establish permanent officials, and to maintain its fleet of ' Indiamen.' It was given a monopoly of trade with Asia, and first challenged the Dutch in the Spice Islands, whence it was expelled after the massacre of Amboyna, in 1623. The English merchants had to be content with the mainland of India, and, after overcoming the Portuguese, some of the first factories were established at Surat in 1612, Madras in 1639, Bombay in 1665, and Calcutta in 1690.

At home there was some criticism of the Indian trade because silver had to be exported to pay for the cotton and the spices (pepper and cloves), for woollen goods were not wanted in these tropical lands.

The *Hudson's Bay Company* was not founded until 1670, and was established to open up the fur trade in Canada.

Similar trading companies were established in France and Spain, but they lasted only for a short time.

Effect of the Companies on British trade

(i) The policy of the Merchant Adventurers was deliberately to restrict the number of their members and the amount of trade which could be done by each member. The effects of the policy was to raise prices, and in the long run this was harmful to British trade and industry.

(ii) The Companies engaged in trade with distant lands often had to work without government protection. They spent a lot of money protecting their trading stations from attack, and naturally resented interlopers who sought to trade without contributing towards the cost of protection. These companies, although they tried to become monopolists, were in the long run beneficial to British trade and industry.

11. CHANGES IN AGRICULTURE IN THE SIXTEENTH CENTURY

IN the sixteenth century important developments in agriculture revolutionized the life of rural England. These changes mark a step from subsistence farming towards capitalist agriculture.

CAUSES

1. The Tudor Age was one in which money and money-making played a dominant part in the life of the country. Money was required to finance the new overseas ventures. Landowners saw no reason why profits derived from land should not be invested in trade concerns, and therefore adopted the best methods for securing the highest profits. A simple way of doing this was to raise rents to the highest possible level.

DIAGRAM 4

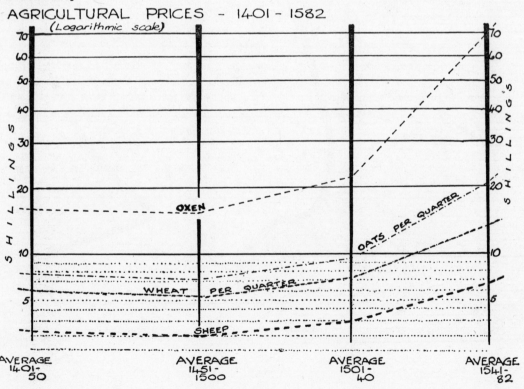

AGRICULTURAL PRICES - 1401 - 1582

MAP 23

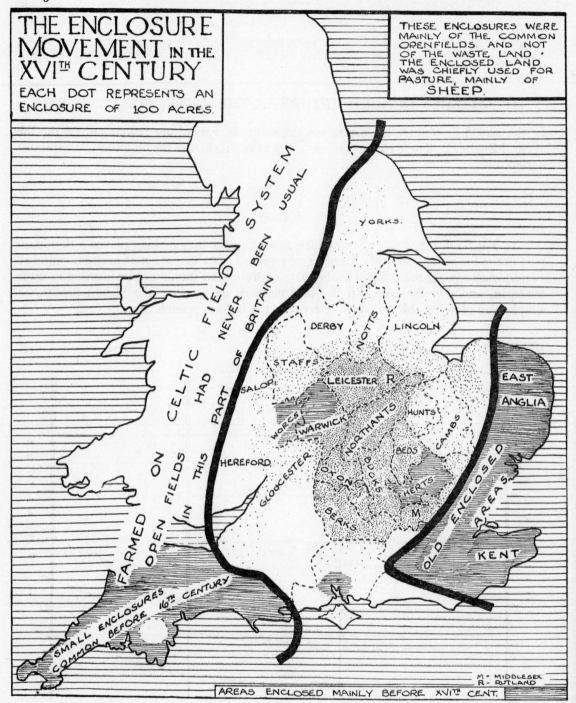

THE ENCLOSURE MOVEMENT IN THE XVIth CENTURY

EACH DOT REPRESENTS AN ENCLOSURE OF 100 ACRES.

THESE ENCLOSURES WERE MAINLY OF THE COMMON OPENFIELDS, AND NOT OF THE WASTE LAND. THE ENCLOSED LAND WAS CHIEFLY USED FOR PASTURE, MAINLY OF SHEEP.

NEVER PART OF BRITAIN HAD BEEN USUAL

CELTIC FIELD SYSTEM

FARMED ON OPEN FIELDS IN THIS

SMALL ENCLOSURES COMMON BEFORE 16TH CENTURY

YORKS.

DERBY   NOTTS   LINCOLN

STAFFS

SALOP   LEICESTER   R   EAST ANGLIA

WORCS   WARWICK   HUNTS

HEREFORD   NORTHANTS   BEDS   CAMBS

GLOUCESTER   OXON   BUCKS   HERTS   OLD ENCLOSED AREAS

BERKS   M   KENT

M - MIDDLESEX
R - RUTLAND

AREAS ENCLOSED MAINLY BEFORE XVITH CENT.

2. In the sixteenth century there was a remarkable rise in prices (see Diagram 4). This had many possible causes—the debasement of the coinage of Henry VIII (the silver content being restored by Elizabeth), the influx of silver from Mexico and Peru towards the end of the century, and the great increase in population after 1500 all played some part. The increase in prices adversely affected landlords, who, ignoring old traditions, tried by every possible means to make more money out of their land.

3. There was a wave of land speculation, because some impoverished landowners were forced to sell their land, and Henry VIII put on sale the monastic lands he had confiscated after the dissolution of the monasteries.

DIAGRAM 5

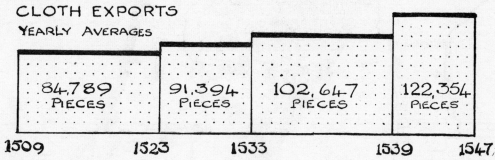

CLOTH EXPORTS
YEARLY AVERAGES

84,789 PIECES — 1509
91,394 PIECES — 1523
102,647 PIECES — 1533
122,354 PIECES — 1539
1547

4. Merchants bought estates as investments from which they hoped to obtain a good revenue. Disregarding the customs of the manor and the rights of their tenants, they demanded exorbitant rents, and resorted to eviction. They turned to sheep-rearing—the most profitable kind of farming, as the demand for wool was increasing with the rapid development of the woollen industry. (Diagram 5 and Map 23.)

AGRICULTURAL CHANGES

1. *Enclosure of the Arable Fields.* There was some change-over from arable farming to pasture, particularly in the Midlands—for example, in Leicestershire, Northampton-shire, Rutlandshire, and south-east Warwickshire. This involved the enclosure of arable land. It was a new feature, and one which was bitterly resented by the peasants.

2. *Enclosure of the Common Land.* There was a considerable enclosure of the common land in other parts of England. The lord took what he regarded as his share of the common land and enclosed it. No compensation was given to the local inhabitants, in spite of considerable hardship that followed the enclosure.

3. *Eviction of Tenants.* All over England leasehold tenants were evicted and rents raised. Smallholdings were enclosed and united into large farms. All this was done mainly by the old process—common in the fifteenth century—of charging high fines when an heir succeeded, turning copyholds into leaseholds, and increasing the rent at the end of the term of the lease. As a result some areas, such as parts of the Yorkshire

MAP 24

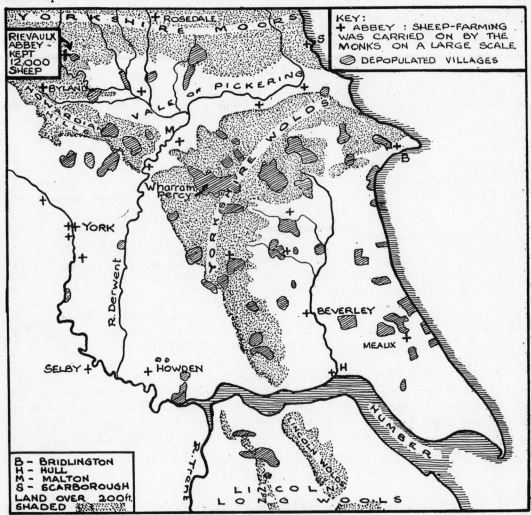

KEY:
+ ABBEY : SHEEP-FARMING WAS CARRIED ON BY THE MONKS ON A LARGE SCALE
DEPOPULATED VILLAGES

RIEVAULX ABBEY KEPT 12,000 SHEEP

B - BRIDLINGTON
H - HULL
M - MALTON
S - SCARBOROUGH
LAND OVER 200 ft. SHADED

THE YORKSHIRE WOLDS TO SHOW DEPOPULATION AFTER
THE ENCLOSURES

Wolds (Map 24), which were formerly well-populated were depopulated, and villages disappeared. There were disturbances in many places, for the peasants who lost their land could find no employment. They became vagrants.

THE ATTITUDE OF THE STATE

The Tudor rulers were primarily concerned with maintaining order, and they were forced to take action with regard to agrarian changes, as discontent led to rebellions, some of which were serious, like Ket's Rebellion of 1549 and the Pilgrimage of Grace of

1536. The Government supported the small tenants and tried to restrain the landlords because :

(i) tenants were the most numerous class, and it was vital that they should be loyal ;

(ii) they were the mainstay of the army of the day—the Yeomen of England had to be prepared to fight in time of war ;

(iii) they contributed to the taxes. Eviction of tenants produced a reduction in the State revenue, for taxes (the subsidies—p. 177) were assessed on farm stock and movable goods.

By a series of statutes the Tudor kings tried to check the enclosures, and even to reconvert pasture to tillage land. They did not expressly prohibit the conversion of arable lands, but aimed at maintaining a certain amount of land under the plough. The enforcement of the statutes was in the hands of the Privy Council, who with the aid of the Star Chamber and other bodies issued orders to local Justices of the Peace. These were unpaid officials, insufficiently trained to carry out this complicated task, and, being landowners, not unsympathetic to those responsible for enclosure. The latter, the wealthiest men in the country, were also able to influence the Privy Council to stop proceedings when they evaded the law.

How far was the State successful ? The Tudor rulers did not succeed in preventing enclosure of land altogether, but they did restrict it. On the other hand, many copyholders suffered eviction. Even so, when the customary rights of the manor were ignored tenants could appeal to the King's courts, which were more sympathetic to them. This, however, was too expensive a step for the majority.

In Stuart times, owing to troubles arising from the Civil War, the Privy Council was not in a position to protect the smallholder. By this time, though enclosure of the land continued, arable land was not usually converted. The population of the country was increasing, and corn-growing became more profitable than formerly.

12. REGULATION OF TRADE IN TUDOR AND STUART TIMES

ELIZABETH and her Ministers were greatly influenced by the theories known as mercantilism. Mercantilism was based on the belief that, as wealth is the basis of the power of a State, the Governments ought to encourage and regulate its production by controlling agriculture, industry, and trade.

The *aims* of Elizabeth and the earlier Stuarts were :

(i) To encourage shipping for the defence of the realm and the promotion of wealth.

(ii) To keep a favourable balance of trade—that is, to prevent an excess of imports over exports so that the State should not be weakened by the export of gold and silver. Tariffs were imposed on foreign imports, and so English agriculture and industry were protected.

(iii) To encourage by monopolies, bounties, and tariffs those industries which were considered beneficial to England, especially those necessary in war-time (such as ship-building and the iron industry). The granting of monopolies was regulated by Statute in 1624 owing to abuse of the right to grant them by the Stuart kings.

(iv) To organize industry and trade in the forms it would be easiest to control. Chartered companies were favoured, and, while the gild system was maintained, regulations were imposed which weakened the gilds. The most remarkable effort to regulate industry was the Act of Apprentices or Artificers, 1562–63.

(v) To encourage foreign workers to come to England to teach their skills to English workmen.

There had been State regulation of wages before this, as in the Statutes of Labourers (see p. 49). From the fourteenth century wages were fixed locally by Justices of the Peace, though Parliament fixed the maximum rates.

By the Statute of 1562–63 :

(*a*) J.P.s were given complete freedom to fix wages—that is, at the maximum rate. This helped employers to resist demands for higher wages.

(*b*) A system of seven years' apprenticeship was made compulsory for all workers.

(*c*) General regulations about industry were made with the object of controlling vagrants who roamed the countryside ; for instance, workers leaving a parish must carry a certificate of character.

THE POOR LAW

The greatest evil of the time was unemployment arising from the break-up of the medieval agricultural system, the disbanding of feudal retainers by the barons, the dissolution of the monasteries, and the widening gap between prices and wages. There was also at times considerable unemployment among the woollen workers owing to fluctuations in the export of woollen cloth.

The Tudor Government was greatly concerned at the alarming increase in the number of " sturdy vagabonds." There had always been the poor to deal with, and their relief was regarded as one of the duties of the Church. In medieval times the monks distributed alms, the gilds supported orphans and widows, and charitable persons left money for hospitals and almshouses.

By the sixteenth century the problem of poverty was acute ; the Government feared the poor would resort to violence and considered the problem from the following points of view :

(i) Relief of the destitute.
(ii) Punishment for the idle.
(iii) Fixing responsible officials to organize the relief.

Many regulations were made imposing harsh punishments for begging, and Houses of Correction, or Bridewells, were established in which the able-bodied were compelled to work and the idle punished. (Bridewell House in London was the first of its kind.) Finally, all the laws were consolidated in the famous Act of 1601 by which :

(i) parishes were to provide work for the unemployed ;
(ii) children of poor persons were to be apprenticed ;
(iii) relief was to be given to the lame, the impotent, and the blind—that is, to those unable to work ;
(iv) idle rogues were to be sent to prisons or houses of correction.

The administration of the Act was given to the Tudor man-of-all-work, the Justice of the Peace, who was given the power to levy a poor rate. Overseers of the Poor were to be appointed to carry out the work of collection and distribution. The Privy Council had the work of the Justices under constant supervision until the outbreak of the Civil War in 1640, when central control broke down, and there followed much local variation in the administration of the Act. Nevertheless, this statute was the basis of all poor-law administration until 1834.

MAP 25

NORTH AMERICA EARLY SETTLEMENTS

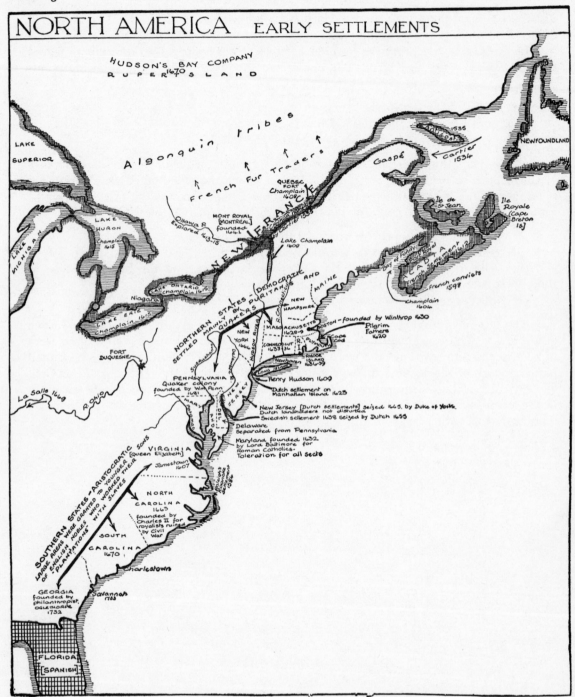

HUDSON'S BAY COMPANY
RUPERT'S LAND 1670

LAKE SUPERIOR

Algonquin tribes

French Fur Traders

LAKE HURON Champlain 1615

LAKE MICHIGAN

NEWFOUNDLAND

Cartier 1535

Gaspé

Cartier 1534

QUEBEC FORT Champlain 1608

Ile de St Jean

Ile Royale [Cape Breton Is]

MONT ROYAL [MONTREAL] founded 1641

Ottawa R. Explored 1613-15

NEW FRANCE

Lake Champlain 1609

Champlain 1604

ACADIA French convicts 1598

Bay of Fundy

Champlain 1604

LAKE ONTARIO Champlain 1615

Niagara

LAKE ERIE Champlain 1615

FORT DUQUESNE

La Salle 1669

OHIO

NORTHERN STATES — DEMOCRATIC AND SETTLED MAINLY BY PURITANS AND QUAKERS

MAINE

NEW HAMPSHIRE

MASSACHUSETTS 1628-9

Boston founded by Winthrop 1630

Pilgrim Fathers 1620

Cape Cod

CONNECTICUT 1633-36

RHODE ISLAND 1636-39

Newhaven

Long Island

NEW YORK 1664

HUDSON RIVER

Henry Hudson 1609

Dutch settlement on Manhattan Island 1623

New Jersey [Dutch settlements] seized 1665. by Duke of York. Dutch landholders not disturbed.

Swedish settlement 1638 seized by Dutch 1655

Delaware separated from Pennsylvania

Maryland founded 1632. by Lord Baltimore for Roman Catholics. Toleration for all sects

PENNSYLVANIA Quaker colony founded by Wm Penn 1681

Susquehanna

NEW JERSEY

MARYLAND

DELAWARE

VIRGINIA [Queen Elizabeth]

Jamestown 1607

Raleigh's Settlement 1586

NORTH CAROLINA 1663 founded by Charles II for royalists ruined by Civil War

SOUTHERN STATES — ARISTOCRATIC LARGE AREAS WERE GRANTED TO YOUNGER SONS OF ENGLISH NOBLES WHO WORKED THEIR PLANTATIONS WITH SLAVES

SOUTH CAROLINA 1670

Charlestown

GEORGIA founded by philanthropist Oglethorpe 1732

Savannah 1733

FLORIDA [SPANISH]

13. COLONIZATION IN THE SEVENTEENTH CENTURY

In the seventeenth century Englishmen emigrated to America to make new homes. The settlers were religious exiles (Puritans, Quakers, Catholics) or the younger sons of the gentry. Many of these new ventures were dependent on the financial support of merchants whose object was to expand their commerce. The Crown assisted them by granting a monopoly of trade.

Map 25 shows that English settlements in North America were confined to the coastal plain from Nova Scotia to Georgia.

A. THE NEW ENGLAND COLONIES

The earliest of the Puritan colonies was Plymouth, founded in 1620 by the Pilgrim Fathers, who were financed by the Plymouth Company, a group of London merchants. The most successful colony was Massachusetts Bay, founded in 1628. In these northern settlements the colonists engaged in agriculture, lumbering, fishing, and shipbuilding. Farming was difficult, for neither the soil nor the climate was favourable. The abundance of lumber and the excellent harbours encouraged the settlers to build ships and to supplement their food supplies with the harvest of the sea.

B. PLANTATION COLONIES

At the southern end of the coastal plain five more colonies developed. Here the climate was much warmer, and suitable for growing tobacco, sugar, and cotton. These were cultivated in plantations, and Negro slaves were brought from West Africa to do the work. The planters became a rich aristocracy.

(i) *Virginia*, founded 1606. The two attempts of Sir Walter Raleigh in 1584 and 1587 to establish a colony failed ; the permanent settlement began in 1606, when the London Company was formed. Jamestown was founded the following year. The Company went bankrupt, and the colonists suffered great misfortunes until 1625 when the tobacco plantations began to prosper.

(ii) *Maryland*, founded in 1632 by Lord Baltimore, a Catholic, who obtained a charter from Charles I making him the proprietor of an area north of Virginia. This colony also grew rich by its exports of tobacco.

(iii) *The Carolinas* were founded in 1663 by leading politicians of Charles II, who obtained a charter to colonize the area south of Virginia. This region was so large that two colonies were formed ; North Carolina developed slowly, but South Carolina, with its cotton plantations, was more successful.

(iv) *Georgia*, founded in 1732 by James Oglethorpe, was the last of the five southern colonies. Slaves were introduced to work the cotton- and rice-fields ; the planters became rich.

COLONIAL TRADE

MAP 26

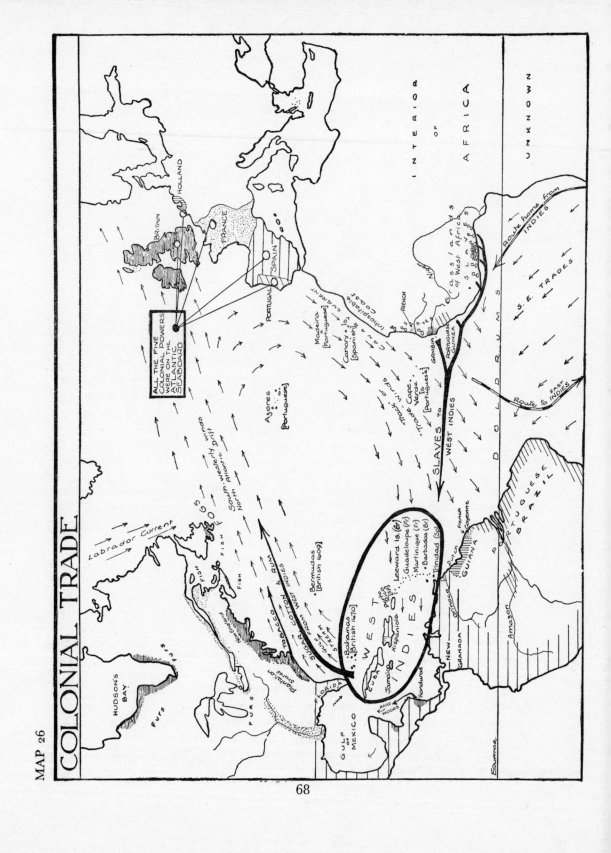

ALL THE FIVE COLONIAL POWERS WERE ON THE ATLANTIC SEABOARD

HUDSON'S BAY

FURS

FURS

Labrador Current

FISH

FISH

FISH

FOGS

New England

Plantation States

GULF OF MEXICO

FLORIDA

GULF STREAM

SUGAR FROM WEST INDIES

TOBACCO & RUM COTTON

Bermudas [British 1609]

Bahamas [British 1670]

WEST INDIES

Cuba

Jamaica [Br]

Hispaniola

Honduras

HARD WOODS

Leeward Is. [Br]

Guadeloupe [Fr]

Martinique [Fr]

Barbados [Br]

Trinidad [Sp]

NEW GRANADA

Dutch & French GUIANA

Cayenne

Amazon

PORTUGUESE BRAZIL

South-westerly winds North Atlantic

Azores [Portuguese]

Madeira [Portuguese]

Canary Is. [Spanish]

Trade Cape Verde Is. [Portuguese]

Trade winds

CANARY CURRENT

Inhospitable Coast

Cape Guinea Coast

GAMBIA

French

Portuguese Guinea

Niger

Grasslands of West Africa

SLAVES

SLAVES to WEST INDIES

Route home from INDIES

DOLDRUMS

S.E. TRADES

Route to INDIES EAST

INTERIOR OF AFRICA

ZONE ?

BRITAIN

HOLLAND

FRANCE

SPAIN

PORTUGAL

EQUATOR

68

C. THE MIDDLE COLONIES

The New England states were separated from the five southern states by three foreign settlements and the Quaker colony of Pennsylvania. Swedes had settled at the mouth of the river Delaware, and the Dutch founded colonies (later New York and New Jersey) at the mouth of the river Hudson. These were seized by the English in 1664. When William Penn, a leading Quaker, obtained a royal charter in 1681, the coast was already occupied, so he sent an expedition inland up the Delaware river. His Quaker colonists made friends with the Indians, and rapidly prospered.

D. OTHER SETTLEMENTS

(i) *Newfoundland.* Annexed by Sir Humphrey Gilbert in 1583, this barren island was inhospitable. Its valuable fisheries made it the most important of all the English possessions in the sixteenth century.

(ii) *Bermudas.* One of the early expeditions to Virginia was shipwrecked on Bermuda, and this led to the establishment of a colony in 1609.

(iii) *West Indies.* The Leeward Islands and Barbados were colonized in 1623 and 1624, and became prosperous when wealthy Cavaliers who left England after the Civil War set up sugar plantations. Jamaica was taken from Spain in 1655, but the settlement was a failure until sugar-planting was introduced in the eighteenth century.

(iv) *Hudson's Bay Company* was founded in 1670 with the object of bringing furs from the lands around the bay which had been explored by Henry Hudson in 1610. This company was interested only in trade, and discouraged settlers.

Map 26 shows the main features of colonial trade in the seventeenth and eighteenth centuries. Note that all the five colonial Powers were on the Atlantic seaboard of western Europe.

14. TRADE POLICY IN THE SEVENTEENTH AND EIGHTEENTH CENTURIES (MERCANTILISM)

THE mercantilist principles which were discussed on p. 64 continued to influence the policy of English Governments in the seventeenth and eighteenth centuries. Laws were passed in the interests of the farmers and for the protection of home industries, navigation Acts to encourage the growth of shipping, and laws concerning the colonies and mother country were also an important part of the trade system. The primary object behind all this legislation was to increase the national wealth and safety.

AGRICULTURE

Farmers were protected by the passing of Corn Laws (the first of this type was in 1663) imposing duties on foreign wheat when the price fell below a stated amount. They were encouraged to export corn by the payment of export bounties.

INDUSTRY

The export of manufactured goods and the import of raw materials required for the home market were encouraged. The import of luxury goods, or of those which competed with home production, was forbidden. Help was given to industries considered necessary to the welfare of the nation. The best example of protective industrial policy may be seen in the cloth industry. Those who exported raw wool were punished severely, and the import of foreign cloth was prohibited altogether after 1660. Foreign textiles such as Chinese silks and Indian calicoes were excluded, so that there was no competition with the home production of woollen cloth. Efforts were made to stimulate trade—for instance, one of the many regulations insisted that university graduates and members of certain professions like judges must wear gowns made of woollen cloth. Similarly, skilled artisans were not allowed to emigrate, while foreign craftsmen were encouraged to make their homes in England. The export of machinery was prohibited.

SHIPPING

Navigation Acts had been passed from the fourteenth century onward with the object of encouraging shipping. The Tudors strongly favoured such a policy. The most famous of all the Navigation Acts, those passed in 1651 and 1660, were passed to enforce the carriage of goods to England in English ships or in ships of the country which had produced the goods.

Not everybody agrees that this policy was to the advantage of England. The object of the Commonwealth Government which passed the Act of 1651 was to destroy the carrying trade of the Dutch, but one probable result was that the English lost much of the Baltic trade to the Dutch.

Foreign Trade

The commercial classes insisted that the Whig Governments who relied on their support should impose restrictions on those countries which sold to us more than they bought from us. Trade with France was discouraged, and that with Portugal favoured : by the Methuen Treaty (1703) duties on Portuguese wine were less than those on French, and English cloth gained almost a complete monopoly in the Portuguese market. Much gold from Brazil found its way to London.

Colonial Regulations

The policy common to all European countries was to regulate the trade of colonies in the interest of the mother country. English colonists were expected to purchase English manufactured goods, and to supply raw materials and other articles which could not be produced in England. (Great value was attached to the West Indies, which produced cane sugar.) The colonists were not permitted to manufacture articles which were made in England, and they were expected to sell certain articles, set down in the Navigation Acts, like tobacco, sugar, naval stores, rice, to England alone. No restrictions were placed on the sale of commodities, such as fish, which were in plentiful supply in England.

The colonists also benefited from this system. They had a stable market for their goods at a time when their commercial development was in its infancy.

MAP 27

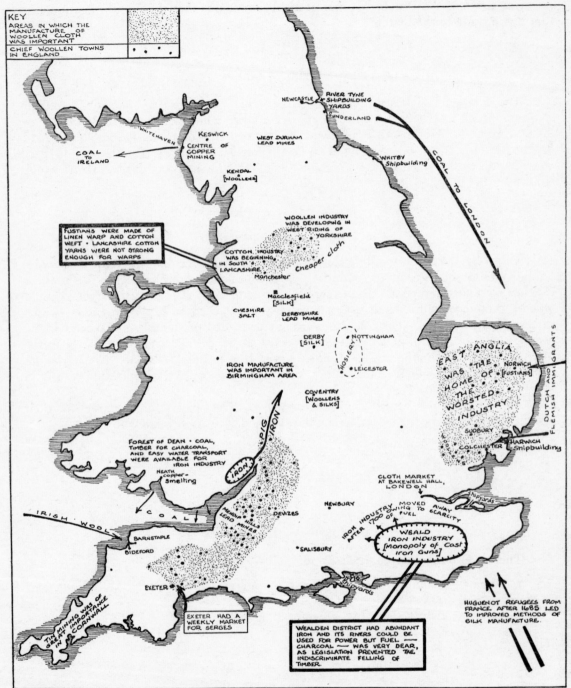

KEY
AREAS IN WHICH THE MANUFACTURE OF WOOLLEN CLOTH WAS IMPORTANT
CHIEF WOOLLEN TOWNS IN ENGLAND

NEWCASTLE
RIVER TYNE SHIPBUILDING YARDS
SUNDERLAND
WHITBY Shipbuilding
COAL TO LONDON

WHITEHAVEN
COAL TO IRELAND
KESWICK CENTRE OF COPPER MINING
WEST DURHAM LEAD MINES
KENDAL [WOOLLENS]

WOOLLEN INDUSTRY WAS DEVELOPING IN WEST RIDING OF YORKSHIRE
Cheaper cloth

FUSTIANS WERE MADE OF LINEN WARP AND COTTON WEFT. LANCASHIRE COTTON YARNS WERE NOT STRONG ENOUGH FOR WARPS

COTTON INDUSTRY WAS BEGINNING IN SOUTH LANCASHIRE
Manchester
Macclesfield [SILK]
CHESHIRE SALT
DERBYSHIRE LEAD MINES

DERBY [SILK]
NOTTINGHAM
hosiery
LEICESTER

IRON MANUFACTURE WAS IMPORTANT IN BIRMINGHAM AREA

COVENTRY [WOOLLENS & SILKS]

EAST ANGLIA WAS THE HOME OF THE WORSTED INDUSTRY
NORWICH [FUSTIANS]
DUTCH AND FLEMISH IMMIGRANTS
SUDBURY
COLCHESTER
HARWICH Shipbuilding

FOREST OF DEAN. COAL, TIMBER FOR CHARCOAL, AND EASY WATER TRANSPORT WERE AVAILABLE FOR IRON INDUSTRY
NEATH copper-smelting
PIG IRON
IRON

CLOTH MARKET AT BAKEWELL HALL, LONDON
Shipyards

IRISH WOOL
COAL
MENDIP HILLS LEAD MINES
BARNSTAPLE
BIDEFORD
DEVIZES
NEWBURY

IRON INDUSTRY MOVED AWAY AFTER 1700 OWING TO SCARCITY OF FUEL
WEALD IRON INDUSTRY [Monopoly of Cast Iron Guns]

SALISBURY
Shipyards

EXETER
TIN MINING WAS OF GREAT IMPORTANCE IN CORNWALL

EXETER HAD A WEEKLY MARKET FOR SERGES

WEALDEN DISTRICT HAD ABUNDANT IRON AND ITS RIVERS COULD BE USED FOR POWER BUT FUEL — CHARCOAL — WAS VERY DEAR, AS LEGISLATION PREVENTED THE INDISCRIMINATE FELLING OF TIMBER.

HUGUENOT REFUGEES FROM FRANCE AFTER 1685 LED TO IMPROVED METHODS OF SILK MANUFACTURE.

ENGLAND BEFORE THE INDUSTRIAL REVOLUTION

PART III: ENGLAND BEFORE THE INDUSTRIAL REVOLUTION

15. INDUSTRIAL ENGLAND ABOUT 1700

In 1700 England was still mainly an agricultural country, but there was, as we have seen, a considerable export trade and many industries, of which the manufacture of woollen cloth was by far the most important. The industry was protected by the Government, for both the export of raw wool and the import of foreign cloth were prohibited. It had benefited from the skill of immigrants, from Flanders in the fourteenth century, from the Netherlands in the sixteenth century, and from France in the seventeenth century.

Woollen cloth was made in practically every village of England, but three areas were particularly important :

(i) Gloucester and Somerset and neighbouring counties in the West of England. This area was famous for its fine cloths and flannels.

(ii) The West Riding of Yorkshire produced cheaper cloths.

(iii) Norfolk and Suffolk and the north of Essex. In these East Anglian districts fine worsteds were manufactured.

The cloth-workers, freed from gild restrictions by their flight from the towns into the villages (see p. 32), became organized in what is known as the domestic (or outwork) system. Employers (clothiers) supplied raw material to workers in their homes and paid them wages. It is, however, interesting to note that even in the fifteenth and sixteenth centuries there were to be found isolated examples of large-scale cloth businesses where many employees worked under one roof. Outstanding among these was John Winchcombe's at Newbury. He was said to have employed over a hundred workpeople. William Stump, of Malmesbury, made use of the Abbey buildings for a factory after the dissolution of the monasteries.

How Cloth is made

There are four principal processes in making cloth :

1. *Carding*—a combing process designed to straighten the fibres by brushing them with wire bristles.

2. *Spinning*—twisting the fibres together to make them stronger. This was performed on the spinning-wheel, worked either by hand or foot. Only one thread could be made at a time ; it was either a warp yarn or a weft yarn. The warp is the thread extending throughout the length of a roll of cloth ; the weft runs across the width of the cloth.

3. *Weaving*—making cloth by interlacing the warps and wefts. The threads of warp pass through a loom and the weft is carried under and over them in a shuttle.

73

The warp is pulled about in the loom, and must, therefore, be stronger than the weft needs to be.

4. *Finishing*—dyeing, bleaching, or printing patterns on the cloth. For these processes soft, lime-free water is necessary.

Wool is made into many different types of cloth, but these may be grouped in two great classes, worsteds and woollens. The former are made from long wools which are generally dyed before they are woven. Woollens, made from short wools, require 'fulling' after they have been woven. The fuller beats the cloth in water mixed with soap or fuller's earth, and this causes it to shrink, and the fibres to felt together, giving the material a smoother finish. Serges are made with long-wool warps and wefts of short wool. Broadcloths, made from the best short wools, were heavily fulled, so that when finished the pattern of the weave was quite invisible. Baizes and kerseys were made from short wools, but they were rough, loose fabrics which needed little fulling.

CLOTH MANUFACTURE IN THE WEST COUNTRY

The clothier was responsible for supervising the manufacture at all stages—the cropping of the wool, the washing, the combing, the spinning of the yarns, the weaving of the cloth, and the finishing processes which perfected the cloth. (Fullers, for instance, washed, cleansed, beat, and stretched the cloth.) The clothier's chief function was trading, and not manufacturing, which was carried on by the spinners and weavers in their homes. He was the organizer of the industry.

As we have seen on p. 43, the richer clothier bought his wool direct from the great sheep-farmers, often buying the year's supply of wool. The 'meaner' clothier purchased it through a middleman, the wool stapler. The poor clothier bought his wool already spun into yarn in the local market.

The yarn was usually spun by women and children. Originally the spinners had worked for themselves, buying their own raw material and selling their yarns to a clothier, but well before 1700 spinners were mostly working for an employer. Spinners of yarn were more numerous than weavers, and were scattered far and wide over the countryside. In general, one weaver could keep ten spinners fully occupied.

Weavers, usually men, worked upon yarn supplied to them by the clothier who paid them so much for each piece of cloth they produced. The looms were owned by the weavers, who worked in their own homes. Generally a weaver did not work for one clothier, but for any number up to six. An apprenticeship system had ceased to be enforced by the local Justices of the Peace long before 1700. Some weavers, however, had an assistant to whom they paid a wage.

Marketing. Rarely was the clothier a merchant exporter ; in general, he took his products to Bakewell Hall, in London, selling them to agents and factors. By 1700 English cloth attracted foreign buyers to London, but some was also sold by Englishmen residing abroad and selling on the instructions of an employer at home. Exeter had an important weekly market for collecting serge.

In the home trade cloth was sold to wholesalers who in turn sold direct to retailers in London or took orders at fairs for those country drapers or travelling chapmen who

MAP 28

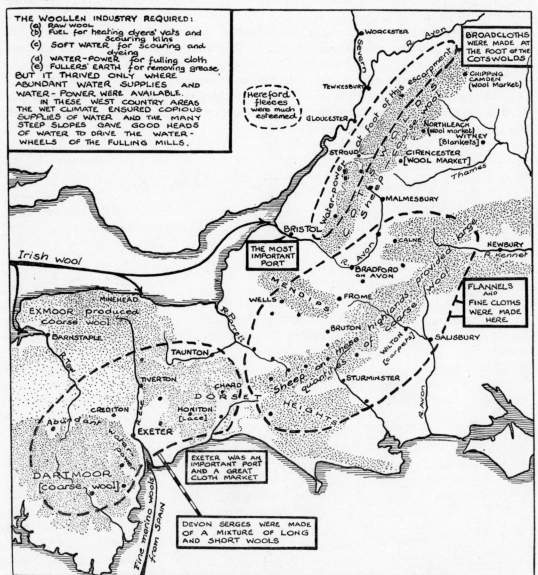

THE WOOLLEN INDUSTRY REQUIRED:
(a) RAW WOOL
(b) FUEL for heating dyers' vats and scouring kilns
(c) SOFT WATER for scouring and dyeing
(d) WATER-POWER for fulling cloth
(e) FULLERS' EARTH for removing grease
BUT IT THRIVED ONLY WHERE ABUNDANT WATER SUPPLIES AND WATER-POWER WERE AVAILABLE.
IN THESE WEST COUNTRY AREAS THE WET CLIMATE ENSURED COPIOUS SUPPLIES OF WATER AND THE MANY STEEP SLOPES GAVE GOOD HEADS OF WATER TO DRIVE THE WATER-WHEELS OF THE FULLING MILLS.

BROADCLOTHS WERE MADE AT THE FOOT OF THE COTSWOLDS

Hereford fleeces were much esteemed

THE MOST IMPORTANT PORT

FLANNELS AND FINE CLOTHS WERE MADE HERE

Irish wool

EXMOOR produced coarse wool

EXETER WAS AN IMPORTANT PORT AND A GREAT CLOTH MARKET

DARTMOOR [coarse wool]

DEVON SERGES WERE MADE OF A MIXTURE OF LONG AND SHORT WOOLS

WOOLLEN MANUFACTURES IN THE WEST COUNTRY

lived in the provinces. The chapmen carried the cloth from town to town on the backs of packhorses.

It should be noted that :

(i) There was much strife between the wealthy clothier and the poor spinners and weavers. Pay rates were often low.

(ii) The hours of labour were excessively long, and much of the work had to be done by dim light.

(iii) Work was irregular, and unemployment common; the clothier could not always provide his men with work. On the other hand, some weavers and spinners stopped working when they did not need the money.

(iv) Children were often employed in bad conditions.

The craftsman working under the Domestic System certainly had his independence, but it is clear that many of the evils usually associated with the Factory System existed long before the Industrial Revolution.

CLOTH INDUSTRY IN THE WEST RIDING OF YORKSHIRE

At the end of the seventeenth century Yorkshire produced chiefly woollens of a quality inferior to West of England cloth and a few worsteds inferior to those woven in

MAP 29

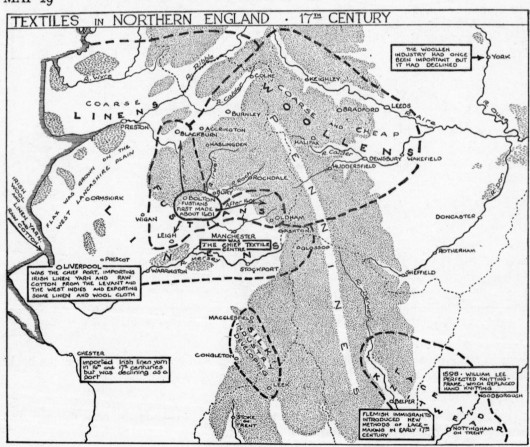

East Anglia. The industry was centred round Halifax, Huddersfield, Bradford, Leeds, and Wakefield. The typical man in the industry was not the clothier or the wage-earning weaver as in the West of England but the small working clothier, who owned the loom on which he worked and the material, the product of his labour. He was not a wealthy capitalist but a workman who sold his cloth one week to buy the raw material for the next week's work. He purchased his raw wool from the stapler and sorted and combed it himself. Usually his wife and children spun the yarn, with help from neighbours and others farther afield. He did his own weaving, with the help of his wife and apprentices. The busiest clothiers had as many as ten assistants and three looms.

Marketing. Originally the amount of cloth produced in the West Riding was small, but in the seventeenth century weekly markets were held. Cloth halls were established in the main towns (Halifax, 1708; Wakefield, 1710; Leeds, 1711), and the products of the small clothiers were sold to local retailers, foreigners, and agents of distant buyers.

Note, in contrast to the West Country system :

  (i) Little capital was required.
  (ii) The output of cloth was comparatively small.
  (iii) It was easy for a man to succeed as a clothier.
  (iv) Conditions were not so bad that friction between master and man was common.
  (v) The Yorkshire clothier was also a farmer doing his weaving in his spare time.

At the end of the seventeenth century West Yorkshire began to make finer worsteds and woollens.

CLOTH MANUFACTURE IN EAST ANGLIA

Though cloth manufacture was widely distributed throughout East Anglia, two areas may be distinguished in which it was specially important. First, in the north of Norfolk, round Norwich, was a region which, lacking water-power, specialized in making worsteds, which did not require fulling. (The name ' worsted ' comes from a village twelve miles north-east of Norwich.) In this area the manufacture of ' new draperies '—light fabrics of the worsted type—was developed by Flemish and Dutch immigrants of the sixteenth century. These ' new draperies ' gained ground at the expense of the older worsteds. Norfolk produced few woollens. A second area was in the south of Suffolk and the neighbouring parts of Essex, in the villages surrounding the towns of Colchester, Braintree, Lavenham, Sudbury, Hadleigh, and Coggeshall. This area originally produced heavier woollens, including broadcloth, which required fulling, but later tended to concentrate on spinning the long wool yarns required by the worsted weavers of Norfolk. The Dutch settled in Colchester and Halstead in the sixteenth century, and the making of new draperies spread to the towns on the Suffolk-Essex border, Colchester being noteworthy for ' bays ' (baizes). The East Anglian woollen industry bore many resemblances to the West Country model. It was organized by rich clothiers, whose handsome houses can still be seen in the towns of the woollen areas. They bought the fine long wools of the Lincoln and Leicester breeds of sheep and distributed them to the homes of the spinners and weavers in the villages.

MAP 30

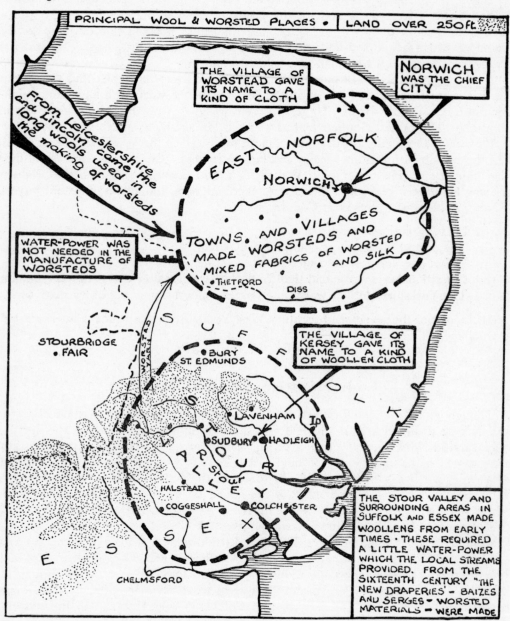

PRINCIPAL WOOL & WORSTED PLACES • | LAND OVER 250 ft

THE VILLAGE OF WORSTEAD GAVE ITS NAME TO A KIND OF CLOTH

NORWICH WAS THE CHIEF CITY

From Leicestershire and Lincoln came the long wools used in the making of worsteds

EAST NORFOLK

NORWICH

WATER-POWER WAS NOT NEEDED IN THE MANUFACTURE OF WORSTEDS

TOWNS AND VILLAGES MADE WORSTEDS AND MIXED FABRICS OF WORSTED AND SILK

THETFORD

DISS

STOURBRIDGE FAIR

SUFFOLK

WORSTEAD YARN

THE VILLAGE OF KERSEY GAVE ITS NAME TO A KIND OF WOOLLEN CLOTH

BURY ST. EDMUNDS

LAVENHAM

Ip

STOUR VALLEY

SUDBURY HADLEIGH

R. Stour

HALSTEAD

COGGESHALL

COLCHESTER

ESSEX

CHELMSFORD

THE STOUR VALLEY AND SURROUNDING AREAS IN SUFFOLK AND ESSEX MADE WOOLLENS FROM EARLY TIMES • THESE REQUIRED A LITTLE WATER-POWER WHICH THE LOCAL STREAMS PROVIDED. FROM THE SIXTEENTH CENTURY "THE NEW DRAPERIES" - BAIZES AND SERGES - WORSTED MATERIALS - WERE MADE

CLOTH MANUFACTURE IN EAST ANGLIA

OTHER TEXTILE INDUSTRIES

Silk. The silk industry owed much to foreign workers, the Huguenots who found homes in Norwich, London (Spitalfields), and Coventry after they were driven from France by the persecution following the revocation of the Edict of Nantes in 1685. Supplies of raw silk came from Italy, China, and Spain, and coarser fibres from Persia and Bengal. There was severe competition from the manufacturers of France and Italy, and silk was not an important industry until after 1719, when a mill was built by Thomas Lombe at Derby using copies of Italian machines. The mill, on an island in the river Derwent, employed three hundred men. Later similar mills, also water-driven, were established at Macclesfield, Stockport, and London.

Hosiery. Hosiery was made, as now, in the Midlands, particularly round Leicester, Nottingham, and Derby and, to a lesser extent, in London. A knitting frame had been invented in 1598 by William Lee : it was not used extensively until the seventeenth century, for it was expensive and unpopular with the workmen, who feared it would create unemployment. The knitters worked in their homes, but did not own the machines, which were the property of the organizers of the industry.

Linen and Cotton. In 1500 Lancashire made coarse woollens and linen. The raw wool was drawn from local sources, Ireland (via Bristol and Liverpool), and the Midlands. The linen industry drew its material from the flax grown in west Lancashire and Ireland.

At the end of the sixteenth century cotton seems to have been introduced to Lancashire—probably by skilled craftsmen from the Netherlands and France. Pure cottons were rare, but the manufacture of fustians (linen warp and cotton weft) grew from 1600.

THE COAL INDUSTRY

Coal as a source of heat had been known for centuries, but was little used before 1500. Until the middle of the eighteenth century it was in demand only for domestic heating in London and the larger towns. The chief mining area was round Newcastle-upon-Tyne, the Northumberland and Durham coalfield, but smaller quantities were obtained from the Midlands, Lancashire, and South Wales and used locally.

Methods of obtaining Coal. The earliest method was to quarry the coal where the seams outcropped at the surface. When these outcrops were exhausted large bell-shaped pits were constructed. If the coal seam outcropped on the side of a hill tunnels were driven into the hillside. Later the pit and adit method was introduced from the Continent. By this method the coal was raised by machines up the mine shaft while the water was drained away by some form of aqueduct to an adit in a valley at a lower level. This new method necessarily led to a deepening of the mines, increasing the danger of fire damp. For ventilation reliance was placed on a down-draught in one shaft and an up-draught in the other, which was at a different level. For the disposal of fire damp the crudest methods were used, which amounted to nothing more than exploding the fatal gas. The problem of lighting was difficult, too. Workings were over a small area round the bottom of the shaft, and more than half the coal was left behind in the form of pillars to support the rocks above. Deep mining was not possible until some better method than chain pumps worked by horses drained the water from the mines.

Shipment of the Coal. Coal was shipped by sea from Tyneside and Wearside to London and the Continent, from Whitehaven, on the West Cumberland coalfield, to Ireland, and from South Wales to Devon and Cornwall. It was also sent to inland towns by river from the coalfields of south Lancashire and Yorkshire and the Midlands, often completing its journey by packhorse.

The coal industry was an example of early capitalist enterprise ; to the owner of the mines it was a venture which might prove highly profitable or the reverse. Early in the seventeenth century the London coal trade was controlled by the Hostmen of Newcastle. They combined to control output and regulate prices in their own interest. The owners of the ships also kept up charges as much as they could. In addition there were men who loaded the coal on lighters and others who conveyed it in the lighters to the ships (keelmen). Unloading by factors and the carrying of the coal to wharves by lightermen in the big towns again added to the expense. The cargoes were bought by wholesalers and distributed in sacks by retailers as they are to-day. There was a steady rise in the price of coal in London during the seventeenth century.

THE IRON INDUSTRY

Production of iron was declining in the seventeenth century because of the inadequate supplies of charcoal, which was used for smelting the ore, and bar iron had to be imported from our colonies and from Russia and Sweden. The forest of the Weald, the earliest iron-making centre, was so depleted that new centres grew up in Shropshire, South Wales, and west Cumberland, where landowners had started to supply the needs of the Navy (ships were then built of wood). The iron industry gravitated to these areas. But there was another side of the iron industry—the manufacture of metal goods, locks, nails, buckles, iron tools. The manufacture of these iron goods developed on the coal-fields, because, once the wrought iron had been produced, coal could be used in the making of the metal products, the demand for which was increasing.

The shortage of timber had an important result. It led to the search for an alternative fuel ; the discovery that coke was a possible substitute brought about tremendous developments in the early eighteenth century.

OTHER METALS

In 1700 lead was still being mined in the Pennines of Derbyshire and north Yorkshire and in the Mendips of Somerset. Of these three areas, Derbyshire was the most important. The ground which contained the lead was granted to those who discovered the lead ore (' free mining '). Crude methods were used. The miner descended a narrow shaft carrying his tools on his back. He also carried up the ore he had mined.

Tin was mined in Devon and Cornwall. By 1700 a system of free mining existed here, and it was carried on sometimes by a single miner and sometimes by a company with hired labour. Shafts were sunk, and the miners met the twin dangers of water and fire damp. The earliest steam-engines were made for use in the Cornish tin mines. By 1700 coal was generally used for smelting.

Copper and brass manufacture made progress in the latter half of the sixteenth century when zinc ore was discovered in the Mendips, and in Gloucestershire and Nottinghamshire. Before Tudor times brass (a mixture of copper and zinc, very much in demand for cannon and for carding boards) was imported, because zinc ore was unknown in this country.

Copper mines were declared royal prerogatives, and a charter was given to the Mines Royal Company (1568) to mine copper; they began operations at Keswick, smelting the ore with peat and charcoal. At the same time a sister company, the Mineral and Battery Company, established works in London and Nottinghamshire to manufacture brass and copper plates ('battery') and wire.

Part of the capital of these two companies was provided by German manufacturers, and German workers were brought over to give technical assistance. Both companies had monopolies until 1689.

GROWTH OF LARGE-SCALE PRODUCTION AND OF CAPITALISM

In the two centuries preceding 1700 there was a noticeable development of large-scale enterprises which required considerable amounts of capital; many of these businesses housed a great number of workers under one roof. As we have seen (p. 74), much of the organization of the West of England cloth industry could be described as capitalistic. In a number of new industries introduced from abroad during the period 1540–1640 (cannon foundries, sugar-refineries, alum and saltpetre works) all the conditions characteristic of large-scale production were to be found.

In the same period some of the older industries were revolutionized by the adoption of new technical methods introduced from abroad, as those of coal (p. 79) and copper-smelting (above). The introduction of the blast furnace about 1500 was of the greatest importance in the iron industry. Coal was substituted for timber in brick kilns, glass-making, and malt-drying. The use of coal instead of wood increased the cost and size of a factory. The size of the market (national and international) was growing, and its needs could be served only by enterprises with large amounts of capital.

16. BANKING AND FINANCE IN THE EIGHTEENTH CENTURY

In Tudor times monarchs and merchants alike made use of the banking facilities of the Continent, negotiating loans from the Flemish or Italian banks, as their predecessors in the Middle Ages had done from the Jews. It was not until the seventeenth century that a banking system grew up in England, though the conditions which gave rise to it existed long before, resulting from the need for money for the great commercial enterprises of the sixteenth century. Much of the wealth which flowed from commerce was invested in land (see p. 61), but the rest had to be deposited somewhere for security. Money was hoarded in chests or used to purchase possessions of value like gold plate. Investment was not possible without some form of banking, and so certain classes of persons lent money and made a profit in doing so. Such classes comprised :

(i) The principal receiver of money deposited for security was the *scrivener*, whose work was to write legal documents and to draw up documents between buyer and seller, lender and borrower. He soon began to take up the money-lending business himself.

(ii) Merchant bankers in London, influential people who lent money to the Governments of European countries, had from 1600 taken the leadership in the field of banking from Antwerp after its fall.

(iii) The goldsmiths in the sixteenth century were primarily engaged in the manufacture and sale of articles of gold, silver, and precious stones. During the Civil War, because they had strong-rooms, the goldsmiths became custodians of money and valuables deposited with them by the merchants. The goldsmith on receiving the deposits issued receipts with a promise to repay (promissory notes). Soon the goldsmith bankers began to lend the money which had been deposited with them, retaining sufficient to meet likely withdrawals. They issued promissory notes payable to bearer, and when these were recognized by Parliament they became in essence bank-notes. In time the goldsmiths took care of deposits without charging for their services, making their profit by obtaining interest on the money they lent. Merchants began the practice of writing an order to the goldsmiths to pay their debts from moneys deposited with them ; this was the origin of the cheque. In 1672 many goldsmiths suffered serious financial difficulties because Charles II temporarily suspended the repayment of loans—' The Stop of the Exchequer.'

Thus, before the foundation of the Bank of England in 1694, the business people of Britain were accustomed to the use of banking facilities, bank-notes, and cheques. But there were certain disadvantages in the system : the rate of interest on loans was high ; many banks were unsafe places of deposit ; the supply of paper money was inadequate, and the gold backing behind it insufficient.

When William III became King (1689) he found the revenue insufficient for his needs, especially in time of war, and he acted upon the suggestion of two Scotsmen, William Lowndes and William Paterson, for raising a loan of money. Parliament authorized the borrowing of a sum of money by public subscription. A group of financiers were permitted to handle the business and to form a joint-stock bank. Thus was set up the business known as ' The Governor and Company of the Bank of England.' The Bank was given the right to issue notes to the value of its total capital, £1,200,000.

In spite of the opposition of the goldsmiths, there was enthusiastic support for the new bank, and the capital was subscribed immediately. William III obtained the money necessary for his wars, and in the economic field important results followed :

(i) The Bank of England encouraged people to deposit their savings.

(ii) The rate of interest on loans began to fall. The Bank charged 8 per cent. on its loan to the Government ; the goldsmiths had charged 12 per cent.

(iii) There was an increased issue of paper money, and this extra currency was of great value to the growing population.

(iv) Bills of exchange were discounted at reasonable rates, and as these included foreign bills, a steadying influence was exerted on the foreign exchanges.

The new Bank could be trusted. It soon gained a reputation for financial strength and security. During the eighteenth century Parliament gradually extended its privileges. Its charter was renewed again and again. It was the chief source of Government loans, and it was also (after 1708) the only joint-stock bank in England and Wales that had the right to issue its own bank-notes. Its activities were, however, confined to London ; in the Midlands and the North of England the Bank's notes were by no means universally accepted.

At the end of the eighteenth century there were also seventy private banks of deposit in London, using Bank of England notes and drawing cheques on their accounts with the Bank.

There were many defects in the monetary system of the eighteenth century, in spite of the fact that in 1696 the Government had issued a new coinage, calling in all the old debased coins. There was an extraordinary lack of small coins, and too few small notes. Until 1793 the Bank of England only issued notes of £10 and upward. It was then that the figure was lowered to £5, and in 1797 to £1 and £2.

These defects created a serious problem for employers when paying wages. Some minted their own coins, others (as in Lancashire) paid men in bills which were honoured by the local shopkeepers. The truck system (payment of goods instead of money) grew up, especially where factories were built in remote places, as a device by which employers paid their work-people.

Country Banks. In order to solve these difficulties, and to meet the needs of new industries in various parts of the country, wealthy merchants and prominent business-men became bankers, issuing their own bank-notes as well as lending money, though by an Act of 1777 no bank could issue notes of less than £5. This rapid growth of country banks gathered speed after 1780, and by 1815 the number (including branches) had grown to about nine hundred. An Act of 1808 required bankers who issued notes to be licensed. Map 57 shows the distribution by counties of these banks in 1815 ; they are found in all parts of the country, and fulfilled the needs of agriculture as well as industry. Lancashire had comparatively few note-issuing banks for bills of exchange were more commonly used (see above).

Country banks were established by men of very varied interests, including scriveners (see p. 82) and industrialists who thus found a means of paying off their debts and building up investments to provide reserve funds. Traders, particularly those who had houses or connexions in London, and tax-collectors also became bankers. Their experience of remitting money to London made their services of particular value to local people. Some of these country banks were unsound, and bankruptcies were not infrequent.

PART IV: THE INDUSTRIAL REVOLUTION

17. THE INDUSTRIAL REVOLUTION

THE period 1760–1830 is often known as the 'industrial revolution' because of the great changes which took place in industry during these years. These changes, however, were not as sudden and dramatic as the coiner of the phrase, Arnold Toynbee, imagined.

Industrial inventions of the greatest importance had occurred before 1760, such as Darby's substitution of coke for charcoal in smelting iron—and there was already large-scale organization in the mining industry (see p. 80). Capitalist employers were not at all uncommon, for instance, in the woollen industry (see p. 74).

It will also become clear in the later pages of this book that the year 1830 did not mark the end of new inventions ; the process of change has continued to the present day. In fact, new ideas, new machines, and new methods of transport have been more numerous and more revolutionary in this later period.

Even during the years 1760–1830, save in the cotton-spinning industry, there was no sudden upheaval. Changes came slowly, and only as demanded by practical necessity. The truth is that at no time does industrial advance proceed uniformly. Periods of stagnation alternate with periods of rapid growth. The years 1760–1830 mark an advance resulting from the slow building up of forces during the preceding centuries.

Not only did the population of England grow in numbers during the eighteenth century but its effective demand for food and other commodities rapidly expanded as wages increased (especially in the new factories) and the standard of living improved. New articles such as cottons and new foods such as wheat, tea, and meat, which had been previously enjoyed only by the upper classes, came into common use. In addition to the rising home demand there was a great increase in the quantities required for export, since British manufactures were the cheapest and best in the world. Inventions did not come by chance, but came when a necessary increase in the production of articles was found difficult due to a shortage of labour, as in the Lancashire cotton-spinning industry, or of material, such as the charcoal required for iron-smelting.

England did not lack people who were willing to invest their money in the expanding industry, for neither the contemporary social code nor the religious precepts of Puritanism condemned the practice of money-making. Noble dukes such as Bridgewater built canals and eminent Quakers such as Darby prospered. The habit of investment had grown since the issue of Government stocks in the early eighteenth century. Plenty of money, in fact, could be borrowed at low rates of interest. The rate of interest fell throughout the eighteenth century.

By this time restrictions on the free movement of labour had disappeared. Workers could move from job to job and from district to district without hindrance. They could also rise in the social scale without meeting the opposition of privileged persons. Successful business-men could reach the highest ranks of society.

The atmosphere of the times encouraged scientific experiment, from which followed practical applications of new ideas ; the current economic philosophy favoured free enterprise as opposed to State regulation. It was a mental climate in which enlightened self-interest could flourish.

18. THE COTTON INDUSTRY

THE people of south Lancashire were poor before the Industrial Revolution. The best soils of the country were undrained fens ; the gritstone moors afforded little opportunity for prosperous agriculture. The farmers and their wives and children naturally turned to the making of woollens and linens (see p. 77). Free from the restrictions imposed by gilds and the restraints of the Weavers Act and the Statute of Apprentices (p. 64), they

MAP 31A

MAP 31B

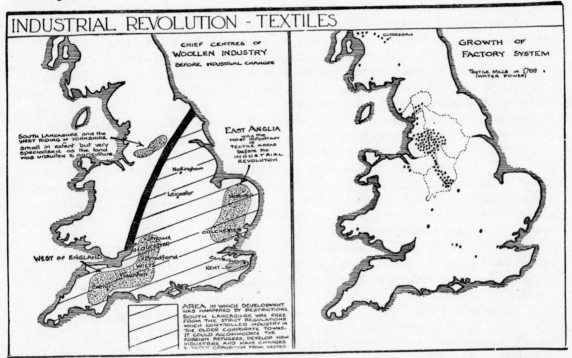

were able to experiment with cotton when it was brought from the eastern Mediterranean by the Levant Company in the late sixteenth century.

By 1700 some poor-quality cotton goods were made, but most of the output until about 1780 was fustians (linen warp and cotton weft) ; they were chiefly manufactured in the Bolton area. The industry was organized on capitalistic lines by merchants or clothiers who distributed work to spinners and weavers. Most of the weavers were now almost full-time operatives, owning but a small plot of land around their cottages ; they concentrated on weaving rather than agriculture.

The production of mixed cotton goods in Lancashire rose steadily in the eighteenth century because :

(i) An increased demand of the New World colonists stimulated the trade.

(ii) Cotton goods, introduced into Europe by the East India Company from India, became popular to such an extent that Parliament, by a series of Acts, 1701, 1721, 1736, prohibited the import, use, or wearing of printed or dyed cottons to safeguard the interests of the woollen industry, but fustians were exempted. The prohibition on pure cottons remained until 1774.

(iii) A remarkable series of inventions in the eighteenth century, resulting from the increased demand, led also to increased production.

At the beginning of the eighteenth century the textile machinery of Lancashire was of the simplest kind. On the weaving side there were two types of loom—the Dutch loom which wove narrow fabrics, but had the advantage of being able to weave about twelve pieces at a time, and the ordinary hand-loom, which was able to weave wide fabrics but only one piece at a time. On the spinning side the only machinery was the ordinary spinning-wheel. Two types were normally in use, the Jersey and the Brunswick wheels. These wheels had the disadvantage that they could only spin one thread at a time, and it was necessary to stop spinning when winding was necessary. The Saxony wheel had also been introduced, and on this machine spinning and winding could proceed simultaneously. The Saxony wheel, however, was not very suitable for cotton-spinning, and was of more use in the linen and woollen industries. Inventions were desperately needed on the spinning side—it had been calculated that one weaver could be kept at work on the yarn produced by four spinners.

Kay. The new inventions involved all the processes of making cloth (see p. 73). John Kay of Bury patented a flying or wheel shuttle in 1733 ; this enabled one person to make broadcloth (that is, double-width cloth), formerly the work of two people, because the weaver threw the shuttle across the loom instead of passing it from one hand to the other. This left a hand free to close up the weft in the cloth.

The fly shuttle was not adopted widely in Lancashire until the sixties, as it was costly and the need for invention on the weaving side was not great. In 1760 an invention of John Kay's son Robert enabled the weaver to use three shuttles, each containing a weft of different colours.

Hargreaves. It was to the spinning side of the industry, however, that the inventors gave most thought, there being a shortage of spinners as compared with weavers. After many unsuccessful attempts by different people James Hargreaves, of Stanhill, near Blackburn, invented about 1763 a machine called a spinning jenny which multiplied many times the yarn that could be produced by one spinner. It was a device easy to operate, and children could handle it, though the yarn it produced was not strong enough to be used as warp. The jenny was not very big, and required little power to work it ; it could be set up in a cottage.

Arkwright. Richard Arkwright, a barber of Bolton, who became one of the great industrialists of his age, in 1769 took out a patent for a water-frame, using a principle of spinning between rollers which had been invented as early as 1738 by Lewis Paul. Power was needed to turn the rollers, and though he had envisaged horse-power, he eventually used the waters of the river Derwent at Cromford, in Derbyshire, where he erected his first factory. The water-frame produced a strong yarn which was suitable for the warp.

His second patent in 1775 was a machine for the carding of cotton into rovings. Again rollers were used.

Arkwright's patents were disputed ; the true inventor of the water frame seems to have been Thomas Highs, of the village of Leigh, near Bolton, and Arkwright heard of the rollers on one of his hairdressing rounds. Nevertheless, he may be regarded as the founder of the modern factory system, for it was his business acumen which recognized the value of the inventions. He built factories at Belper and Matlock, in Derbyshire, and later, in 1776, in Lancashire.

Crompton. Although Arkwright's patent was a great advance, it had the defect of producing uneven yarn. By combining the merits of the jenny and the frame, Samuel Crompton in 1779 succeeded in constructing a machine known as a mule, which produced yarn of even and smooth quality—suitable, say, for making muslins. At first the mule was worked by hand in the cottages, but in 1790 water-power was applied to mule spinning at Dale's work, New Lanark. Within a few years a mule with four hundred spindles was constructed and the machine was used more and more in factories and less and less in cottages. The factories were necessarily constructed by the side of streams, hence they were called ' mills ' ; this name continued after 1790, when steam was increasingly used in new power-driven machinery.

Britain now manufactured muslins and fine cotton goods and was able to compete in the Eastern markets.

Cartwright. In the last twenty years of the eighteenth century the demand for good-quality cottons so increased that the weavers experienced great prosperity. There had been no technical improvement in weaving since Kay's flying shuttle. The manufacturers were anxious to find a power-driven loom, and in 1785 Edmund Cartwright, a clergyman, patented a loom which could be worked by water-power. It was clumsy and unsuccessful. Improvements, made by Horrocks in 1803 and Roberts in 1813, overcame technical difficulties, but the looms were only slowly adopted, and hand-loom weaving remained important until 1830.

The older textile industries of wool and linen did not adopt these inventions so rapidly, and they did not become factory industries until the middle of the nineteenth century. By 1835 four times as many people were employed in cotton manufacture as in wool.

Side by side with inventions in spinning and weaving industrial chemists improved methods of bleaching, dyeing, and colour printing. The ancient method of bleaching cloth was to expose it to the rays of the sun, together with frequent steepings in sour milk. In 1798 Tennant, of Glasgow, began to make chlorine bleaching powders using the method Berthollet had discovered in 1774. This reduced the period of bleaching from months to days. The process of dyeing changed when vegetable dyes were replaced by those manufactured from minerals. Printing of calicoes, which was done by engraved blocks pressed by hand on the cloth, was slow and expensive, and was replaced in 1783 by Thomas Bell's device of printing by revolving cylinders.

The factories at first were located on the edge of the Lancashire moors, where the fast-flowing streams provided power and where the weather was frequently damp—for a humid atmosphere is helpful in cotton-spinning, and lessens the risk of the fibres breaking as they are attenuated in the spinning process. After 1789 steam-engines were introduced for spinning, and the cotton industry settled in the south Lancashire coalfield.

MAP 32

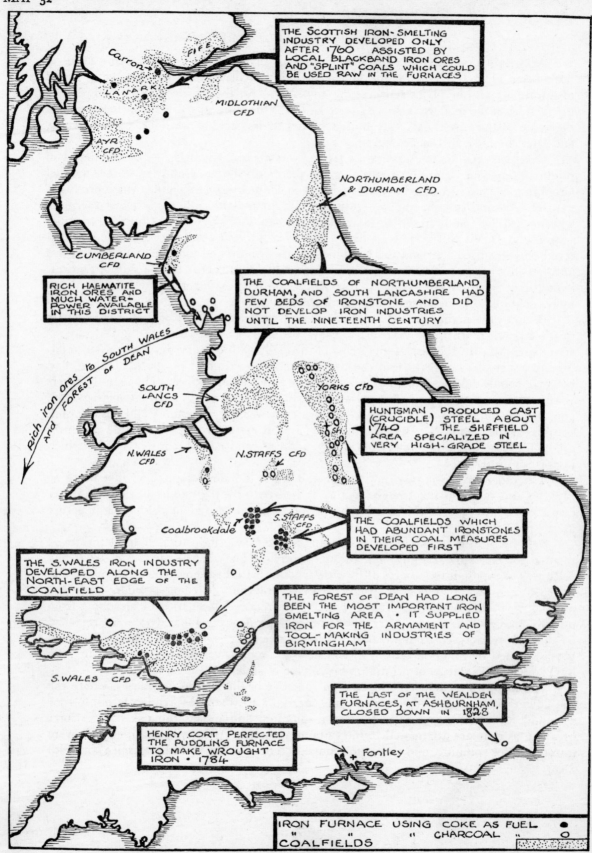

THE SCOTTISH IRON-SMELTING INDUSTRY DEVELOPED ONLY AFTER 1760 ASSISTED BY LOCAL BLACKBAND IRON ORES AND "SPLINT" COALS WHICH COULD BE USED RAW IN THE FURNACES

NORTHUMBERLAND & DURHAM CFD.

CUMBERLAND CFD

RICH HAEMATITE IRON ORES AND MUCH WATER-POWER AVAILABLE IN THIS DISTRICT

THE COALFIELDS OF NORTHUMBERLAND, DURHAM, AND SOUTH LANCASHIRE HAD FEW BEDS OF IRONSTONE AND DID NOT DEVELOP IRON INDUSTRIES UNTIL THE NINETEENTH CENTURY

rich iron ores to South Wales and FOREST of DEAN

SOUTH LANCS CFD

YORKS CFD

HUNTSMAN PRODUCED CAST (CRUCIBLE) STEEL ABOUT 1740 THE SHEFFIELD AREA SPECIALIZED IN VERY HIGH-GRADE STEEL

N.WALES CFD

N.STAFFS CFD

Coalbrookdale

S.STAFFS CFD

THE COALFIELDS WHICH HAD ABUNDANT IRONSTONES IN THEIR COAL MEASURES DEVELOPED FIRST

THE S. WALES IRON INDUSTRY DEVELOPED ALONG THE NORTH-EAST EDGE OF THE COALFIELD

THE FOREST OF DEAN HAD LONG BEEN THE MOST IMPORTANT IRON SMELTING AREA · IT SUPPLIED IRON FOR THE ARMAMENT AND TOOL-MAKING INDUSTRIES OF BIRMINGHAM

S. WALES CFD

THE LAST OF THE WEALDEN FURNACES, AT ASHBURNHAM, CLOSED DOWN IN 1828

HENRY CORT PERFECTED THE PUDDLING FURNACE TO MAKE WROUGHT IRON · 1784

+ Fontley

IRON FURNACE USING COKE AS FUEL ●
" " " CHARCOAL " ○
"COALFIELDS"

THE IRON INDUSTRY

19. THE IRON INDUSTRY

Iron-making involves two distinct processes :

(i) Ironstone or iron ore is taken from the ground and is burned to remove the impurities ; the product is called pig iron.

(ii) Pig iron is the raw material from which cast iron, wrought iron, and steel are made. Cast iron is obtained by forming a mould in sand and pouring in the molten iron. Wrought or malleable iron is produced by burning out more impurities until the metal is practically pure iron. Steel is made by refining the pig iron and then adding small amounts of carbon, which hardens the metal. Small additions of other elements give the steel special properties of toughness (by adding manganese) or rustlessness (by adding chromium).

MAP 33

STAGES IN THE DEVELOPMENT OF THE IRON AND STEEL INDUSTRY

As we have seen (p. 80), by the seventeenth century the demands of the iron and ship-building industries had led to a scarcity of timber. The iron industries in the Weald and the Forest of Dean declined rapidly owing to the shortage of fuel. Sheffield cutlers had to buy bar iron from Sweden.

Three inventions transformed the iron industry :

1. *The Discovery of a Substitute for Charcoal.* Coal had long been used in furnaces for other manufactures (see p. 81) but had not been used for smelting iron because it contained sulphur and other impurities which made the iron brittle. Efforts to use coal, the supply of which was plentiful, began in the seventeenth century, but it was not till 1709 that Abraham Darby, of Coalbrook-

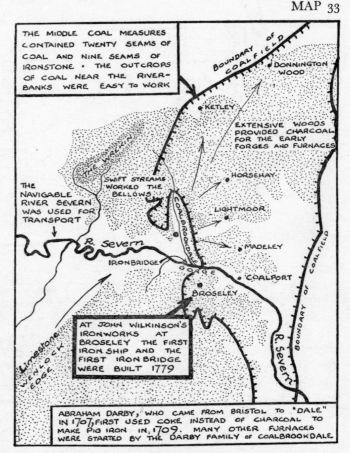

THE MIDDLE COAL MEASURES CONTAINED TWENTY SEAMS OF COAL AND NINE SEAMS OF IRONSTONE · THE OUTCROPS OF COAL NEAR THE RIVER-BANKS WERE EASY TO WORK

BOUNDARY OF COALFIELD

DONNINGTON WOOD

KETLEY

EXTENSIVE WOODS PROVIDED CHARCOAL FOR THE EARLY FORGES AND FURNACES

HORSEHAY

THE WREKIN

THE NAVIGABLE RIVER SEVERN WAS USED FOR TRANSPORT

SWIFT STREAMS WORKED THE BELLOWS

COALBROOKDALE

LIGHTMOOR

R. Severn

MADELEY

IRONBRIDGE

GORGE

COALPORT

BOUNDARY OF COALFIELD

BROSELEY

LIMESTONE

WENLOCK EDGE

R. Severn

AT JOHN WILKINSON'S IRONWORKS AT BROSELEY THE FIRST IRON SHIP AND THE FIRST IRON BRIDGE WERE BUILT 1779

ABRAHAM DARBY, WHO CAME FROM BRISTOL TO "DALE" IN 1707, FIRST USED COKE INSTEAD OF CHARCOAL TO MAKE PIG IRON IN, 1709. MANY OTHER FURNACES WERE STARTED BY THE DARBY FAMILY OF COALBROOKDALE.

COALBROOKDALE

dale, Shropshire, found a practical method of producing pig iron smelted by coke. At first the method was employed only at Coalbrookdale ; the coal of Shropshire (clod coal) was particularly suited for making coke, whereas coal in other areas was less successful. His invention was only useful in making cast iron. Pig iron made in this way was considered to be too impure for the forge. After 1760 a water-driven bellows was used to increase the blast, and the quality of the pig

MAP 34

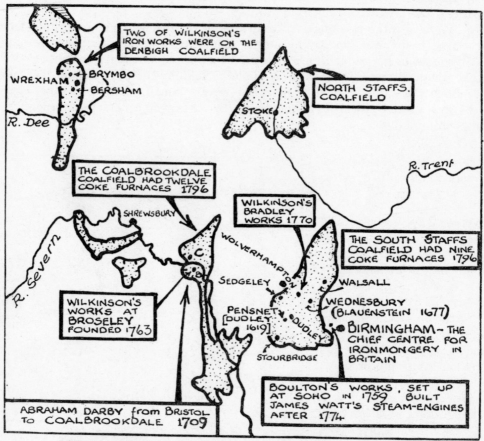

JOHN WILKINSON'S WORK IN THE WEST MIDLANDS

iron improved. The development of the use of coke was slow, though cast iron began to replace wrought iron in the eighteenth century. The Coalbrookdale foundries made the Newcomen engines (see p. 93). Ironworks near by, at Broseley, were set up by 'Iron-mad' Wilkinson, who found many new uses for iron, such as the first iron bridge, iron boats, and iron monuments. In 1774 he also invented a new method of boring cannon. John Roebuck established the Carron ironworks near Falkirk in 1759.

The use of coke led to the concentration of the iron industry on the coalfields. Britain was doubly fortunate in having many coalfields with seams of iron as well as coalfields near navigable water, and she soon became the world's greatest producer of iron. 2. *The Discovery of New Methods of Iron Manufacture.* During this period a considerable number of experiments were made to find a better method of converting pig into wrought iron than that of beating out the impurities with heavy hammers in an open hearth furnace with charcoal while the pig iron was in a molten state. It was not until 1783 that Henry Cort discovered a method of removing the carbon which remained in the pig iron. He had the idea of puddling it—that is, of heating it in another furnace together with clinkers rich in iron oxide, and stirring the molten iron so that the oxide united with the carbon impurities and escaped as gases. The purified metal was taken out of the furnace and passed through rollers. The invention of the rolling mill obviated hammering ; rolling could be done in a tenth of the time previously required for

MAP 35

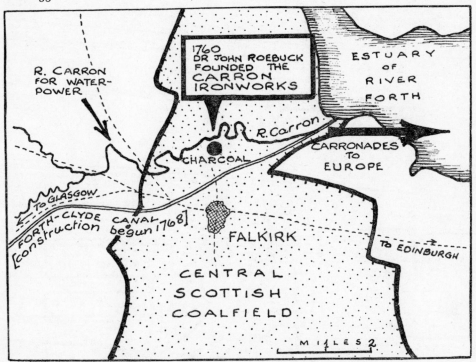

THE CARRON IRONWORKS AT FALKIRK

hammering. Homfray, of Pen-y-Daren, improved Cort's invention, and the new rolling and puddling processes therefore developed chiefly in South Wales (Map 36).

Further improvements in the technique of iron manufacture resulted from experiments at the Carron ironworks. Dr Roebuck found that by increasing the strength of the blast certain kinds of coal could be used instead of coke. James Neilson in 1828–29 had the idea of heating the air before it entered the furnace : this hot-blast process greatly reduced the cost of production.

3. *Technical Progress in the Steel Industry.* In 1740 Benjamin Huntsman, of Sheffield, had discovered a way of producing cast steel by melting the iron together with powdered charcoal and ground glass, which acted as reagents, in a sealed crucible at a very high temperature. Steel of much better quality was obtained, but the quantities made were small, and steel was still used only for luxury articles.

The general results of technical progress in the iron and steel industry were that

MAP 36

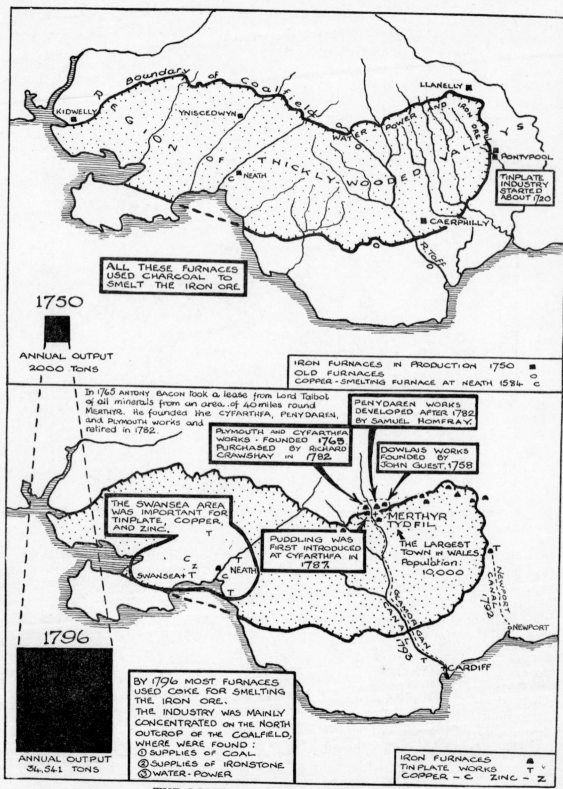

1750

ALL THESE FURNACES USED CHARCOAL TO SMELT THE IRON ORE.

TINPLATE INDUSTRY STARTED ABOUT 1720

ANNUAL OUTPUT 2000 TONS

IRON FURNACES IN PRODUCTION 1750 ■
OLD FURNACES ○
COPPER-SMELTING FURNACE AT NEATH 1584 ○c

In 1765 ANTONY BACON took a lease from Lord Talbot of all minerals from an area of 40 miles round MERTHYR. He founded the CYFARTHFA, PENYDAREN, and PLYMOUTH works and retired in 1782.

PENYDAREN WORKS DEVELOPED AFTER 1782 BY SAMUEL HOMFRAY.

PLYMOUTH AND CYFARTHFA WORKS · FOUNDED 1765 PURCHASED BY RICHARD CRAWSHAY IN 1782

DOWLAIS WORKS FOUNDED BY JOHN GUEST, 1758

THE SWANSEA AREA WAS IMPORTANT FOR TINPLATE, COPPER, AND ZINC.

MERTHYR TYDFIL
THE LARGEST TOWN IN WALES Population: 10,000

PUDDLING WAS FIRST INTRODUCED AT CYFARTHFA IN 1787

1796

BY 1796 MOST FURNACES USED COKE FOR SMELTING THE IRON ORE.
THE INDUSTRY WAS MAINLY CONCENTRATED ON THE NORTH OUTCROP OF THE COALFIELD, WHERE WERE FOUND:
① SUPPLIES OF COAL
② SUPPLIES OF IRONSTONE
③ WATER-POWER

ANNUAL OUTPUT 34,541 TONS

IRON FURNACES ▲
TINPLATE WORKS T
COPPER - C   ZINC - Z

THE SOUTH WALES IRON INDUSTRY

Britain was no longer dependent on Swedish and Russian iron—a matter of importance to the country during the Napoleonic wars, and production of pig iron, no longer dependent on timber supplies, became located on the coalfields. Iron goods became cheaper, and greatly increased in number and variety : the whole of British industry, from railways to cotton-spinning, and from ship-building to engineering, depended upon cheap iron and steel in large quantities. By 1800 the technique of this production had been mastered.

4. *The Invention of the Steam-engine.* The extensive development of large-scale industrial production by mechanical means was impossible without some effective kind of motive power. Water-power has many disadvantages. Factories had to be located near running streams. The water supply was not always reliable, sometimes scarce in summer and subject to floods and frosts in winter. Reservoirs had to be constructed to store water.

Steam-power had been known from ancient times but it was not used in this country for industrial purposes until the seventeenth century, when the increasing depths of the tin and copper mines of Cornwall necessitated the employment of some easy means of raising the water from the bottom of the mines. Captain Thomas Savery in 1698 patented a steam engine for this purpose. The construction of his engines was imperfect, and explosions were common. Great improvements in efficiency and safety were made by Thomas Newcomen, and after 1712 his engines were used to pump the water from the deepest mines. The Newcomen engines were wasteful of fuel because they depended upon the alternate heating and condensation of the apparatus ; only near coal-pits could they be profitably used in industry.

It was in 1765 that James Watt produced improvements to the Newcomen engine, and the first modern steam-engine relatively economical in the use of fuel was patented by him in 1769. By his invention of a condenser for the steam it was no longer necessary to cool the cylinder each time. At first Watt's engines were used only to pump water from mines and into factory tanks. In the manufacture of his steam-engines Watt had to overcome many difficulties :

(i) He wanted cylinders bored sufficiently accurately to prevent the escape of steam. He achieved this about 1774 with the assistance of John Wilkinson, the ironmaster.

(ii) He needed the help of men willing to risk their capital. Dr Roebuck, of the Carron Iron Works, and, later, Matthew Boulton, of Soho, Birmingham, the foremost iron manufacturer of Europe, came to his aid.

(iii) He needed skilled workers, and these were found at Boulton's Soho works.

In 1781 Watt took out his second patent, in which he used steam-power to turn a wheel, and so drive a machine. He owed much to the work of William Murdoch, his foreman.

Watt's new machine was first used at the Soho works, but subsequently most of the great ironmasters ordered engines to work their bellows, hammers, and rolling mills. The breweries and flour mills followed, and later the textile mills, particularly the cotton-spinning factories. The first spinning mill to be worked by steam was erected at Popplewick, Nottinghamshire, and between 1775 and 1800 out of 287 steam-engines erected all over the country, 88 went to cotton mills, mostly in Lancashire.

The new steam-power had important results. Factories were now built on coalfields, and industry for a long time to come was harnessed to coal. The increased power available facilitated methods of large-scale production and cheapened the costs of making goods.

DIAGRAM 6

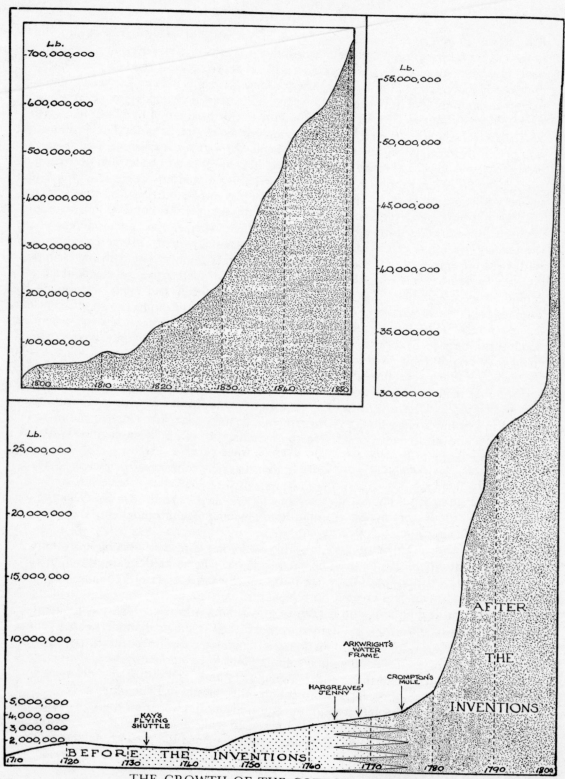

Lb.
700,000,000
600,000,000
500,000,000
400,000,000
300,000,000
200,000,000
100,000,000

1800 · 1810 · 1820 · 1830 · 1840 · 1850

Lb.
55,000,000
50,000,000
45,000,000
40,000,000
35,000,000
30,000,000

Lb.
25,000,000
20,000,000
15,000,000
10,000,000
5,000,000
4,000,000
3,000,000
2,000,000

AFTER THE INVENTIONS

ARKWRIGHT'S WATER FRAME

HARGREAVES' JENNY

CROMPTON'S MULE

KAY'S FLYING SHUTTLE

BEFORE THE INVENTIONS

1710 · 1720 · 1730 · 1740 · 1750 · 1760 · 1770 · 1780 · 1790 · 1800

THE GROWTH OF THE COTTON INDUSTRY

94

20. THE FACTORY SYSTEM AND ITS RESULTS

THE introduction of machinery, and especially of machines worked by steam power, led to the concentration of industry in factories. Large-scale businesses grew up for which large capital resources were needed. In the early days of the Industrial Revolution comparatively poor men succeeded in building up large enterprises. They ploughed back all their profits into their businesses and set up bigger factories. As the size of the factory units grew it became more difficult for the poor workman ever to own or control the capital—machines, buildings, material—with which he worked. The gulf between the industrialist who provided the capital and the labourers who did the work steadily grew wider and deeper. Whereas the manufacturers prospered greatly, the workers suffered great hardships in the factories and the mines.

Men, women, and children worked long hours in unwholesome and dangerous conditions at monotonous tasks for low wages. The hand workers, craftsmen whose skill was no longer required, lost status. Hand-weavers, for instance, who had been so prosperous when the spinning machines were first introduced, had to accept miserably low wages in the 1830's. Children and women, who provided the cheapest form of labour, were exploited.

The rapid development of the new industries on the coalfields of the North and Midlands, where no traditions of civic life existed, led to overcrowding in barrack-like and unplanned towns. The squalor caused by bad sanitation, no street lighting, and an insufficient supply of water spread disease and vice. Builders, however, worked under great difficulties. The pressure of population, the influx of casual labour, the duties on timber and bricks, and the window tax all prevented better-living conditions.[1]

As production depended on the fluctuations of the market, work became irregular ; unemployment cast its shadow over the lives of wage-earners. Bad relationships developed between workers and employers ; industrial strife became a feature of the factory system.

It is difficult to say whether the hardships were inherent in the change-over from the domestic to the factory system. Conditions of labour before the industrial changes were also bad ; long hours of work, monotonous jobs, unemployment and antagonism between worker and industrialist were common under the Domestic System (see p. 76), but in the factories there was in addition the burden of a harsh and ruthless discipline.

The effect of the Napoleonic Wars (see p. 130) was at the least a strongly complicating factor. The wars themselves created hardships, but more than that, they prevented the Government from dealing with the hardships growing up at home. The Government, fearful of revolution, was unsympathetic or even ignorant of the evils which existed.

The changes of the period were not in the long run calamitous, for the growing wealth led to substantial improvements in the standard of living of the people.

[1] Many industrialists—*e.g.*, Arkwright and Robert Owen—did a great deal for the housing of their workers.

MAP 37

CANALS

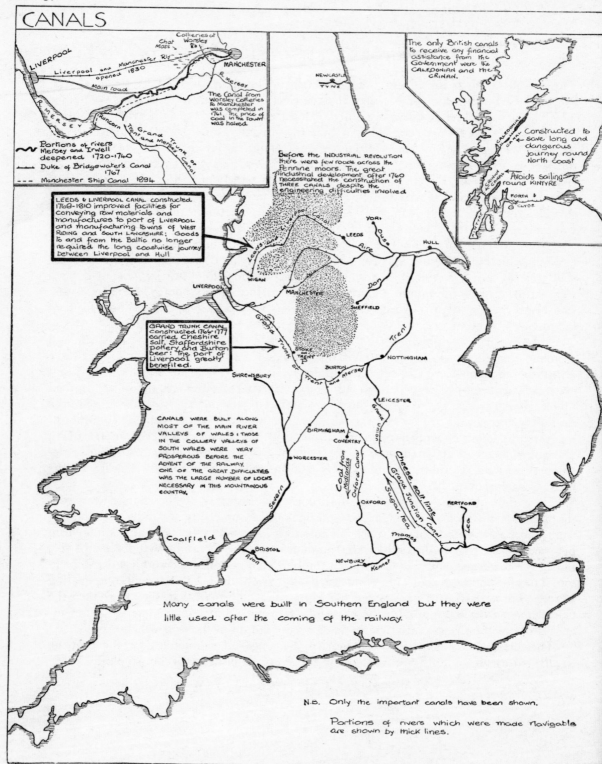

The only British canals to receive any financial assistance from the Government were the CALEDONIAN and the CRINAN.

Constructed to save long and dangerous journey round North coast

Avoids sailing round KINTYRE

Colleries of Worsley

Chat Moss

LIVERPOOL

Liverpool and Manchester Rly. opened 1830

MANCHESTER

R. Mersey

The Canal from Worsley Collieries to Manchester was completed in 1761. The price of coal in the town was halved.

Main road

R. MERSEY

Runcorn

Grand Trunk or Trent and Mersey Canal

Portions of rivers Mersey and Irwell deepened 1720-1740

Duke of Bridgewater's Canal 1767

Manchester Ship Canal 1894

LEEDS & LIVERPOOL CANAL constructed 1768-1810 improved facilities for conveying raw materials and manufactures to port of LIVERPOOL and manufacturing towns of WEST RIDING and SOUTH LANCASHIRE; Goods to and from the Baltic no longer required the long coastwise journey between Liverpool and Hull

Before the INDUSTRIAL REVOLUTION there were few roads across the Pennine moors. The great industrial development after 1760 necessitated the construction of THREE CANALS despite the engineering difficulties involved

NEWCASTLE

TYNE

YORK

OUSE

Leeds and Liverpool Canal

LEEDS

AIRE

HULL

WIGAN

LIVERPOOL

MANCHESTER

DON

SHEFFIELD

GRAND TRUNK CANAL constructed 1766-1777 carried Cheshire salt, Staffordshire pottery and Burton beer: the port of Liverpool greatly benefited.

Grand Trunk or Trent and Mersey

STOKE on TRENT

BURTON

TRENT

NOTTINGHAM

SHREWSBURY

LEICESTER

CANALS WERE BUILT ALONG MOST OF THE MAIN RIVER VALLEYS OF WALES; THOSE IN THE COLLIERY VALLEYS OF SOUTH WALES WERE VERY PROSPEROUS BEFORE THE ADVENT OF THE RAILWAY. ONE OF THE GREAT DIFFICULTIES WAS THE LARGE NUMBER OF LOCKS NECESSARY IN THIS MOUNTAINOUS COUNTRY.

BIRMINGHAM

COVENTRY

Grand Union

WORCESTER

Coal from Midlands

Oxford Canal

Cheese salt line

Grand Junction Canal

Sugar, tea

OXFORD

HERTFORD

LEA

SEVERN

Thames

Coalfield

BRISTOL

AVON

NEWBURY

KENNET

Many canals were built in Southern England but they were little used after the coming of the railway.

N.B. Only the important canals have been shown.

Portions of rivers which were made navigable are shown by thick lines.

THE development of trade is at all times closely connected with the means of communication available, and in the eighteenth century the revolution in industry would have made little progress if the problems of transport had not received attention.

Inland communications were completely inadequate to deal with the great expansion of industry. From the times of the Romans until the seventeenth century Britain's seas and rivers were more important than roads for the transport of goods and people ; many roads were mere tracks suitable only for packhorses. Most English rivers were navigable for barges for a part of their course, and heavy goods were transported either on the rivers or by sea (for example, coal from Newcastle to London). Towns which were near navigable rivers were centres for distributing goods, and those on estuaries carried on foreign trade as well, as did London and Bristol. Rivers such as the Thames, Lea, Severn, Wye, and the Great Ouse were of the utmost importance for transport. Even in the sixteenth century attempts were made to improve the waterways by dredging and widening and cutting off awkward bends. From making artificial cuts in rivers it was only a short step to constructing canals to connect rivers.

CANALS

The Need for Canals

1. Road transport was difficult and expensive (see p. 101).

2. River transport was inadequate even on the sections where the river channels had been deepened.

3. The growing population of the country required more food, and the industries more coal. The first canals were built to meet special needs. The demand for canals came first from that part of industrial England which was growing faster than any other, south Lancashire.

The Provision of Canals

1. *The Bridgewater Canal.* In 1759[1] the Duke of Bridgewater, the owner of large coal-mines at Worsley, ten miles north-west of Manchester, obtained Parliamentary permission to construct a canal to connect the two places. The work was carried out under the supervision of an engineer of genius, James Brindley. An extension from Manchester to Runcorn was opened in 1767. This made an alternative water route from Manchester to the Mersey.

2. *The Grand Trunk Canal* was undertaken to meet the needs of the rising pottery industry of north Staffordshire, which required china clay from Cornwall and flints from the coast of the English Channel as well as coal from local mines. Canal transport was very suitable for fragile pottery. The canal, which was cut from the Mersey to the Trent, and was opened throughout its entire length in 1779, also benefited the salt

---

[1] An earlier canal in Great Britain was the Sankey Brook Navigation (1757) linking St Helens with the Mersey.

MAP 38

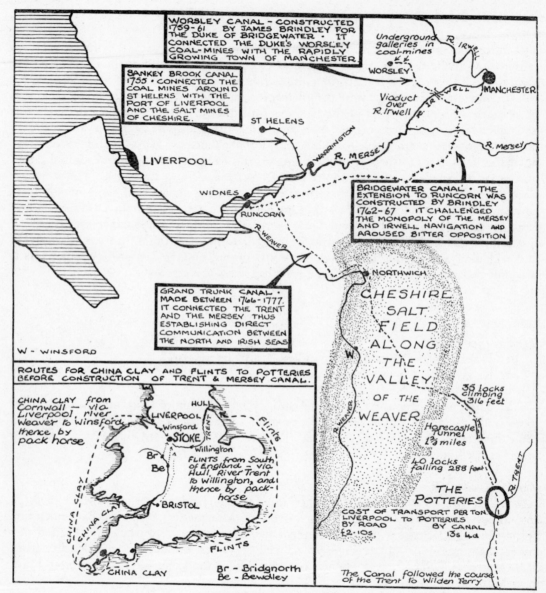

WORSLEY CANAL - CONSTRUCTED 1759-61 BY JAMES BRINDLEY FOR THE DUKE OF BRIDGEWATER · IT CONNECTED THE DUKE'S WORSLEY COAL-MINES WITH THE RAPIDLY GROWING TOWN OF MANCHESTER

Underground galleries in coal-mines

R. IRWELL

WORSLEY

Viaduct over R. Irwell

MANCHESTER

R. IRWELL

SANKEY BROOK CANAL 1755 · CONNECTED THE COAL MINES AROUND ST HELENS WITH THE PORT OF LIVERPOOL AND THE SALT MINES OF CHESHIRE.

ST HELENS

WARRINGTON

R. MERSEY

R. Mersey

LIVERPOOL

WIDNES

RUNCORN

R. WEAVER

BRIDGEWATER CANAL · THE EXTENSION TO RUNCORN WAS CONSTRUCTED BY BRINDLEY 1762-67 · IT CHALLENGED THE MONOPOLY OF THE MERSEY AND IRWELL NAVIGATION AND AROUSED BITTER OPPOSITION

NORTHWICH

CHESHIRE SALT FIELD ALONG THE VALLEY OF THE WEAVER

GRAND TRUNK CANAL · MADE BETWEEN 1766-1777. IT CONNECTED THE TRENT AND THE MERSEY THUS ESTABLISHING DIRECT COMMUNICATION BETWEEN THE NORTH AND IRISH SEAS

W - WINSFORD

W

R. WEAVER

35 locks climbing 316 feet

ROUTES FOR CHINA CLAY AND FLINTS TO POTTERIES BEFORE CONSTRUCTION OF TRENT & MERSEY CANAL.

CHINA CLAY from Cornwall — via Liverpool, river Weaver to Winsford, thence by pack horse

HULL

LIVERPOOL

TRENT

Flints

Winsford

STOKE

Willington

FLINTS from South of England — via Hull, River Trent to Willington, and thence by pack-horse

Br

Be

Harecastle Tunnel 1⅔ miles

40 locks falling 288 feet

THE POTTERIES

R. TRENT

CHINA CLAY

BRISTOL

FLINTS

COST OF TRANSPORT PER TON LIVERPOOL TO POTTERIES
BY ROAD   BY CANAL
£2-10s   13s 4d

CHINA CLAY

CHINA CLAY

Br - Bridgnorth
Be - Bewdley

The Canal followed the course of the Trent to Wilden Ferry

'THE DUKE'S CANALS'

industry of Cheshire and the iron industry of the Severn valley. As its name suggests, the Grand Trunk Canal was the main artery, to which smaller canals were connected. Liverpool and Hull were now linked by waterway, and their trade grew rapidly.

The financial success of the early canals and the obvious advantages to trade led to the construction of canals in all parts of the country (see Map 37).

It will be noticed on Map 37 that the canals linked the estuaries of the four main rivers of England. There was, however, no scientific planning from a national point of view, and no Government assistance (except for two canals in Scotland which were not constructed for the purpose of inland trade), and this accounts for the lack of uniformity in size, depth, and distribution. They were often made in face of the opposition of landowners, river improvement boards, and turnpike trustees. The physical features of Britain presented many natural difficulties, but the early engineers—even when illiterate like Brindley—showed that these could be overcome by making tunnels and viaducts. A new class of navvies (that is, navigators) was created, and new techniques adopted, which were later applied to the improvement of roads and the making of railways.

The Effects of Canal Construction

1. They provided a speedier, cheaper, and more reliable system of transport for goods than the country had ever known. The rate per ton for goods from Liverpool to the Potteries in 1777 was £2 10s. by road and 13s. 4d. by canal.

2. The volume of trade was greatly increased. Perishable and fragile articles could be safely carried. Trade in wheat before the canal era was mainly local ; wheat could be carried by canal a hundred miles for 5s. a quarter.

3. Cheaper and more efficient transport enabled the town population to grow. The area from which their food supplies were drawn was greatly extended.

4. The farmers in particular benefited, for areas which before could not be profitably cultivated were now brought under the plough to supply the needs of the increased population.

5. Canal construction stimulated the development of ports, especially Liverpool, by enlarging the hinterlands to and from which the imports and exports came.

6. Goods could be taken across country to avoid a long coastal journey. The Leeds and Liverpool Canal became a highway from Liverpool to the Baltic.

The Decline of Canals

The canals met a real need, and were amazingly successful. Although the cost of transport was generally reduced to a quarter of what it had been, the canal companies made large profits. No obstacles were too great to be overcome. By the end of the eighteenth century three canals had been constructed across the Pennines.

The coming of the railways marks the end of the canal era.

1. Improved organization would have checked their decline. The lack of uniformity in size, and depth, the absence of through rates, and their unsuitability for mechanical transport are examples of defects which could have been remedied.

2. The hilly character of Britain, necessitating frequent locks which create delay, remained an insuperable obstacle.

3. Many of the canal companies opposed the construction of railways and were bought out by the new railway companies.

E.H.—D

MAP 39

ROADS

IN THE SCOTTISH HIGHLANDS
Telford constructed
920 miles of road and
over 1000 bridges

MACADAM ADVOCATED NEW
METHODS FOR ROAD REPAIRS
—Use of angular instead
of round stones value of
a good foundation —
HIS WORK RESULTED IN
THE IMPROVEMENT OF ROADS
ALL OVER THE WORLD.

MACADAM
b 1756

Telford's Glasgow - Carlisle road

TELFORD
b 1757

NEWCASTLE

PORT
PATRICK

Mail to
Donaghadee
[IRELAND]
every evening

CARLISLE
in
41 Hours

WHITEHAVEN

I.O.Man
Mail Packet
once weekly

JOHN
METCALFE 1717-1810
improved roads in
the West Riding and
neighbouring counties

HOLYHEAD

Dublin
Mail Packet
Six times weekly

LIVERPOOL
in
32 Hrs

MANCHESTER
in
28 Hours

Mena. Bridge

Telford's Holyhead
road

POSTAGE RATE FOR A SINGLE LETTER
FROM LONDON TO PLACES WITHIN
THIS BELT WAS 8D

YARMOUTH
in
21 Hours

Mail to
Cuxhaven [Elbe]
twice weekly

Mail Coach

Mail Coach

BIRMINGHAM
in
16 Hours

HARWICH

Mail to
Holland
twice weekly

MILFORD
HAVEN

Waterford
[IRELAND]
Six times weekly

LONDON

BRISTOL

DOVER

Calais mail
Four times
Weekly

PLYMOUTH

Mail Packet
Halifax, N.S and
New York: once a
month

FALMOUTH

West Indies
twice monthly

Lisbon
once a week

Channel Islands
Mail
Once a week

METCALF'S ROADS SHOWN +++++
TELFORD'S ROADS SHOWN oooooooo
POSTAL INFORMATION TAKEN FROM
PATERSON'S ROAD BOOK OF 1803

ROADS

A. *Before the Industrial Revolution*

The Roman roads fell into disuse, and in the Middle Ages most roads were no better than ' rights of way.' If one track became too poor for use a detour over adjoining land was made. It was supposed to be the duty of the manorial lord and his tenants to maintain the roads, but as time went on the only road work which was done was undertaken as a religious duty. Bequests of land, money, houses, and oxen were left to monasteries for the purpose. Towns, with their surrounding villages, were practically self-sufficing, and only limited demands were made upon the roads, which no doubt were adequate for the local needs.

By the sixteenth century the state of the roads had deteriorated, and the dissolution of the monasteries made matters worse. The repair of the roads by the Statute of 1555 was made a local concern. Each parish was to elect two unpaid surveyors each year ; landowners were to supply horses, and all other inhabitants four days' labour. This system was the basis of all road administration until 1835, but it was not effective.

In the seventeenth century the increase in traffic, and especially in the use of

MAP 40

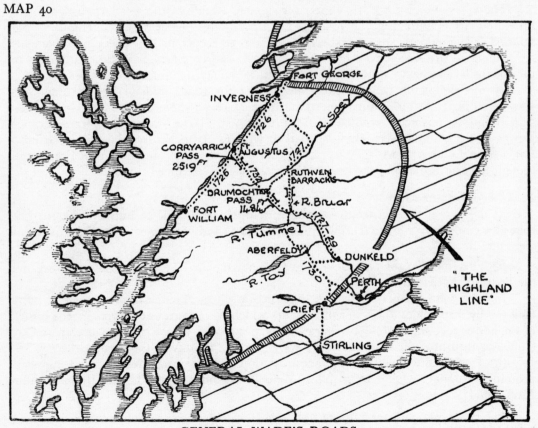

GENERAL WADE'S ROADS

cumbersome wheeled wagons drawn by eight horses, showed up the inadequacy of the roads. In 1660 stage-coaches plied between London and the larger towns, yet transport, according to contemporary writers, was difficult, dangerous, and slow. Strings of pack-horses carried most of the goods, and the animals floundered knee-deep in mud.

The Turnpike System. The expansion of trade in the seventeenth century led to a demand for better roads. In 1663 the first turnpike trust was formed, and the first effective toll-gate was fixed at Wadesmill, in Hertfordshire. The turnpike trusts were set up under a private Act of Parliament by groups of merchants to keep the roads in better condition, and they were authorized to levy tolls from road-users to pay for the cost of upkeep.[1] Most of the trusts were created between 1750 and 1830. Three areas benefited most by these Turnpike Acts : (i) The Midlands around Birmingham ; (ii) Yorkshire, Lancashire, and Cheshire ; (iii) the counties adjoining London.

The mileage administered by each trust was usually very small, and limited to the neighbourhood of large towns. Roads in the country away from large centres were still repaired by forced labour. A given stretch of road might be administered by many different trusts without a common policy. London in 1818 had twelve turnpike trusts for about two hundred miles of road ; north of the Thames there were eighty-seven toll gates within four miles of Charing Cross.

The efficiency of the trusts varied very much. Some of the smaller trusts did very little towards maintaining the roads ; the larger ones engaged skilled engineers and salaried permanent officials and experimented in road repair, making great improvements.

Financial arrangements were often far from satisfactory. Sometimes interests on their loans was so heavy that the trusts had little money remaining for repair.

By the eighteenth century the condition of the roads, judged by our standards, was appalling ; Arthur Young (see p. 110) pronounced them to be ' terrible.' Those near London, however, compared favourably with those of contemporary France. Towns in the country were often isolated in winter. It took three days for a coach to travel from London to Manchester in 1760 and between ten and twelve to Edinburgh, though towards the end of the century ' flying coaches ' reduced the time.

B. *After the Industrial Revolution*

At the end of the eighteenth century attempts were made to improve the roads so that they could carry the increasing amount of goods and passengers. The improvements were due to :

(i) The initiative of two Government departments—the General Post Office and the Board of Agriculture.

In 1783 John Palmer, of Bristol, suggested a scheme for the improvement of postal facilities by dispatching the mails on coaches which were to run at express speeds instead of on horseback, the cost to be defrayed by passengers who wished to travel quickly. Thus was instituted the mail-coach era which had its heyday in the decade 1820-30.

(ii) Improved technique in road construction and repair acquired by road engineers, prominent among whom were John Metcalf, Thomas Telford, and John Loudon McAdam.

[1] The earlier trusts of the seventeenth century in Hertfordshire, Cambridge, and Huntingdon were in fact administered by Justices of the Peace.

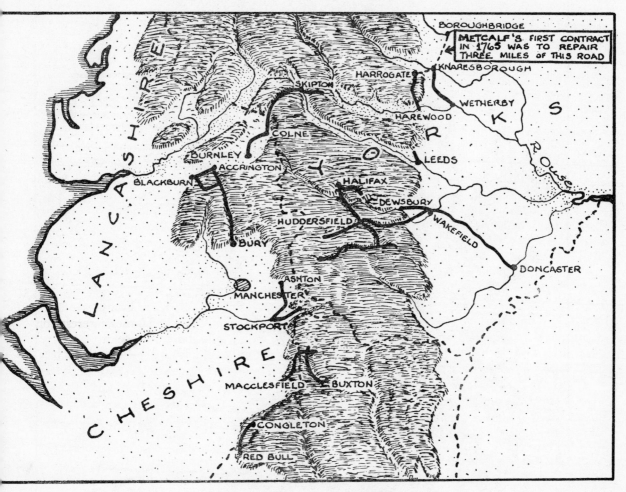

THE WORK OF METCALF

Metcalf ('Blind Jack of Knaresborough') constructed 180 miles of road in the Pennine areas of Yorkshire, Lancashire, Cheshire, and Derbyshire. He showed great skill in improving the foundations and drainage of the roads.

Telford began highway construction in 1803, building 920 miles of road and 1200 bridges in the Highlands of Scotland. His most famous projects were the Glasgow-Carlisle road (1814–25) and the London to Holyhead road, begun in 1810 for the Post Office. This was completed, together with the Menai and Conway bridges, in 1830. Telford planned his routes carefully, and chose solid foundations for his roads. He paid great attention to efficient drainage, and, unlike Metcalf, who was content to use only local stone, selected his materials very carefully.

MAP 42

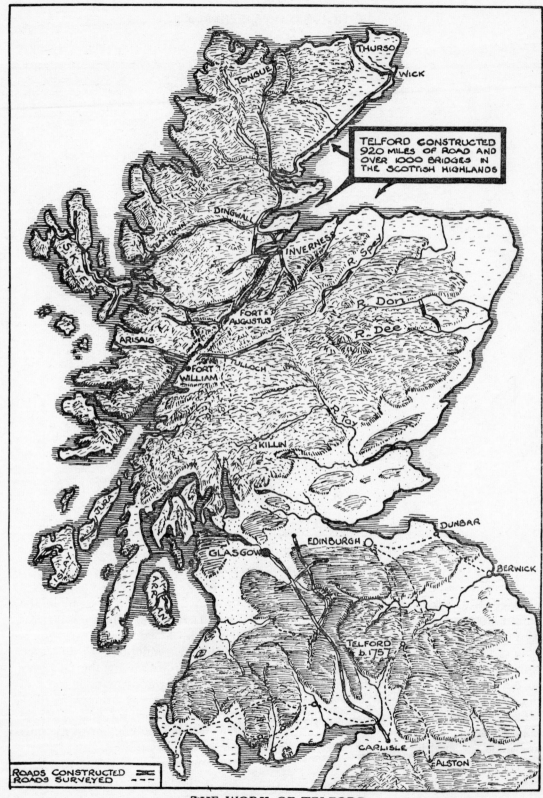

TELFORD CONSTRUCTED 920 MILES OF ROAD AND OVER 1000 BRIDGES IN THE SCOTTISH HIGHLANDS

THURSO
WICK
TONGUE
DINGWALL
SKYE
INVERNESS
R. SPEY
R. Don
FORT AUGUSTUS
R. Dee
ARISAIG
TULLOCH
FORT WILLIAM
R. Tay
JURA
KILLIN
ARRAN
DUNBAR
EDINBURGH
GLASGOW
BERWICK
TELFORD b.1757
CARLISLE
ALSTON

ROADS CONSTRUCTED
ROADS SURVEYED

THE WORK OF TELFORD

McAdam. The President of the Board of Agriculture, Sir John Sinclair, realized that it was of little use increasing food supplies unless they could be transported to the growing towns and cities. From 1810 to 1836 John McAdam was the expert adviser to the Board, advocating the repair of the roads of the country on scientific principles.

MAP 43

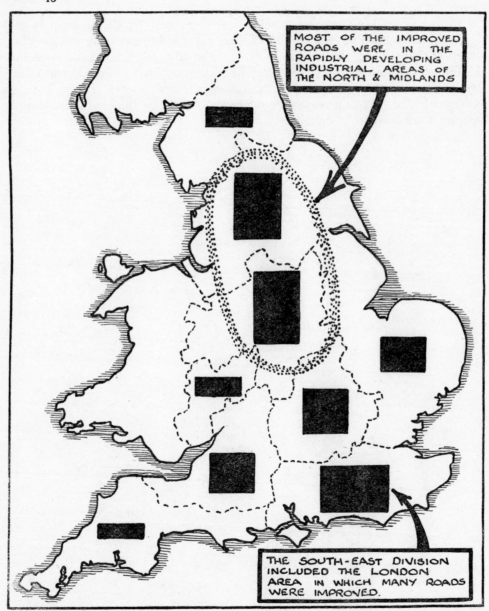

ENGLAND: TO SHOW WHERE ROAD IMPROVEMENTS WERE MADE

In 1815 he was appointed General Surveyor to the large Bristol Turnpike Trust, and later became adviser to other trusts. In 1827 he was given the post of Surveyor-General of the Highways of Britain. He thought that Telford laid too much stress on the firm foundations of his roads and not enough on a good road surface. McAdam's method was to put down small angular blocks of stone of equal size. The traffic pressed them into a hard surface, and made the metalled road we still describe as ' macadamized.'

C. *Improvements in the Administration of Roads*

On the advice of McAdam many reforms were made. By the General Highways Act 1835 compulsory labour was abolished, and rates were levied by the parishes for the upkeep of their roads. By various later Acts the administrating unit was enlarged, until in 1888 the County Council became the main authority. The Turnpike Trusts lost their revenues with the coming of the railways, which soon attracted both goods and passenger traffic. Their powers were not renewed, and by 1896 not a single turnpike remained on a public road in Britain.

22. AGRICULTURAL CHANGES IN THE EIGHTEENTH CENTURY

ALTHOUGH England was becoming the leading commercial and industrial State of Europe at the beginning of the eighteenth century, it was still mainly an agricultural country. Even those people who were engaged in the manufacturing industries such as spinning and weaving sometimes worked in the fields for part of the year.

The agriculture of the seventeenth and early eighteenth centuries had the following characteristics :

(i) Villages were largely self-supporting. They produced their own food, brewed their own beer, and made their own clothes and agricultural implements.

(ii) Methods of farming were still backward, especially in the North of England, where wheaten bread was a luxury.

(iii) Despite the enclosures that had been going on continuously for centuries the greater part of the Midland counties still maintained the open field system.

(iv) Small farmers predominated. There were some freeholders among them, but most of the peasants held land by copyhold or short leases which were generally renewed. Copyholders paid rent, but this was low, and the land was practically their own.

(v) There was little experiment in agriculture ; few winter crops were grown and cattle were pastured from autumn to spring or killed off in November if pasture was scarce. There was no adequate system of drainage. Most of the land was drained by alternating ridges and depressions, which led to waste of good land. Where there had been no consolidation of strips much time was lost by the farmers, who had to go from strip to strip. The system of common pasture for animals spread disease among the cattle and sheep.

(vi) There had been a considerable amount of voluntary enclosure and strip consolidation since the fourteenth century (p. 61) ; much of the waste had been reclaimed, though fully a quarter of England and Wales consisted of moorland, heathland, and forest. The fenlands around the Wash had been drained by a Dutchman, Vermuyden, in the seventeenth century.

Conditions were favourable to change at the beginning of the eighteenth century :

(i) During the Civil War forced sales of land and sequestrations led to great transfers of estates. The new purchasers were eager to make profits and ready to apply new methods. Encouraged by low interest rates, older aristocracy were busy buying land.

(ii) Merchants who bought land could afford to make experiments, for they had money they had made in business.

(iii) The earlier enclosure had been successful from the landowners' point of view : profits and rents were higher. After 1688 the landowners controlled Parliament and influenced the Government to encourage enclosure.

(iv) Pioneers in new methods of farming among the landed gentry had demonstrated the value of the new methods, and others were encouraged to adopt them.

MAP 44

AGRARIAN CHANGES

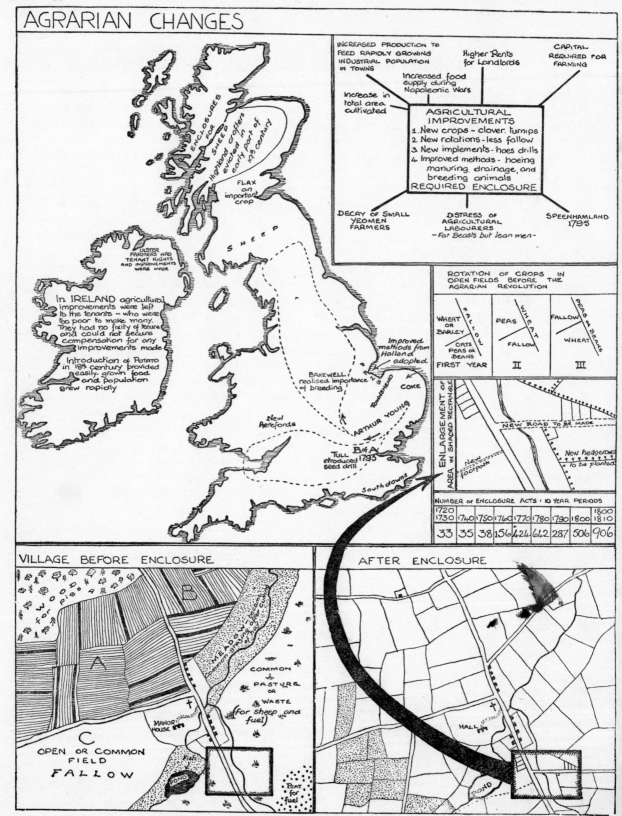

INCREASED PRODUCTION TO FEED RAPIDLY GROWING INDUSTRIAL POPULATION IN TOWNS

Higher Rents for Landlords

CAPITAL REQUIRED FOR FARMING

Increased food supply during Napoleonic Wars

Increase in total area cultivated

AGRICULTURAL IMPROVEMENTS
1. New crops – clover, turnips
2. New rotations – less fallow
3. New implements – hoes drills
4. Improved methods – hoeing manuring, drainage, and breeding animals
REQUIRED ENCLOSURE

DECAY OF SMALL YEOMEN FARMERS

DISTRESS OF AGRICULTURAL LABOURERS – Fat Beasts but lean men –

SPEENHAMLAND 1795

ENCLOSURES FOR SHEEP

Highland crofters evicted in early part of 19th century

FLAX an important crop

SHEEP

ULSTER FARMERS HAD TENANT RIGHTS AND IMPROVEMENTS WERE MADE

In IRELAND agricultural improvements were left to the tenants – who were too poor to make many. They had no fixity of tenure and could not secure compensation for any improvements made

Introduction of Potato in 18th century provided easily-grown food and population grew rapidly

Improved methods from Holland adopted

BAKEWELL realised importance of breeding

TOWNSHEND

COKE

ARTHUR YOUNG

New Herefords

TULL introduced 1795 seed drill

B of A

Southdowns

ROTATION OF CROPS IN OPEN FIELDS BEFORE THE AGRARIAN REVOLUTION

WHEAT OR BARLEY / FALLOW / OATS PEAS OR BEANS — **FIRST YEAR**	PEAS / WHEAT / FALLOW — **II**	FALLOW / PEAS & BEANS / WHEAT — **III**

ENLARGEMENT OF AREA IN SHADED RECTANGLE

NEW ROAD TO BE MADE

New footpath

New hedgerows to be planted

NUMBER OF ENCLOSURE ACTS : 10 YEAR PERIODS

1720 1730	1740	1750	1760	1770	1780	1790	1800	1800 1810
33	35	38	156	424	642	287	506	906

VILLAGE BEFORE ENCLOSURE

WOOD for pigs

B

A

MEADOW Common grazing after crops of hay cut

COMMON PASTURE OR WASTE (for sheep and fuel)

MANOR HOUSE

C

OPEN OR COMMON FIELD **FALLOW**

Fish POND

PEAT for fuel

AFTER ENCLOSURE

HALL

POND

(v) The growing urban population increased the demand for home-grown food and improved communications enabled farmers to supply more distant markets.

(vi) The Napoleonic Wars aggravated the position by cutting off European supplies; the high prices during the war encouraged farmers to introduce the new methods which would increase production. The heavy duties on corn after the war had the same effect.

TECHNICAL IMPROVEMENTS IN FARMING METHODS

1. *New Machinery.* Jethro Tull (1674–1740) published his *Horse-hoeing Husbandry* advocating the planting of seed in furrows. He invented a drill for sowing, and advised hoeing the land between the furrows, for which purpose he invented the horse-hoe. He was a crank, however, in certain respects, and farmers were slow to adopt his drill. Very slowly metal was substituted for wood in the framework of farm machinery.

2. *New Crops.* About 1650 the turnip was introduced from Holland. Turnips provided food for cattle; sown in rows, the crop could be a means of cleaning the fields from weeds. About 1700 white clover, lucerne, and other leguminous plants were sown. The roots of these plants enriched the soil with nitrogen, while the crops themselves provided food for cattle. Potatoes were increasingly grown.

3. *New Rotation of Crops.* The chief advantage of the new crops was that there was no longer any need for the fallow field. Lord Townshend practised the fourfold or Norfolk system of rotation—that is, wheat, turnips, oats or barley, and clover or grass.

4. *Systematic Breeding of Animals.* Until the middle of the eighteenth century sheep were kept mainly for their wool and not for mutton, and cattle were reared for milk, and as draught animals to pull the ploughs. Horses were bred for racing rather than for pulling carts. Robert Bakewell (1725–95) a Leicestershire farmer, experimented in the breeding of sheep for mutton, and he was so successful that his New Leicesters swept aside all competitors. The brothers Colling applied Bakewell's methods to the breeding of cattle, and they reared famous herds of Durham Shorthorns. Bakewell's methods were soon adopted by other farmers.

5. *New Methods of Drainage.* The problem of drainage was not successfully solved until the introduction of pipe drainage in the nineteenth century, but Joseph Elkington's use of deep trenches in Warwickshire fields after 1764 was adopted by many farmers.

6. *Diffusion of Knowledge.* The improvements in farming methods interested the landlords and the big tenant farmers. The smallholders were either too sceptical or too poor to adopt the new techniques. George III ('Farmer George'), the Duke of Bedford (at Woburn Abbey), Lord Townshend (at Rainham), and, above all, Thomas Coke, of Holkham, Norfolk, were some of the large capitalist farmers who made their mark on the farming of the age. Thomas Coke (1752–1842) was efficient and successful, although some of the improvements attributed to him were actually introduced by predecessors. Coke did, however, improve the covenants in the leases to his tenants. He was by this means able to force his tenants to rotate the crops on their land, and look after their property generally. But he is also remembered for his agricultural meetings, 'Coke's Clippings,' held at sheep-shearing time to demonstrate his methods

of farming to landowners, tenant farmers, and farmers from all over Europe. By these means he contributed to the diffusion of knowledge of the new methods.

Arthur Young (1741–1820) wrote on agricultural matters and did much to spread knowledge of the new methods. He began a tour of the country in 1767, recording the agricultural life of England, and later went to Ireland and France. He edited a monthly publication for farmers. When in 1793 Pitt founded the Board of Agriculture Arthur Young was chosen as Secretary, and organized the collection of information on agricultural conditions in different counties. He contrasted the farming under the open-field system with the work of the capitalist farmers, and was a strong advocate of enclosure.

The Enclosure Movement

The driving force behind the enclosure movement after 1750 was the urgent need to increase food production rather than the propaganda of the enthusiasts.

The Necessity for Enclosure

1. The new methods required enclosed fields. In the open field the conservative majority could prevent individual attempts to make improvements.

2. The open field was wasteful of time and labour (see p. 25).

3. Map 44 shows how the holdings of scattered strips were consolidated into compact farms. At the same time the common meadow, the common pasture, and waste were enclosed and divided in proportion to a man's holding of arable land.

(N.B. The enclosures of the sixteenth century had often been for sheep-rearing ; the new enclosures of the eighteenth century affected all branches of farming.)

The Method of Enclosure

At the beginning of the eighteenth century larger landowners had been busily enclosing land, either by agreement or by coercing the smaller man. The latter part of the eighteenth century saw enclosure by Act of Parliament.

A petition for permission to enclose was made to Parliament by a local landowner of some standing in the parish, and a private Bill was introduced into Parliament only when the petition had been supported by owners of three-quarters of the land concerned. As the value of the land was considered, and not the number of holders, a single large landowner could overcome the opposition of numerous small villagers.

Commissioners were sent to the village to re-allot the land, and the new village with its roads and fields was mapped out on the basis of the claims accepted by the Commissioners. These maps and the detailed information which accompanies them are of great value for reconstructing the past history of a village.

A general enclosure Act in 1801 simplified the procedure and reduced the cost.

The Necessity for the Creation of Large Farms let on Long Leases

The new agricultural methods required larger farms and the abolition of short leases. They affected, therefore, freeholders and leaseholders alike. The freeholders whose holdings were small found it was not economical to use the new and more elaborate and expensive machinery, even if they could find the money to buy it. The leaseholders, who frequently held their lands on short leases of one or two years, realized that any improvements they made resulted in the landlords increasing their rent. If evicted the tenants received no compensation for any improvements they might have made to the farms.

The Results of the Agrarian Changes

A. *Increased Production*

English farming became the best in the world. There was more food, and cheaper food, and this made possible the growth of industrial towns, and saved a growing population from starvation during the Napoleonic Wars.

Not all parts of Britain were affected to the same degree. Low prices involved the contraction of the cultivated area, but this did not mean that production ceased where the crop yields had been lowest. Sometimes land which had provided high yields went out of cultivation, for it was profitability rather than quantity of wheat per acre which determined the farmer's policy. For example, the clay lands of the Midland plain yielded more bushels of wheat per acre, but because they were heavy soils, and needed more labour to work them, they were not as profitable to work as the lighter soils of East Anglia, where labour costs were lower.

B. *Social Effects*

1. *The Big Landowners and the Large Tenant Farmers.* These people had enterprise and capital. They wanted enclosure and profited by it. They had the Government behind them, for up to 1832 Parliament was controlled by landowners.

There had been a remarkable concentration of land-ownership in the seventeenth century, so that even before 1750 much of the land of England was owned by relatively few people, who increased their income by leasing it to tenants. By means of a legal device (the entail) large estates were preserved intact : in this way family pride was satisfied and the political power of the great landlords was increased.

2. *The Small Owners (Yeomen) and the Small Tenants.* The small owner-occupier was declining between 1700 and 1750. The purchase of land by the aristocracy during this period was often for the purpose of enclosure and lease to a large tenant farmer. The small owner-occupier stood in the way of the big man's schemes, and he was bought out. Often he became a tenant farmer, for he could not afford the legal charges, cost of fencing, and other expenses entailed in enclosing land or the adoption of new methods requiring capital he did not possess. Sometimes he set up as a small manufacturer.

MAP 45

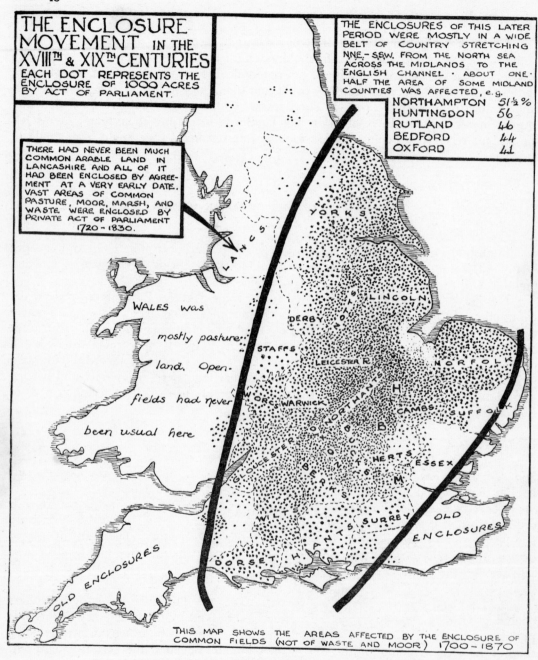

THE ENCLOSURE MOVEMENT IN THE XVIIIᵀᴴ & XIXᵀᴴ CENTURIES
EACH DOT REPRESENTS THE ENCLOSURE OF 1000 ACRES BY ACT OF PARLIAMENT.

THE ENCLOSURES OF THIS LATER PERIOD WERE MOSTLY IN A WIDE BELT OF COUNTRY STRETCHING NNE.–SSW. FROM THE NORTH SEA ACROSS THE MIDLANDS TO THE ENGLISH CHANNEL · ABOUT ONE-HALF THE AREA OF SOME MIDLAND COUNTIES WAS AFFECTED, e.g.

NORTHAMPTON	51½ %
HUNTINGDON	56
RUTLAND	46
BEDFORD	44
OXFORD	41

THERE HAD NEVER BEEN MUCH COMMON ARABLE LAND IN LANCASHIRE AND ALL OF IT HAD BEEN ENCLOSED BY AGREEMENT AT A VERY EARLY DATE. VAST AREAS OF COMMON PASTURE, MOOR, MARSH, AND WASTE WERE ENCLOSED BY PRIVATE ACT OF PARLIAMENT 1720–1830.

WALES was mostly pasture land. Open fields had never been usual here

THIS MAP SHOWS THE AREAS AFFECTED BY THE ENCLOSURE OF COMMON FIELDS (NOT OF WASTE AND MOOR) 1700–1870

During the period of Parliamentary enclosure there was at first some tendency for this progress to continue, but during the Napoleonic Wars the number of yeomen actually increased. Farming was then very profitable, and both large and small men did well. During this prosperous period some small owner-occupiers were able to buy more land, but with the slump in 1815 the decline of the yeoman farmer again continued. Only the big men were able to weather the storm.

The truth is that, though the small owner-occupier (the yeoman) and the small tenant farmer may have been social assets, economically they were out of date. Farming was no longer carried on to provide food for the local people (subsistence farming) but to provide crops for those markets where the grower could get the highest profit. The farmer was therefore exposed to the laws of supply and demand, and had to be ready to expand or contract production of particular crops as the price fluctuations of the market dictated. The new system called for greater mobility of labour, and for workers who were ready to go from one place to another and from one type of work to another. It demanded greater elasticity of method and a readiness to switch from one crop to another as the prices changed. A small man with a few acres was quite unfitted for a place in the new competitive agriculture, where prices were determined by costs of production in different parts of the country and, later, in other parts of the world.

3. *The Agricultural Labourer—the Cottager—the Squatter*. In the pre-enclosure village the cottager usually had a small plot round his cottage, a few strips in the open fields, a cow, and some poultry. He generally worked for wages on the farm of the large owner or tenant. There were many 'squatters' who had settled on the waste without any legal right and had proceeded to cultivate it.

When the enclosure took place, if the cottager had a legal right to his land he was in the redistribution, given his rights but very little more. He may have been provided with poor land, but he received something. Note on the map the tiny corner patches the cottagers were awarded.

The treatment of the man with no legal right (the squatter) varied from one enclosure to another. Sometimes his cottage was burned and sometimes he received a small plot of land. The lot of such a man was made worse by the fact that part-time employment in cottage industries such as weaving disappeared with the development of the factory system. It must be stressed that there was no mass eviction or mass unemployment after the village had been enclosed. The growing population of the countryside was absorbed by the many opportunities for employment in the new commercialized farms, and by the industries in the towns.

The agricultural revolution broke up the old village community. In its place was the prosperous landowner, receiving high rents from wealthy farmers who rented large farms on long leases, and the labourers, or wage-earners dependent on the tenant farmer for a livelihood.

DIAGRAM 7

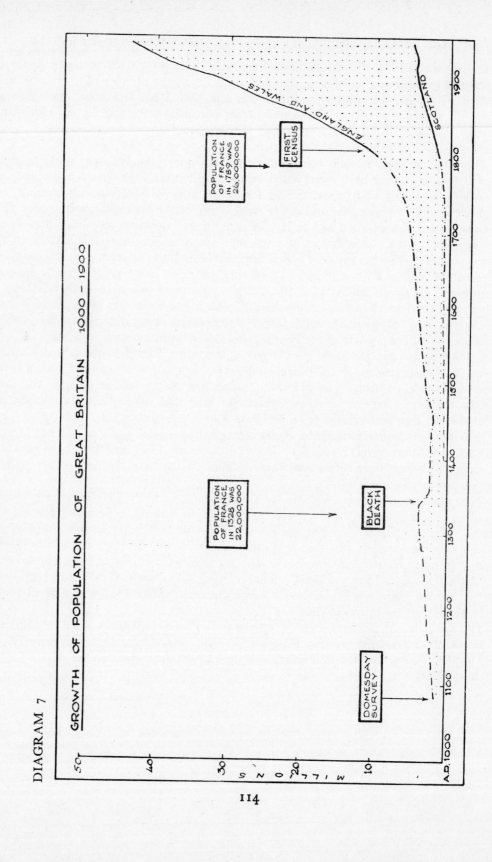

GROWTH OF POPULATION OF GREAT BRITAIN 1000 - 1900

23. POPULATION CHANGES 1700–1850

A. The Rise in Population

IT is a matter of great significance that from 1700 onward the population of England grew rapidly. There is little doubt that there was a labour shortage in certain areas of England in the middle of the eighteenth century, as is shown by the fact that in London and other industrial areas wages were rising. The increase in the number of inventions suggests that some attempt was being made to deal with this shortage by the use of machines.

Diagram 7 illustrates the growth of the population; from 5,800,000 in 1700 to 18,000,000 in 1851. In one hundred and fifty years the population had more than trebled itself. In the first fifty years, as Diagram 7 shows, it increased by half a million, and between 1800 and 1850 by nearly ten millions.

The growth of a country's population is determined by the relation of the number of births to deaths, and to a lesser extent by emigration and immigration. Early records of this country's population are not very accurate.

Birth Rate

The number of births per thousand people was high between 1750 and 1850 as compared with the preceding century and the century following. From 1700 to 1790 there was a slight but definite rise, a gradual fall until 1840, and a more decided fall after 1840 (see Diagram 8).

It has sometimes been stated that the rise in population was due to:

(i) The large number of children who worked in certain industries, such as cotton-spinning and mining. Large families, it was stated, meant a larger family income. There is probably little truth in this statement. The number of cotton-workers was but a small proportion of the total population, and at the beginning of the nineteenth century was less than those employed as female domestic servants.[1]

(ii) The Speenhamland system of poor relief, between 1795 and 1834 (see p. 135). It was supposed that these payments encouraged early marriage and led to large families. There may be some truth in this, but during those years when the system was at its height, from 1811 to 1831, the increase in population was greater in those counties north of the Trent, in which this form of poor relief was largely non-existent, than in those southern counties most affected by it.

The dominant factors which led to a rise in the birth rate appear to have been:

(i) *A Decline in the Apprenticeship System.* Previously the apprentice, living in his master's house, had to postpone marriage until he had completed his contract. By the eighteenth century the Act of Apprentices (see p. 64) was less strictly enforced. The machines of the early industrial period did not require a long and expensive training.

[1] Nevertheless it is admitted that some manufacturers—*e.g.*, Arkwright—did advertise for men with large families for their mills.

MAP 46

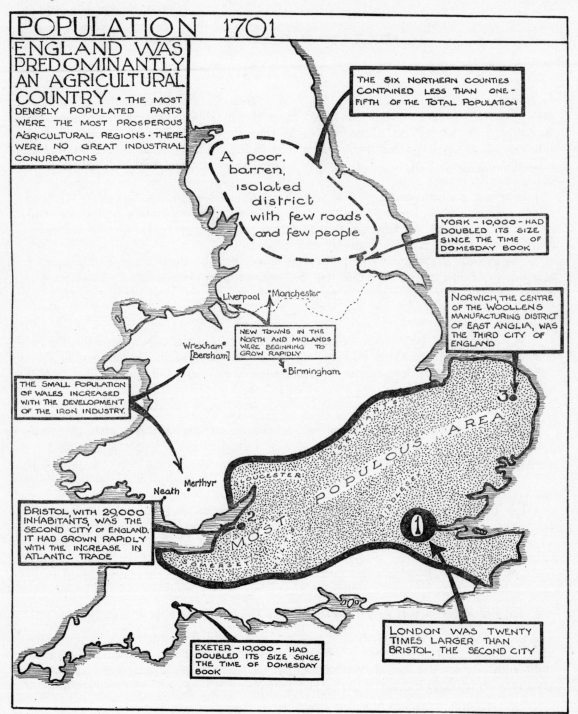

POPULATION 1701

ENGLAND WAS PREDOMINANTLY AN AGRICULTURAL COUNTRY · THE MOST DENSELY POPULATED PARTS WERE THE MOST PROSPEROUS AGRICULTURAL REGIONS · THERE WERE NO GREAT INDUSTRIAL CONURBATIONS

THE SIX NORTHERN COUNTIES CONTAINED LESS THAN ONE-FIFTH OF THE TOTAL POPULATION

A poor, barren, isolated district with few roads and few people

YORK – 10,000 – HAD DOUBLED ITS SIZE SINCE THE TIME OF DOMESDAY BOOK

NORWICH, THE CENTRE OF THE WOOLLENS MANUFACTURING DISTRICT OF EAST ANGLIA, WAS THE THIRD CITY OF ENGLAND

NEW TOWNS IN THE NORTH AND MIDLANDS WERE BEGINNING TO GROW RAPIDLY

THE SMALL POPULATION OF WALES INCREASED WITH THE DEVELOPMENT OF THE IRON INDUSTRY.

BRISTOL, WITH 29,000 INHABITANTS, WAS THE SECOND CITY OF ENGLAND. IT HAD GROWN RAPIDLY WITH THE INCREASE IN ATLANTIC TRADE

EXETER – 10,000 – HAD DOUBLED ITS SIZE SINCE THE TIME OF DOMESDAY BOOK

LONDON WAS TWENTY TIMES LARGER THAN BRISTOL, THE SECOND CITY

Liverpool · Manchester · Birmingham · Wrexham [Bersham] · Merthyr · Neath · MOST POPULOUS AREA

116

(ii) *The Growth of Industries in which Workmen received their Maximum Wages at a comparatively Early Age.* Many of the new jobs did not involve great skill, such as coal-mining and iron-working. Semi-skilled and unskilled labour was used in the construction of canals, roads, and railways.

(iii) *Change in living Conditions.* The labourer who once lived with the farmer and his family ceased to do so after the agrarian changes of the eighteenth century.

Increasingly, therefore, marriage took place at an earlier age than formerly.

Death Rate

The steep decline in the death rate was the most important cause of the increase in population during the period. It fell rapidly after 1730, and was mainly due to a check in infant mortality. A large number of the babies born survived.

Many causes contributed to an improvement in the health of the nation :

(i) The better quality of food and the greater quantity of it which resulted from the new farming methods. The introduction of root crops and the winter feeding of animals gave increased supplies of meat and milk.

(ii) Better conditions in the towns. Progress towards healthier surroundings started in London and spread into the provinces. Most towns until the eighteenth century retained medieval conditions of sanitation, bad when there was a small population, but fatal when the numbers began to grow as they did in the Industrial Revolution.

In 1613 Hugh Myddleton constructed an artificial waterway, the New River, twenty-seven miles long, to bring the water of Hertfordshire to London. There were improved houses and paved streets, a new system of laying sewage pipes, and carting of garbage was forbidden. Provincial towns began to follow London's example. They obtained rights from Parliament (by means of private Acts) to improve streets, water-supply, and sanitation. But conditions deteriorated 1800–50.

(iii) Improvements in medicine. There were more hospitals—an increase from two to eleven in London from 1720 to 1760—and whereas before 1720 there were only two hospitals outside London (Rochester and Bath), by the end of the century most provincial cities built hospitals. Dispensaries, a useful aid to hospitals in distributing medicines, first constructed in Red Lion Square, London, in 1769, rapidly grew in numbers both in London and in the provinces. There were twenty-three in London alone by 1800.

The qualifications of doctors were higher owing to the stricter supervision exercised by the Society of Apothecaries and the College of Physicians, founded in the eighteenth century, and to the teaching of medicine organized in the hospitals. Instead of ignorant women, skilled midwives assisted at the birth of children, minimizing the risk of death for mother and child. There was a phenomenal saving of life as a result.

More diseases were diagnosed and cured. The gradual introduction of green vegetables and lemon juice in the normal diet was a preventive to illness, and scurvy practically disappeared. A striking example of the blotting out of disease relates to smallpox, a scourge of the early eighteenth century, dealt with by a method of vaccination introduced by Edward Jenner in 1798.[1]

---

[1] The effects of these improvements must not be exaggerated, surgery was often primitive, anæsthetics unknown, and medicines often used incorrectly.

MAP 47

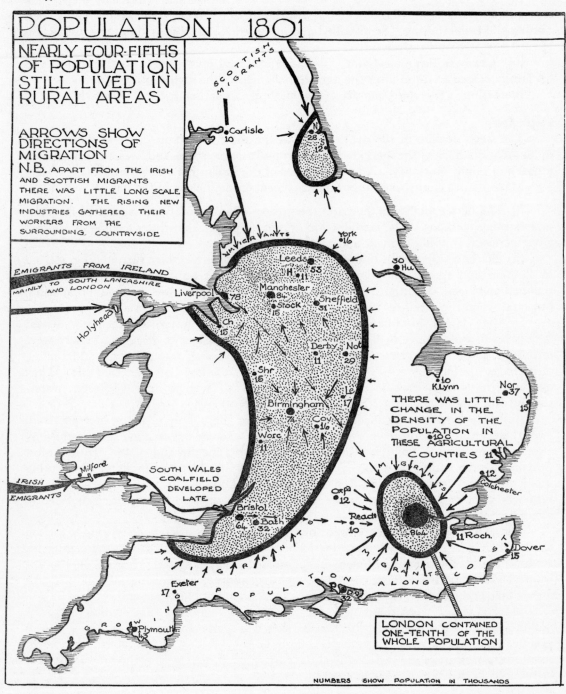

POPULATION 1801

NEARLY FOUR·FIFTHS OF POPULATION STILL LIVED IN RURAL AREAS

ARROWS SHOW DIRECTIONS OF MIGRATION

N.B. APART FROM THE IRISH AND SCOTTISH MIGRANTS THERE WAS LITTLE LONG SCALE MIGRATION. THE RISING NEW INDUSTRIES GATHERED THEIR WORKERS FROM THE SURROUNDING COUNTRYSIDE

SCOTTISH MIGRANTS

Carlisle 10

28 N
12 S

IRISH MIGRANTS

York 16

30 Hu.

Leeds 53
H. 11

Manchester 84
Stock. 15

Sheffield 31

EMIGRANTS FROM IRELAND MAINLY TO SOUTH LANCASHIRE AND LONDON

Liverpool 78

Holyhead

Ch. 15

Derby 11
Not. 29

Shr. 15

Le. 17

K.Lynn 10

Nor. 37

Y 15

THERE WAS LITTLE CHANGE IN THE DENSITY OF THE POPULATION IN THESE AGRICULTURAL COUNTIES 11

Birmingham 7
Cov. 16

Worc. 11

10 C

12

Colchester

Milford

IRISH EMIGRANTS

SOUTH WALES COALFIELD DEVELOPED LATE

Bristol 64
Bath 32

Oxf. 12

Read. 10

864

MIGRANTS

11 Roch.

Dover 15

Exeter 17

POPULATION

32

MIGRANTS ALONG

GROWN

Plymouth

LONDON CONTAINED ONE-TENTH OF THE WHOLE POPULATION

NUMBERS SHOW POPULATION IN THOUSANDS

DIAGRAM 8

BIRTHS AND DEATHS

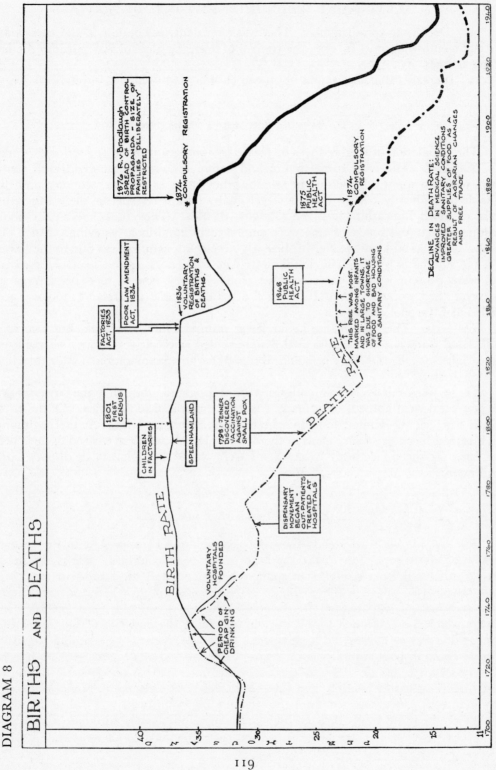

(iv) Decline in gin-drinking. This was prevalent in London in the early part of the eighteenth century. In 1751 the control of licensing alcohol was put into the hands of magistrates.

(v) Increased use of soap and improved clothing led to higher standards of hygiene.

B. Immigration and Emigration

The population of England was increased by immigrants from Ireland and Scotland.

The Irish. The Irish came to England before the end of the eighteenth century, but, except for a few who settled in London, they came as seasonal workers, and rarely to settle permanently. After 1800, however, many Irishmen settled in the manufacturing areas of south Lancashire and the Glasgow district. They took lower-paid posts in building canals and roads. Some were employed in hand-loom weaving. Much of the distress of the hand-loom weaver in the early nineteenth century was due to the lowering of wage standards by the Irish immigrants who came to England to avoid starvation, and were content with a bare standard of life. They tended to depress wage rates wherever they worked. In 1847, after the potato famine in Ireland, 300,000 people landed at Liverpool alone.

The Scots. The Scots came in far fewer numbers than the Irish, but also at first as seasonal workers. Those who settled were skilled workers, and many became leading industrialists, such as M'Connell and Kennedy, who manufactured cotton machinery in Manchester.

There were relatively few emigrants from England, though some artisans defied the law [1] and went abroad. But many Irishmen emigrated to America. Of the 127,000 people who left the United Kingdom in 1842, 90,000 were Irish. At the beginning of the nineteenth century many glens in the Scottish Highlands were cleared of their people and used for sheep-farming. Many Scots were forced to emigrate to distant parts of the Empire.

C. Redistribution of Population

Side by side with the steady increase of population came a shift in the centres of population, hitherto largest in the southern and eastern counties. The northern areas were transformed from stretches of solitary heathland and mountains to areas where large towns grew up. On the coalfields of North and South Wales and the Midlands more and more people deserted the country for the town, and this set in motion a social change which has continued to this day, transforming the majority of Englishmen from country-dwellers to citizens of large towns. This was evident by 1800, and by 1851 a third of Britain's population lived in towns of over 20,000 inhabitants (see Map 48).

Few workers in the older industrial centres migrated to the North. Those from East Anglia drifted to London, and those from the West Country to South Wales. The new industrial areas were fed from the surrounding countryside. Workers living near at hand on the farms were attracted by higher wages in industry, and these were replaced

[1] From 1719 to 1825 the emigration of skilled British workmen was prohibited.

MAP 48

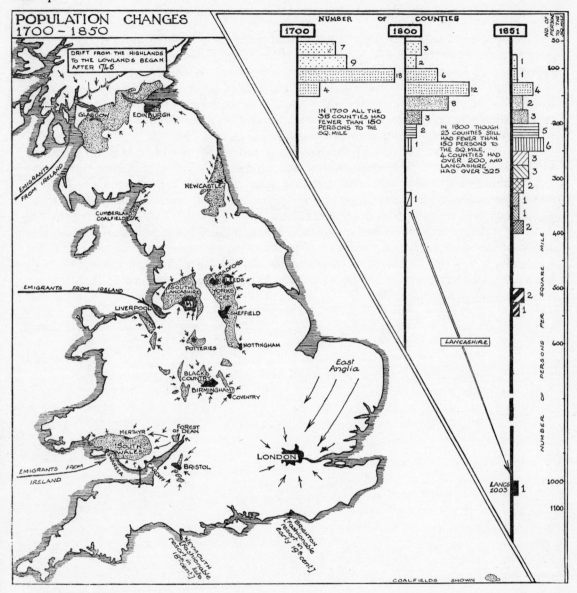

on the farms by workers from still farther afield. Thus a series of migrations from the countryside of Lancashire and Cheshire, together with some immigrants from Ireland, supplied the needs of the rising Lancashire cotton industry. The West Riding woollen industry drew its labour from the farms of Yorkshire, and the factories of the Black Country drew from Staffordshire, Warwickshire, and Worcestershire. But in the years of depression there was often a backflow of population.

D. Thomas Robert Malthus (1766–1834)

Although he made important contributions to the theory of rent and prices, Malthus is chiefly remembered for his *Essay on the Principle of Population as it affects the Future Improvement of Society* (1798). He considered that society could never be perfect ; there was always a tendency for the population, growing in a geometrical ratio, to increase faster than the means of subsistence which grew in an arithmetical ratio. The population of a country, however, never did outgrow the means of subsistence because numbers were kept down by the positive checks of war, famine, and disease.

In 1803 a second edition of the *Essay* was published in which Malthus modified his original doctrine. The emphasis on the geometrical and arithmetical ratios was largely abandoned, and it was admitted that other influences kept down the growth of population. There were preventive checks (moral restraint), such as the postponement of marriage and restraint from having children.

The writings of Malthus had a profound effect, influencing greatly both law-makers and poor-law administrators. Some of the reluctance to introduce measures of reform was undoubtedly due to the belief, inspired by Malthusian pessimism, that, if one evil was cured, a worse problem might arise ; for instance, people rescued from pestilence would only die from starvation.

PART V : THE NINETEENTH CENTURY
24. BRITAIN IN THE WORLD OF 1800

The nineteenth century was the age of Britain's commercial supremacy. She was the pioneer of industrial changes, afterwards adopted throughout the world. Export of her manufactured goods, their carriage, and investment of her wealth in developing industry and transport overseas paid the import of raw materials and vast quantities of food needed for the ever growing population which the farmers could no longer support. And in addition to the natural advantages of Britain—her insular position on the Atlantic seaboard, a coastline with excellent harbours, mineral wealth, and a temperate climate—there were other political and social factors which gave her pre-eminence in the commerce of the world.

1. *An Overseas Empire.* The most important of these was the possession of an empire overseas. By 1800 there were no serious rivals to her colonial expansion. She had struggled with Spain, Holland in the seventeenth century, throughout the eighteenth century with France for supremacy in Canada and India : struggles which ended in triumph.

Britain had lost the American colonies in 1783, but the foundations of her new empire were already laid. The United Empire Loyalists settled in and strengthened her hold on Canada, the defeat of the French made her predominant in India, while Captain Cook's expeditions opened up a new sphere of activity in Australia and New Zealand. Coastal settlement in Africa enabled her to penetrate into the interior of the Continent, and the West Indies, the most cherished of all her possessions, supplied her sugar, rum, cotton, tobacco, and hardwoods, the staple commodities of overseas trade.

Colonies were a source of raw materials and food which could not be grown in temperate latitudes (p. 67)—a secure market for the sale of manufactured goods (p. 71).

The expansion of British colonial territory in the eighteenth century and after the Napoleonic Wars (see Map 49) increased her trade, encouraged inventions and led to the introduction of large-scale methods of production to meet the increased demand.

2. *Command of the Sea.* Britain was supreme on the seas. The Royal Navy was able to protect British shipping in all parts of the world.

3. *Her Rivals engaged in Political Struggles.* In the nineteenth century possible rivals were more concerned with wars and internal revolt than with economic progress. While Europeans struggled for democracy or fought for freedom, Britain remained neutral, sold them arms, clothes, etc., captured their trade, and carried their goods.

4. *Form of Government and Social System.* Britain had a stable constitutional Government which could keep order and maintain the legal rights and property of the British people. There was a comparative absence of the social barriers and class distinctions which divided the people of Europe. Men were free to move about and work where they wished to a degree unknown on the Continent, where feudal restrictions still fettered the people. Dispossessed agricultural workers found employment in the towns. They provided a supply of cheap labour to work the new machines. In countries where the peasantry remained on the land there was difficulty in attracting labour to the factory.

5. *Internal Economic Conditions.* Internal barriers to trade had long been swept away, and the medieval gild, with its conservative restrictions, exercised no control over the new industrial development. The accumulated profits derived from trade and commerce in the past two centuries provided capital to finance the changes in industry and agriculture

123

MAP 49

BRITISH ACQUISITIONS DURING NAPOLEONIC WARS

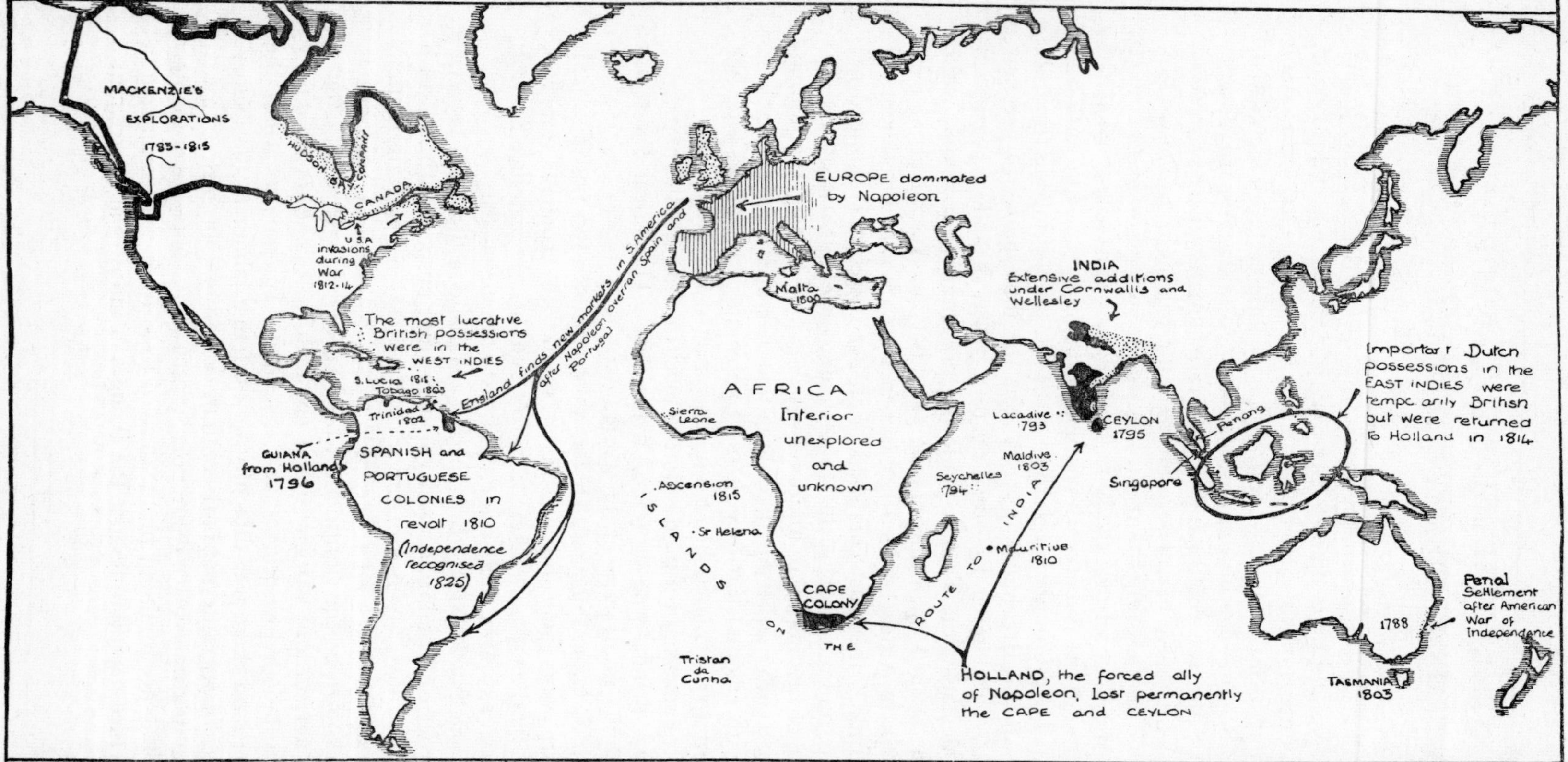

MACKENZIE'S EXPLORATIONS 1793-1815

Important Dutch possessions in the EAST INDIES were temporarily British but were returned to Holland in 1814.

Penal Settlement after American War of Independence

1788

TASMANIA 1803

INDIA Extensive additions under Cornwallis and Wellesley.

EUROPE dominated by Napoleon

CEYLON 1795

Singapore

Laccadive 1793

Maldive 1805

Seychelles 1794

Mauritius 1810

ON THE ROUTE TO INDIA

HOLLAND, the forced ally of Napoleon, lost permanently the CAPE and CEYLON

AFRICA Interior unexplored and unknown

CAPE COLONY

Sierra Leone

Malta 1800

Ascension 1815

St Helena

Tristan da Cunha

ISLANDS

Portugal

After Napoleon overran Spain and Portugal

HUDSON BAY Co

CANADA

U.S.A. invasions during War 1812-14

The most lucrative British possessions were in the WEST INDIES

St Lucia 1814

Tobago 1803

Trinidad 1797

GUIANA from Holland 1796

SPANISH and PORTUGUESE COLONIES in revolt 1810 (Independence recognised (1826)

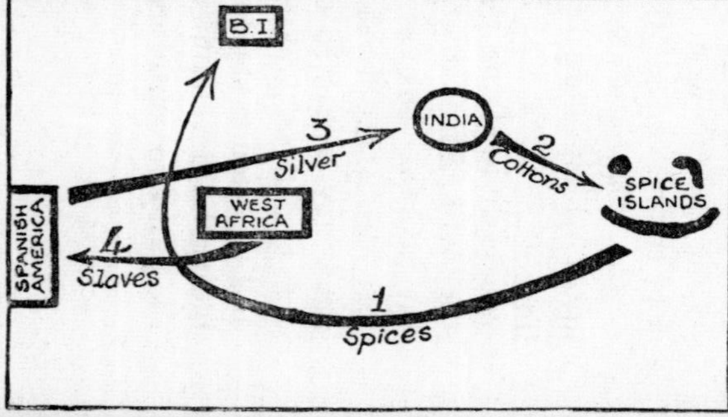

CAUSES OF BRITISH EXPANSION

TRADE	WARFARE	EMIGRATION	EXILE	LOVE OF ADVENTURE & DISCOVERY
e.g. East India Co. British South African Coy	e.g. Canada Cape India	e.g. U.S.A. all dominions in Temperate lands	e.g. convicts and political prisoners XVII Barbados & W.Indies XVIII U.S.A. XIX Australia	Cook to Australia. Missionaries to Africa.

HOW THE EIGHTEENTH CENTURY DEMAND FOR SPICES TO PRESERVE FOOD WAS SATISFIED.

B.I.

SPICE ISLANDS

INDIA

Cottons 2

Silver 3

Spices 1

WEST AFRICA

Slaves 4

SPANISH AMERICA

25. FROM 'LAISSEZ-FAIRE' TO THE WELFARE STATE

THE DECLINE OF MERCANTILISM

THE Industrial Revolution produced a new manufacturing class whose commercial doctrine was *laissez-faire* ('leave alone'). This was the advice said to have been given by a French merchant when asked by a statesman what the Government of France should do for industry.

Mercantilism, the economic theory which had governed State policy from Tudor times (see p. 64), had long survived its usefulness, and had become discredited and unpopular.

1. When industry spread out from the towns to the countryside it was difficult for the State to enforce its regulations, and in many cases the regulations were merely devices for protecting old-established enterprises from the competition of newcomers.

2. The value of the Navigation Acts and the old colonial policy which had culminated in the loss of the American colonies was also questioned.

3. The protection of the home industry by imposing taxes on foreign imports—such as the Corn Duties of 1815—led to high prices which were of advantage only to the privileged few.

4. The system of collecting Customs duties was cumbrous and inefficient, involving the employment of a large number of officials, so that the cost of collection was disproportionate to the amount of money obtained ; high duties yielded only a small revenue.

5. The high tariffs made smuggling profitable. An estimate of 1783 placed the number of smugglers at 40,000.

THE MOVEMENT TOWARDS 'LAISSEZ-FAIRE'

The sweeping away of mercantilist restrictions on the freedom of trade and industry was due to :

(i) The political agitation of the rising class of merchants, manufacturers, and professional people who represented a moneyed interest which opposed the landed interest of the aristocracy.

The new manufacturing class wanted cheap food for the work-people and cheap raw materials for their factories, and therefore, they opposed duties on imports. They wanted to pay low wages. They believed that men, if free to do so, would leave any badly paid job. They opposed regulations designed to check the manufacture of inferior goods ; competition, they believed, would drive out of business anybody who made goods of poor quality.

(ii) The teachings of the economists, chief of whom were Adam Smith, Malthus, and Ricardo.

In his *Wealth of Nations*, published 1776, Adam Smith taught that men, when left free to pursue their own interests in the way they consider best, will, although unintentionally, promote the public good. Private enterprise, he asserted, was superior to Government action.

The Rev. Thomas Malthus declared that ' man's self-interest is God's providence,' and that it was better for everybody if men were free to make as much money as they could.

Though his book *Principles of Political Economy*, published in 1817, is less well-known than *The Wealth of Nations*, David Ricardo was the most important of the economists who championed the cause of the manufacturing classes against the landed interests. To buy in the cheapest and sell in the dearest market was regarded by Ricardo as a divine law. He believed that the new industrialization of Britain was both inevitable and desirable and saw *laissez-faire* as the ' natural economic order.'

(iii) The work of the utilitarians, a group of political philosophers who, like the economists, believed in individual freedom. They were followers of Jeremy Bentham, who taught that all laws should be subjected to one simple test—the greatest happiness of the greatest number of people. When laws failed to promote this it was time to reform them.

Bentham and his followers were practical-minded people who strove actively for reform. Bentham himself worked hard to reform the barbarous legal and penal systems of his day. Francis Place worked for the repeal of the Combination Acts, which had hampered the formation of trade unions (see p. 141). Edwin Chadwick initiated public health legislation (see p. 140).

The Reaction against ' Laissez-faire '

Laissez-faire suited the times. Britain's industry, trade, and wealth grew rapidly. By the middle of the nineteenth century she became the most powerful and influential country in the world, but opposition was growing to both the economic and the political aspects of *laissez-faire*. All too frequently it operated unfairly against the poorest people —for example, though in theory masters and men were free to fix high wages and short hours of labour, in practice workers had to accept low wages and long hours or starve. It became apparent to thoughtful people that the policy of *laissez-faire* was too harsh in its operation.

The early reformers were moved by humanitarian impulses. They included :

(i) Romantics, such as poets and writers like Burns and Wordsworth, who believed that *le cœur a ses raisons*.

(ii) Revolutionaries, like Thomas Paine and William Godwin, who presented lofty ideals concerning the dignity of man. Among Paine's ideas were compulsory education, old-age pensions and children's allowances, young-age pensions and a united nations organization.

(iii) Radicals, such as William Cobbett, whose weekly journal, *The Political Register*, was influential among the labouring classes, and Major Cartwright, who founded Hampden Clubs.

(iv) Early socialists, like Robert Owen, who considered a man's character depended on his environment, and who advocated reform in an endeavour to improve mankind (p. 138).

(v) Philanthropists, like William Wilberforce, who attacked slavery, and Lord Shaftesbury, who attacked the evils of child labour in the new factories (see p. 138).

The Government largely ignored the early agitators because they accepted the economists' doctrine that wages could not be raised or hours of labour reduced without disaster to both employer and employee, and they believed, with Malthus, that an improved standard of living would lead to a too rapid increase in the population, and that philanthropic effort, therefore, was futile and dangerous.

The Movement towards State Action

The reaction from *laissez-faire* was complete in the second half of the nineteenth century, during which there was an ever-increasing control over manufacturers to prevent their doing as they pleased. By the end of the century, public opinion had been converted to the idea that the State had a responsibility for social and industrial conditions.

The changed outlook was due to (1) the influence on our government of social reformers, and (2) a result of the growth of State socialism in Germany.

(i) The mid-Victorian novelists and poets, like Dickens, Reade, and the Brownings, conscience-smitten by the horrors of child-oppression, destitution, and ignorance, thoroughly opposed *laissez-faire*.

(ii) Christian socialists, like the Rev. Charles Kingsley, regarded *laissez-faire* as contradictory to Christian principles. Literary socialists, like John Ruskin and William Morris, objected to the social injustices and ugliness of modern industry and preached a kind of idealistic communism. Socialists, like Karl Marx, emphasized a materialist outlook on life.

(iii) Bismarck increased the power of the militarist Prussian State, intervening in every sphere of German life—agriculture, industry, trade, and education. The military and industrial success of Germany dazzled other countries and encouraged them to copy many of the methods first successfully introduced in Germany—compulsory education, work-people's insurance against sickness, accidents, and old age, and the nationalization of railways. France and Britain later met increased foreign competition by the intro-duction of protective tariffs and systems of colonial preference (see p. 184).

By the end of the century the movement toward State socialism had been successful. A series of Factory Acts, Mines Acts, Workmen's Compensation, and Truck Acts promoted industrial welfare. Trade and industry were regulated by statute, as in the Merchant Shipping Acts, Merchandise Marks Acts, and Railway Regulation Acts. A series of enactments by the Liberal administration from 1906 to 1912 began a new programme of social reforms. See p. 149.

MAP 50

ARTIFICIAL PROSPERITY DURING NAPOLEONIC WARS

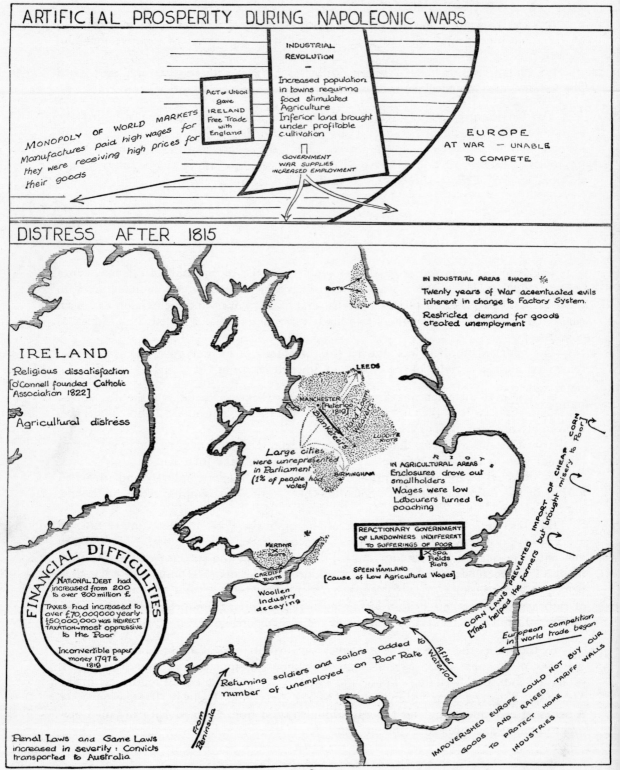

INDUSTRIAL REVOLUTION
—
Increased population in towns requiring food stimulated Agriculture
Inferior land brought under profitable cultivation

ACT of UNION gave IRELAND Free Trade with England

MONOPOLY OF WORLD MARKETS
Manufactures paid high wages for they were receiving high prices for their goods

GOVERNMENT WAR SUPPLIES INCREASED EMPLOYMENT

EUROPE
AT WAR — UNABLE TO COMPETE

DISTRESS AFTER 1815

RIOTS

IN INDUSTRIAL AREAS SHADED
Twenty years of War accentuated evils inherent in change to Factory System.
Restricted demand for goods created unemployment

IRELAND
Religious dissatisfaction
[O'Connell founded Catholic Association 1822]

Agricultural distress

LEEDS

MANCHESTER [Peterloo 1819]
Hand Loom Weavers
Blanketeers
LUDDITE RIOTS

Large cities were unrepresented in Parliament (1% of people had votes)

BIRMINGHAM

R I O T S
IN AGRICULTURAL AREAS
Enclosures drove out smallholders
Wages were low
Labourers turned to poaching

CORN LAWS PREVENTED IMPORT OF CHEAP CORN
[They helped the farmers but brought misery to Poor]

REACTIONARY GOVERNMENT OF LANDOWNERS INDIFFERENT TO SUFFERINGS OF POOR

X Spa Fields Riots

SPEEN HAMLAND
[Cause of Low Agricultural Wages]

MERTHYR X RIOTS

CARDIFF RIOTS

Woollen Industry decaying

European competition in world trade began

IMPOVERISHED EUROPE COULD NOT BUY OUR GOODS AND RAISED TARIFF WALLS TO PROTECT HOME INDUSTRIES

FINANCIAL DIFFICULTIES
NATIONAL DEBT had increased from 200 to over 800 million £.
TAXES had increased to over £70,000000 yearly £50,000,000 was INDIRECT TAXATION—most oppressive to the Poor
Inconvertible paper money 1797 to 1819

Returning soldiers and sailors added to number of unemployed on Poor Rate
After Waterloo

From Peninsula

Penal Laws and Game Laws increased in severity : Convicts transported to Australia

26. DISTRESS IN 1815

THE factors which contributed to the misery and distress of the English people after 1815 resulted from the industrial and agricultural changes (see pp. 95, 111), the Napoleonic wars and their after-effects, and the unsympathetic attitude of the Government.

A. THE FRENCH REVOLUTIONARY AND NAPOLEONIC WARS (1793–1815) AND THE ANGLO-AMERICAN WAR (1812–14)

Direct effects : (a) on Industry

1. The Continental Blockade inaugurated in 1806 by Napoleon's Berlin Decrees interfered with trade and led to unemployment. Unemployed workmen in the Midlands and the North smashed machinery believing it was responsible for their miseries (the Luddite Riots, 1811–12).

2. Conflict with America ending in war (1812–14) also interfered with trade. The non-importation Act 1807 passed by American Congress prohibited British imports, and the war brought about a complete stoppage of trade between America and Britain. The Lancashire cotton industry suffered from the shortage of raw cotton.

On the other hand, war needs stimulated production in certain industries, such as metal and wool, and the dislocation of industry and trade on the Continent gave British manufacturers a virtual monopoly of the markets of the world. English cotton and woollen goods were smuggled even into France.

Direct effects : (b) on Agriculture

The outbreak of war interfered with the import of corn, and a number of bad harvests made matters worse. The price of wheat rose. The poor suffered as the wages of agricultural labourers remained low. The Speenhamland system (see p. 135) prevented a rise in wages.

On the other hand, the war years were a time of great prosperity to farmers (profits) and landlords (high rents), who benefited both from the restrictions on imports and from the increased demands of the home market. So keen was the demand for corn that much unsuitable land was brought into cultivation. Enclosure Acts were hurried through Parliament regardless of the hardships to the poor farmers incurred by the changes.

Indirect Effects

Social. The energy of the Government was devoted to winning the war instead of to solving social problems, so the questions of child labour and factory conditions were pushed aside because more production was needed.

Political. The fear of revolution profoundly embittered industrial relations. Workers' agitation for reform was followed by repressive measures, such as the Six Acts, or Gag

Acts of 1819, which seriously interfered with the liberty of the citizen. Workmen were prevented from taking united action to demand higher wages or better conditions by the enforcement of the Conspiracy Laws and the enactment of the Combination Laws of 1799 and 1800.

Financial : (i) Suspension of cash payments (see p. 171). (ii) The cost of the war was very considerable, especially as Britain financed the Continental coalitions against Napoleon. Money was raised by loans, and taxes were high. In 1799 Pitt imposed the income tax for the first time, but this was not the main basis of taxation, and yielded much less than the taxes on foodstuffs, drink, and raw materials. The burden of taxation fell less heavily on the rich than on the poor ; one-half of a workman's earnings went to the Government.

Effects resulting from the End of the War

1. Returning soldiers and sailors found difficulty in getting employment, for large numbers were suddenly released on the labour market.

2. The Government's orders for arms and clothing ceased in 1815, so dislocating the metal and woollen industries. Prices fell, and so did wages. Foreign customers, too, were impoverished ; they began to develop their own manufacturing industries.

3. The income tax was repealed, but indirect taxation continued to be high.

4. Peace brought an end to the artificial prosperity of the farmers, and a decline in agricultural prices (Diagram 15) ruined the less efficient. A series of bad harvests increased their difficulties. Many farms were abandoned and much land turned over from corn to pasture. The chief sufferers were those who cultivated the heavy clays (as in the Midlands), which were less suitable for growing turnips or the four-course rotation. Though clay lands are naturally more fertile and yield heavier crops, they require more labour and more horse-power and better drainage than do lighter soils, and they are more liable to complete crop failures.

The Corn Law of 1815 (see p. 133), enacted to protect the farmers, was ineffective in its attempt to prevent disaster.

The Napoleonic wars took place during the important period of transition from domestic to factory industry, and it is difficult to distinguish between the hardships caused by the economic changes and the effects of the wars. The wars caused more rapid change, and thus intensified the inevitable distress that such great transformations in agricultural and industrial methods must involve.

Reforms

The acute distress which the nation suffered in the period 1815–30 demanded far-reaching reforms in the British political, social, and economic systems.

27. THE RISE OF FREE TRADE

THE Younger Pitt in the ten years (1783–93) before the outbreak of the war with France, strongly influenced by the ideas of Adam Smith (see pp. 125–126), reduced the duties on tea (1784) and negotiated a commercial treaty with France (the Eden Treaty of 1786) by which France reduced duties on British manufactures, while in return Britain lowered the duties on French wines. Trade developed rapidly, but the outbreak of the wars with France in 1793 put an end to Pitt's schemes. But many English manufacturers had been converted to the free trade views ; they no longer feared competition from foreigners, and aimed to extend their markets abroad rather than to seek protection for industry at home. At the end of the French wars in 1815 their demands, such as the Petition of London Merchants, 1820, began to influence the Government.

1. THE REFORM OF THE FISCAL AND TARIFF SYSTEM

At the beginning of the nineteenth century indirect taxes provided the greater part of the national revenue ; there were some 1500 articles on the Customs and Excise lists. Some articles like silk were prohibited from entering the country altogether. Smuggling was prevalent, and a large army of officials tried in vain to prevent it.

The fiscal system was reformed by William Huskisson, Robert Peel, and William Gladstone. Huskisson, by virtue of his position as President of the Board of Trade and M.P. for Liverpool, was impelled to examine the question of smuggling and the complaints of the merchants who demanded a remedy. He swept away high tariffs, aiming at a maximum rate of duty on imports of 30 per cent. This rate, he calculated, would make smuggling unprofitable. Silk and paper, formerly prohibited, were admitted, silk at a tax of 30 per cent., and paper at a low rate. Raw wool, the export of which had not been permitted, was now allowed to be sent out, though with an export duty of 1d. per pound. Similarly the export of machinery was permitted under licence.

Huskisson also lowered the tariff on a large number of articles, particularly raw materials, to 20 per cent., and with the help of Robinson codified the thousand separate Customs Acts into a single consolidated tariff. Other inland revenue taxes, such as those on windows, shops, and servants, were repealed or reduced during the period 1822–27.

Peel was influenced by the Report of the Committee on Import Duties (1840), pointing out that over 94 per cent. of the total revenue of the Customs for the year 1838–39 had been produced from seventeen articles. He aimed at securing a surplus of revenue over expenditure in order to pay off the National Debt.

He therefore advocated moderate tariffs, and reduced duties on manufactured goods to 20 per cent., on semi-manufactured goods to 12 per cent., and on raw materials to 5 per cent. in his Budget of 1842. In 1845 he lowered duties still further and abolished some five hundred altogether. To make up for the lost revenue in 1842 he reimposed income tax for three years at 7d. in the £ on incomes over £150.

Gladstone completed the work of his predecessors. He levied duties only on a few

DIAGRAM 9

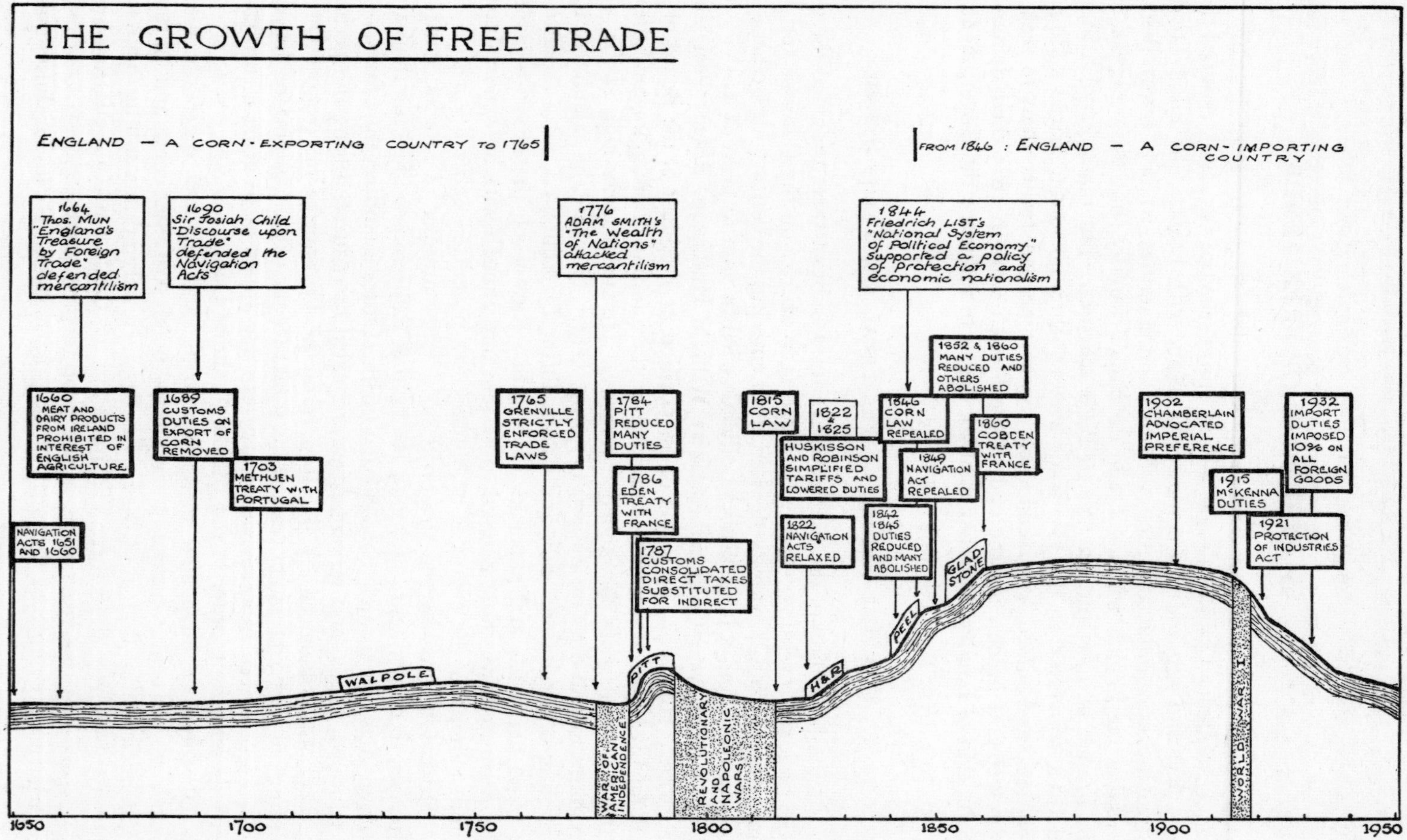

THE GROWTH OF FREE TRADE

ENGLAND – A CORN-EXPORTING COUNTRY TO 1765

FROM 1846: ENGLAND – A CORN-IMPORTING COUNTRY

Boxes (left to right / by period):

- 1644 Thos. Mun "England's Treasure by Foreign Trade" defended mercantilism
- 1690 Sir Josiah Child "Discourse upon Trade" defended the Navigation Acts
- 1776 Adam Smith's "The Wealth of Nations" attacked mercantilism
- 1844 Friedrich List's "National System of Political Economy" supported a policy of protection and economic nationalism

- 1690 Meat products and dairy products from Ireland prohibited in interest of English agriculture
- 1689 Customs duties on export of corn removed
- 1703 Methuen Treaty with Portugal
- Navigation Acts 1651 and 1660

- 1765 Grenville strictly enforced trade laws
- 1784 Pitt reduced many duties
- 1786 Eden Treaty with France
- 1787 Customs consolidated direct taxes substituted for indirect

- 1815 Corn Law
- 1822 & 1825 Huskisson and Robinson simplified tariffs and lowered duties
- 1822 Navigation Acts relaxed
- 1846 Corn Law repealed
- 1849 Navigation Act repealed
- 1842 1845 Duties reduced and many abolished
- 1852 & 1860 Many duties reduced and others abolished
- 1860 Cobden Treaty with France

- 1902 Chamberlain advocated imperial preference
- 1915 McKenna Duties
- 1932 Import duties imposed 10% on all foreign goods
- 1921 Protection of Industries Act

Timeline: 1650   1700   1750   1800   1850   1900   1950

River/statesmen labels: WALPOLE · PITT · PEEL · GLADSTONE

Wars: WAR OF AMERICAN INDEPENDENCE · REVOLUTIONARY AND NAPOLEONIC WARS · WORLD WAR I

132

imports of general consumption such as tea, spirits, and tobacco, and these for the purpose of revenue only. This made for economy in collecting import duties. After his budgets of 1853 and 1860 there were approximately fifty articles on the Import List as compared with one thousand five hundred in 1820. He promised to abolish the income tax, and did reduce it to 2d. in the £.

In 1860 was concluded Cobden's Treaty with France, by which England abolished all duties on French manufactured goods and reduced those on wine and brandy, while France removed her prohibition of British imports, imposing 30 per cent. duty on them. A 'most favoured nation' clause in the Treaty enabled Britain to secure the benefits which France gave to other countries.

THE REFORM OF THE CORN LAWS

Before 1815 England was generally self-supporting, and it was only in times of bad harvests, when the price of corn rose high, that imports of corn were allowed from the Baltic lands and from the countries of eastern Europe, while exports were prohibited. When the price was low bounties were given to farmers who exported corn, and imports were not permitted. These laws, which could prevent both imports and exports according to the price of corn, were known as 'corn laws.' In 1815 a corn law was enacted with the definite aim of protecting agriculture ; the import of corn was prohibited until the price rose to an average of 80s. per quarter for wheat. In 1828 this was replaced by a sliding scale of duties—as the price of corn rose the rate of duty decreased.

The Anti-Corn-Law League. The manufacturing classes objected to tariffs on corn. They knew that the high cost of food caused suffering to the workers, and that a great expansion of trade would follow the repeal of the corn laws : agricultural countries could only buy English manufactures if they could pay for them in corn. In 1839 the Anti-Corn-Law League was formed. Its leaders, Richard Cobden and John Bright, used their gifts of oratory inside and outside of Parliament. The success of the league was due to the great wealth behind the agitation and its excellent propaganda.

The Irish Famine of 1845 and 1846 caused by the failure of the potato harvest convinced Peel that corn must be imported without the payment of a heavy duty, and in 1846 he repealed the Corn Laws.

The British farmer feared ruin, but it was not until 1860 that corn was imported in very large quantities, and not until 1870 that the British farmer began to suffer from the competition of American corn.

THE NAVIGATION ACTS

(i) Famous Navigation Acts were passed in 1651 and 1660 (see p. 70).

(ii) These Acts were connected with colonial policy. The American colonies had revolted in 1775, and Britain's colonial policy needed to be revised.

(iii) They were also a means of stimulating the building of ships which were needed in times of war. After 1815 it became clear that the Acts served little useful purpose.

(iv) In 1823 Huskisson carried through Parliament the Reciprocity of Duties Bill which enabled treaties to be made with other countries lowering pilotage and anchorage dues in ports. He was able to negotiate these treaties of reciprocity, or mutual concession, with most countries : Holland was an exception.

(v) In 1849 all restrictions on foreign ships bringing cargoes to Britain were removed ; British coastal shipping was, however, reserved to British ships until 1854.

The British people for the most part supported free-trade principles throughout the nineteenth century, and regarded them as the key to their prosperity.

28. REFORM ACT 1832 : POOR LAW, FACTORY LEGISLATION, PUBLIC HEALTH

THE Reform Act of 1832 brought the new class of manufacturers into Parliament ; the landowning interests were quite prepared to support some changes, such as The Factory Acts, which were opposed by the manufacturing interests.

The three great reforms of the reformed Parliament were :

(i) The Poor Law Amendment Act, 1834.
(ii) The Factory Act, 1833.
(iii) The Municipal Corporations Act, 1835.

A. THE REFORM OF THE POOR LAW

The Need for Reform. The Poor Law in the early nineteenth century was still based on the Act of 1601 (see p. 65). After the Civil War each parish administered its relief without any supervision from the central Government, entrusting the work to untrained, unpaid, and unwilling officers. The difficulties after 1750 could not be met in this way.

The Settlement Acts. A Settlement Act passed in 1662 enabled parish officers to remove any persons from their parishes if they were likely to be chargeable on the rates. This provision interfered with workers passing easily from one part of the country to another. But a later Act in 1697 enabled a man to move from one parish to another if the authorities first agreed to accept him back should he become chargeable on the rates. Young men without families could obtain certificates of readmission without difficulty.

Indoor Relief. Shelter was given in the poorhouse to all persons, infirm or destitute, who required help. In the newer workhouses of the seventeenth century the residents were set to work and the produce of their labour sold to cover the cost of their upkeep. The workhouse might be in private hands or under the direct control of the parish. If under the latter's control, it was made as repellent as possible to keep the poor rates low. By an Act of 1723 J.P.s could refuse outdoor relief to those who would not go to the workhouse.

Gilbert's Act. The desperate condition of the agricultural worker led the Government in 1782 to revise the system of Poor Law relief. Gilbert's Act authorized groups of parishes to unite to build workhouses to be used by all except the able-bodied, to whom relief was to be given. Few parishes took advantage of its provisions.

Outdoor relief. This took the form either of small weekly doles of money or of a system of billeting out of the unemployed upon ratepayers who could employ them. Children were apprenticed to masters, and, at the end of the eighteenth century, to cotton-mill owners (see p. 95).

Speenhamland. In 1795 the Justices of the Peace of Speenhamland, in Berkshire, decided to supplement the wages paid by the local farmers out of the rates. The amount

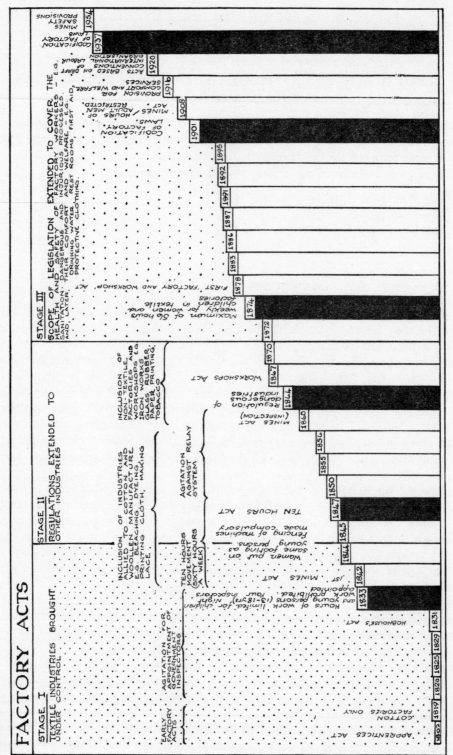

DIAGRAM 10

FACTORY ACTS

of the subsidy depended upon the price of corn and the size of the labourer's family. (When the price of the quartern loaf was 1s. the man was allowed 3s. a week, together with 1s. 6d. for his wife and each child.)

This system was copied by other parishes, and it spread over the South of England. It was never very common in the North. It resulted in a large increase in the poor rate, improvident marriages, and general pauperization of the agricultural labourer.

Another similar scheme was the *Roundsman system*, where the farmers employed paupers and the parish subsidized their low wages. The pauper was given a ticket by the parish, and this he took round to the farmers who employed him. In other districts farmers agreed to employ a certain quota of paupers according to the rateable value of their property. Farmers preferred subsidized pauper labour to free labour. It was cheaper. The independent labourers were frequently dismissed, and in time became paupers. People grew accustomed to accepting relief, and demoralization spread. Farmers too suffered because of the heavy burden of the poor rates.

The Poor Law Amendment Act (1834)

The Reform Parliament set up a Royal Commission in 1832 to inquire into the administration of Poor Relief. The Commission recommended sweeping changes. These changes were based upon two principles :

(i) *The Principle of the Workhouse Test.* All outdoor relief for able-bodied persons was to be abolished. Relief was to be given in the workhouse.

(ii) *The Principle of Less Eligibility.* The position of the able-bodied person receiving relief in the workhouse was to be less desirable (less eligible) than that of the humblest worker outside the workhouse.

Parliament accepted these principles, and passed the Act of 1834. The Act set up new administrative machinery. In place of the unpaid parish official three paid Government Commissioners with a paid secretary (Edwin Chadwick) had the implied duty of administering the poor law in accordance with the two principles of the Royal Commission. The Poor Law Commissioners established by the Act of 1834 had the power to issue directives to boards of guardians elected by ratepayers. The boards of guardians were to represent not a single parish but groups (unions) of parishes, thus making Gilbert's Act (p. 135) compulsory.

The Act was a triumph for the ideas of Bentham and Malthus. The latter had condemned outdoor relief, as leading to an over-populated countryside. Bentham was responsible for the birth of new administrative methods. Pauperism declined, and the burden on the rates was lowered, but sometimes at the cost of great suffering. Fortunately, good harvests in the middle thirties, the expansion of industry, and the building of railways mitigated this suffering. The Royal Commission did not make a diagnosis of the fundamental causes of poverty. It was assumed that pauperism was solely the result of defective administration. No account was taken of the agricultural changes in the country, or the industrial changes in the towns. The Act did not deal with the causes of poverty, but merely improved the administrative machinery for the granting of relief. A scientific investigation into the problems of poverty was not made until the appointment of the Poor Law Commission of 1909.

The Poor Law Commissioners of 1834 had little opposition in implementing the Act in the South of England. The new Union workhouses were built, but it was still found necessary to grant a great deal of outdoor relief to able-bodied persons. But when the three Commissioners (the ' three kings of Somerset House ') commenced to build workhouses (nicknamed ' Bastilles ') in the North of England they met fierce resistance. The Speenhamland system had never been common in the North. Before 1834 the unemployed in the North had received relief from parish officers. After 1834 they were forced into workhouses housing all types of inmates. The Chartist Movement (p. 149) drew some of its strength from the opponents to the Act of 1834.

In 1847 the Commissioners were replaced by a Poor Law Board with a President who was a member of the Government and of Parliament.

B. FACTORY LEGISLATION (1800–50)

Many manufacturers maintained that the restriction of hours of labour would ruin their trade and put them at a disadvantage with foreign competitors. A group of reformers insisted that it was in the interest of all to protect factory workers, more especially the women and children.

Up to 1830 the most influential of the reformers were Sir Robert Peel the elder and Robert Owen. Sir Robert was himself a cotton-mill owner, and Owen, in his cotton mill at New Lanark, put into practice his own ideas, reducing the hours of work to twelve a day, and refusing to employ children under the age of ten. He showed, by example, that employers need not be ruined if they concerned themselves with the happiness of their employees.

The Pauper Apprentices Act (1802) applied solely to pauper apprentices, and prohibited night work or employment for more than twelve hours a day. The duty of enforcing the Act rested on the Justices of the Peace, many of whom were mill-owners themselves. They were not interested, and even if they had been it was difficult to exercise control where the mills were remote and scattered. Those mills which were built later on the coal-fields could command a plentiful supply of child labour, as parents were only too anxious to send their children into factories to increase the family income. As the Act only concerned paupers it had little effect.

Factory Act (1819). Robert Owen in 1816 enlisted the support of Peel, then President of the Board of Trade. The investigations of a Committee set up by Peel resulted in the Act of 1819 by which

(i) No child under nine years was to be employed.

(ii) Children between nine and sixteen were to be employed for not more than twelve hours.

This Act covered free as well as pauper labour and was subject to enforcement by Justices of the Peace. It applied only to cotton factories.

Factory Act (1833). After 1830 the reformers had the sympathy of the Tories, who were prepared to accept any legislation in opposition to the manufacturers. Richard Oastler, a Yorkshire bailiff, denounced ' Yorkshire slavery,' and demanded a ten-hour day for all under twenty-one years. Michael Sadler introduced a Bill into Parliament to this end, and though the Bill was rejected, public attention had been aroused. Sadler later lost his seat in Parliament, and it was Lord Ashley (later Shaftesbury) who devoted himself to the cause of factory reform, and successfully carried through the Act of 1833 which applied to all textile mills :

(i) No child under nine years was to be employed.

(ii) Children between the ages of nine and thirteen were not to be employed more than nine hours a day in the factory, and were to spend two hours at school.

(iii) Children and young persons between the ages of thirteen and fifteen were not to be employed for more than twelve hours a day.

(iv) There was to be no night work for children under thirteen.

(v) A clause authorized inspectors to enter factories to see that the law was enforced (the most important part of the Act). The factory inspectors' reports became the basis for future reforms.

The Ten Hours Movement. The Factory Act of 1833 was a disappointment to those who advocated a ten-hour day. By this time men in factories realized that by supporting the limitation of the hours of women and children they were helping themselves. The agitation continued. When Peel the younger was returned to power in 1841 he introduced the Factory Act of 1844, limiting the hours of women to twelve a day, but reducing the age at which a child might be employed in a factory to eight. Provisions were made for the fencing of dangerous machinery. Lord Ashley resigned from Parliament in 1846, and his place as leader of the reformers was taken by John Fielden, a manufacturer, who in 1847 introduced a further Ten Hours Bill which was passed without difficulty. It reduced the hours of women and young persons to ten a day. The results were at first disappointing. The Factory Inspectors complained that the Acts were being evaded. The working day was from 5.30 A.M. to 8.30 P.M., and the employers worked the women and children in relays, frequently obtaining more than ten hours of work from them. A further Act in 1850 limited the working day inclusive of meals (1½ hours) for women and young persons to twelve hours to run from 6 A.M. to 6 P.M. (or 7 A.M. to 7 P.M.), and in 1853 the same applied to children.

Though nothing was done for men, in practice, however, the ten-hour day for men became operative because they could only work with the assistance of women and children. After this there was little opposition to factory reform on the part of mill-owners, and reforms were carried through from time to time. By 1867 the principles of Factory Acts were imposed on all factories and workshops, and not merely on textile factories. Rules concerning safety, ventilation, and sanitation were later imposed, and the minimum working age was raised in 1901 to 12 years, and in 1919 to 14 years.

Regulations in the Mines

Lord Shaftesbury's agitation for factory reform was extended to the mines. In 1840 he was able to secure the appointment of an investigating committee. Its report in 1842, written in vivid language and illustrated for the first time in the history of blue-books, shocked the British public. Children were employed opening trap-doors (to work the ventilating system) and drawing trucks of coal. They often worked in complete darkness. Parish apprentices had been used in this inhuman system, and there had been no one to protect them.

The Mines Act of 1842 prohibited the employment of women and boys under ten years underground, and appointed Government inspectors to report regularly on conditions in the mines. This Act was important, but it was only a beginning. In 1850 further provisions were made for the inspection of mines, and twenty years later more detailed regulations were drawn up.

In 1908 the working-day for miners was limited to eight hours.

C. PUBLIC HEALTH (1800–55)

While the death-rate was falling in the first half of the century over the country as a whole, it was rising in many of the large towns.

Improvement in the health of the people depended on better conditions in these towns. That is why the third major reform of the 1830's, the Municipal Corporations Act of 1835, was of such great importance, for by its provisions a Council elected by the ratepayers could do much to rid the towns of their squalor. Though the Act applied only to towns possessing charters, provision was made for unchartered urban areas to benefit from the Act, and most towns had done so by 1870.

Edwin Chadwick (1800–91) was one of the great social reformers of his age. When studying the conditions making for poverty (as secretary of the Poor Law Commission) he concluded that much was due to unemployment which resulted from sickness and disease. He maintained that the high death-rate in the towns was due to bad sanitation, and also that disease could not be wiped out by individual action. It must be done by the State. Chadwick advocated a central body to supervise the work of local authorities. The Report of the Poor Law Commission published in 1842 was mostly Chadwick's work ; it had a profound effect on the Government and the public, though it was not until 1848, following an outbreak of cholera, that a Public Health Act was passed, setting up a Central Board of Health.

After an inquiry, in areas where the death rate was high, this Board could create a local board of health. The Central Board, however, was unpopular, and it was dissolved in 1858, with the disappearance of cholera, and its functions taken over by the Privy Council and the Home Office.

THE WORKERS' ATTEMPTS AT ALLEVIATING THEIR DISTRESS (1790–1850)

DURING this period radical reformers agitated for better conditions for the workers. Much of the history of the labour movements is bound up with the careers of (i) Francis Place, the tailor of Charing Cross, whose shop provided a centre for the discussions of social reforms, and (ii) Robert Owen, a factory-owner, who had opportunities to put his radical ideas into practice.

The workers themselves united to improve their lot in (i) Trade Unions, (ii) Co-operative Societies, (iii) the Chartist Movement.

A. *Trade Unions : Early Years*

There were associations of workmen in the eighteenth century. Trade clubs grew up in skilled trades like printing and weaving. They were formed to enforce apprenticeship and other laws, rather than to enforce demands for improved conditions from the masters. These clubs were not looked upon with disfavour until the outbreak of the French Revolution, when fear of disorder led to the repression of all working-class associations.

In forming labour associations workers suffered from :

(i) fear of prosecution for conspiracy, for which a heavy sentence was imposed ;
(ii) the Combination Acts of 1799 and 1800, which prohibited unions of both masters and men. Masters were rarely prosecuted, but proceedings were sometimes taken against workmen. The policy of the Government drove the workers' unions underground

The Movement for the Repeal of the Combination Laws, 1824–25. Francis Place was the driving force behind this movement both in and outside Parliament. He had the support of Joseph Hume, a Radical M.P., who influenced Huskisson to set up a Parliamentary committee to inquire into the Combination Laws. Place's effective work behind the scenes resulted in a report favourable to repeal, and in 1824 the Laws were repealed. Unfortunately an epidemic of strikes followed, and the law was amended in 1825. In its final form the Act permitted workmen to combine to regulate wages and hours of labour, but it was difficult to act without committing the new statutory crimes of ' obstruction ' and ' molestation.' Trade unions had ceased to be illegal, but it was not possible to secure a wage increase by strike action.

Progress to 1850. The unions which developed in the next decade became linked to the new Utopian socialism of Robert Owen. The ultimate object was to form not a number of trade unions, one for each industry or craft, but rather one trades union comprising all workers. A number of such unions were formed, such as the Grand National Union of all the Operative Spinners of the United Kingdom and the Grand National Consolidated Trades Union. The latter was founded by Robert Owen in 1833–34. It was a revolutionary organization which aimed at replacing private employers

141

MAP 51

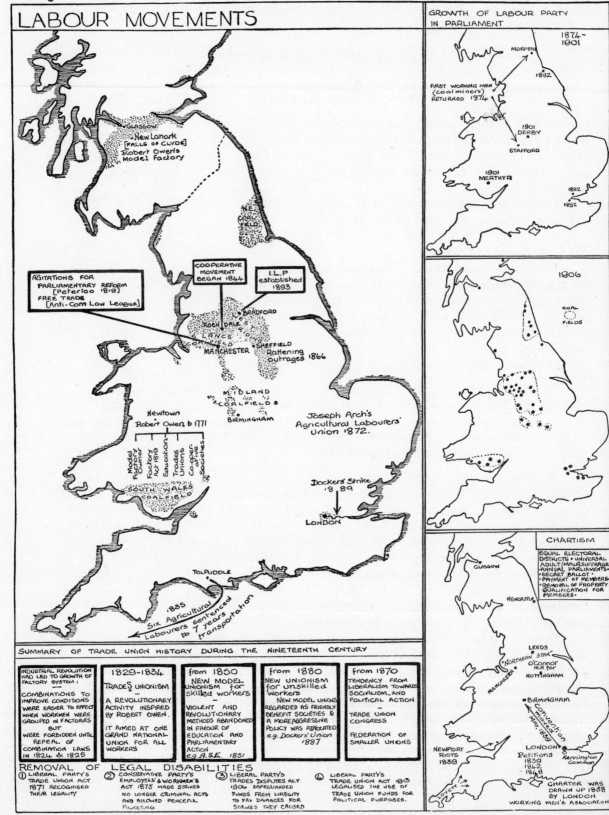

by a system of workers' control : parliamentary government was to be superseded by the rule of the 'Grand National.' Half a million enthusiastic workers joined, but the employers took speedy action. They presented a 'document' to their employees, forcing them to declare they did not and would not belong to the trades union, and threatened a lock-out. Efficient management of these monster organizations was lacking. Owen was not a successful leader. The men were not willing to fight for great ideals, but were concerned only with their local grievances.

DIAGRAM 11

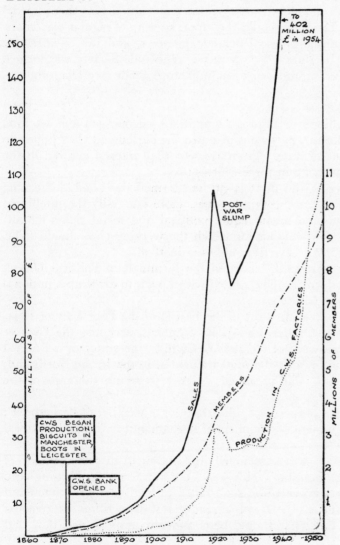

THE GROWTH OF THE CO-OPERATIVE
WHOLESALE SOCIETY

The Tolpuddle Martyrs. The Government and the Press supported the employers against the unions. The attitude of authority was shown by the case of the six Dorset labourers who in 1834 tried to form a branch of the Agricultural Labourers' Union at Tolpuddle. They sought to increase their weekly wage of 7s. to 10s. a week. In doing so they administered a number of oaths, as was customary, though contrary to an Act of 1797. They were prosecuted and transported overseas for seven years. After this the trade union movement declined until about 1850.

B. *The Co-operative Movement*
The co-operative movement developed between 1815 and 1850, partly as an attempt to escape from the truck system, whereby employers paid wages in goods instead of money and partly as a means of finding work for the unemployed.
Producers' Co-operatives. Groups of workers collected money to found villages such as Harmony Hall, East Tytherly, Hampshire, where crops were to be raised by co-operative production. They were influenced by the socialistic ideas of Robert Owen. Producers'

co-operatives were not successful because of difficulties they experienced in selling their goods.

Consumers' Co-operatives. In 1827 Dr King and members of the Brighton and other Mechanics Institute founded the Brighton Co-operative Society with the object of selling goods retail. The modern co-operative movement began with the formation of the Rochdale Pioneers' Society, which opened a shop in Toad Lane, Rochdale, Lancashire, in 1844, to sell groceries. The ultimate object was to found an Owenite Co-operative community. There were twenty-eight members paying 2*d.* a week. By 1851 the society had a capital of £1100. Branch shops were opened, and the range of goods extended. Its success was due to the fact that dividends were paid not on capital (as other societies had done) but upon purchases. The shops could rely upon a group of regular customers. Many societies followed the example of the Rochdale pioneers, and the co-operative movement developed steadily. In 1863 a Co-operative Wholesale Society was formed to buy goods in bulk. In 1877 it commenced to manufacture goods (see Diagram 11).

C. *The Chartist Movement (1832–48)*

The failure of the trade unions to improve conditions encouraged the working classes to agitate for political reform. By means of power in Parliament they hoped to pass laws to improve their economic state. From 1832 to 1848 interest centred in the Chartist movement. Chartism grew up in three centres :

(i) *In London.* William Lovett, who in 1835–36 had formed the London Working Man's Association (aim—to educate the working classes, more especially the intelligent artisans, and to seek by constitutional means equal political and social rights for all) and Francis Place drew up a list of demands for which the working class should fight. These formed the basis of the People's Charter, published in 1838.

(ii) *In Birmingham.* Thomas Attwood, leader of the Birmingham Political Union, which had agitated for political reform in 1832, united with Lovett to draw up a national petition embodying the aims of the Charter.

(iii) *In the North.* A movement arising out of the hatred of the Poor Law of 1834, and led by John Fielden, Richard Oastler, and J. R. Stephens, accepted the Charter as a means of setting aside oppressive laws. Fergus O'Connor, the editor of a Radical newspaper, *The Northern Star*, soon became the most influential leader in the North and, ultimately, of the whole movement. He preached violence to secure the ends of the Charter, which were :

(i) Manhood suffrage ; (ii) No property qualifications for a Member of Parliament ; (iii) Annual Parliaments ; (iv) Payment of Members of Parliament ; (v) Equal electoral areas ; (vi) Vote by secret ballot.

In 1839 a Chartist Convention was summoned in London to discuss methods of securing demands set down in the petition. This was later transferred to Birmingham. Lovett and the moderates (' Moral Force Chartists ') failed to hold back O'Connor and his associates (' Physical Force Chartists '). It was agreed that if the petition was rejected by Parliament (i) a national one-day strike should be considered, and (ii) that they had the right to arm.

The petition was rejected, but in the end the Convention broke up, both leaders and delegates realizing the impossibility of persuading all workers to strike. There was a rising in Newport, Wales, where John Frost and two others, held responsible for trying to release an imprisoned Chartist, were transported for life.

During the years 1840–42 O'Connor and his followers obtained the ascendancy. Another petition was presented in 1842, and failed. Strikes followed in the North, and troops were called out. Many Chartists were imprisoned. Lovett had secured a new supporter, Joseph Sturge, and hoped to secure middle-class support. The movement was splitting up into groups.

During the 1842–48 period there was some improvement in the condition of the working classes. The Corn Laws were repealed in 1846, and the Ten Hours Act was passed in 1847. O'Connor had become M.P. for Nottingham in 1847, and the following year decided to organize another national petition, but false signatures exposed the whole movement to ridicule.

The programme of Chartists was sensible, and in the course of time was adopted by all parties. Most of the points of the Charter have been put into legislation (though electoral areas are not exactly equal, and annual elections to Parliament are not held —they would hardly be practicable), but the movement failed because :

(i) Their ideas of Parliamentary reform were too sweeping for the times.

(ii) Their leadership was poor, and their followers uneducated and undisciplined. Ranged against them were wealthy and ably led manufacturers and landowners.

(iii) The Chartists were divided among themselves. There were personal antagonisms and groups with divergent aims.

(iv) The incentive for action died out with the better conditions which resulted from the reforms of the 1840's.

The Chartist Movement inspired the more responsible leaders of society to inquire into and to improve the lot of the working people.

The Development of Trade Unionism (1850–73)

In this Golden Age of Victorian prosperity there was a steady improvement in the condition of the working classes. Both money wages and real (that is, what the money could buy) wages rose considerably. The trade union movement, which had diminished in strength after the collapse of the Grand National Consolidated Trades Union, recovered and grew strong in the period 1850–73. But the New Model Unionism of this time was quite different from Robert Owen's Utopian scheme for a reconstruction of society. The new unionists accepted society as it was and set out to bargain with the employers for increased wages and better conditions.

The Amalgamated Society of Engineers, formed in 1851, was the typical union of the period. Its secretary was William Allan.

1. The members belonged to a skilled trade.

2. It aimed not only to improve wages and conditions but also to act as a friendly society, giving help to its members in times of sickness, unemployment, and old age.

3. Its leaders were paid officials who gave whole-time service to the Union. They were moderate men, and became experienced in negotiation.

4. It was a national union, with a central executive which made the rules and alone

could authorize strike pay. District committees administered their own funds, and could negotiate agreements with local employers, but could not call out men on strike.

It is not surprising that the employers of the engineers formed an opposing association, and when there was a dispute at Oldham the men were locked out for a period of three months. The Amalgamated Society spent £43,000 in strike pay. Although the men

DIAGRAM 12

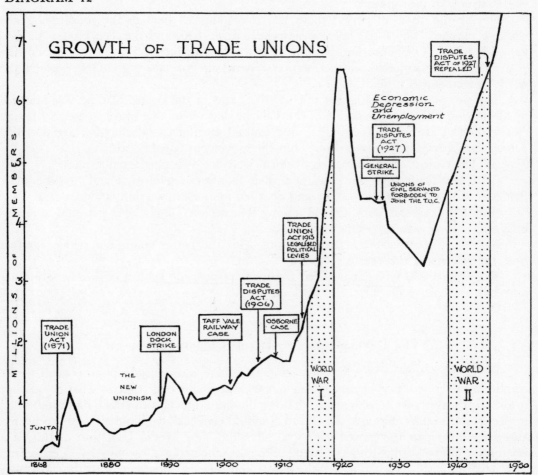

were ultimately forced back to work, publicity brought the Society an increase of members.

Many other trade unions were formed on the model of the Engineers, one of the most important being the Amalgamated Society of Carpenters and Joiners. Its secretary was Robert Applegarth.

The Junta. Between 1860 and 1870 there developed in London an unofficial cabinet of the trade union movement known as the Junta. The secretaries of the five leading unions met informally and decided matters of trade union policy.

They agreed not to spend large sums of money on unnecessary strikes, but to gain their ends by conciliation and peaceful bargaining, building up large funds for the payment of benefits.

They agitated for political reform, hoping by an extension of the franchise to secure their economic aims and better educational opportunities for all.

Most important of all, they pressed the Government to improve the legal position of the trade unions. The Junta was influential in securing the passing of the Master and Servant Act (1867). This gave the employee who had broken his contract fairer treatment. His offence was dealt with in the courts as a civil one and no longer as a criminal offence, except when his action caused loss of life or serious damage to property.

The Sheffield Outrages. There was strong opposition to trade unions among the middle and upper classes, and incidents in Sheffield during 1866 aroused strong feeling. Workers in the Sheffield district who had refused to join a strike were subjected to rattening by their fellow-workers; their tools were hidden, and sand was placed in their machines. A worker's house was blown up. At this time too, the judges made an unfavourable decision against trade unions in the law courts.

The Law Court Decision of 1867 (Hornby v. Close). The Boilermakers' Society tried to prosecute one of its branch treasurers who had stolen union funds. The Courts refused to admit the right of a trade union to sue in the law courts, because, though it was not (since 1825) a criminal organization, it had objects in restraint of trade—that is, the union could call a strike in order to obtain an increase in wages. Agitation, organized by the Junta, forced the Government to appoint a Royal Commission in 1869, and to pass the Trade Union Act (1871), which provided that :

(i) unions were not illegal merely because they were ' in restraint of trade ' ;

(ii) their funds were protected by law.

But in the same year the Criminal Law Amendment Act was passed which strengthened the law of conspiracy by making picketing, molestation, and obstruction during strikes criminal offences. The workers were incensed, and the Junta at once organized resistance, especially among the householders in towns, who had had a vote since 1867. As a result the Conspiracy and Protection of Property Act of 1875 was passed, allowing peaceful picketing. These Acts established the power of trade unions, which henceforth could organize strikes if bargaining failed to secure their demands.

Trade Councils and the Trade Union Congress. After 1860 Trade Councils or meetings of representatives of the local unions grew up in the larger towns and in 1868 delegates of the most important unions met together in a Trade Union Congress to consider the general policy of the Unions. While the Trade Union Act of 1871 was under discussion the Congress used its influence with members of Parliament.

Arbitration developed as a method of settling disputes. This was particularly due to the work of Mundella, an industrialist of Nottingham.

THE TRADE UNION MOVEMENT (1875–96)

From 1870 onward trade unionists became much more interested in politics as a means of increasing their influence. The period is also notable for the growth of the " New Unionism," when unions of unskilled labourers were formed.

Political Activities (see pp. 144-145). There were few working-men in Parliament up to 1870. But after this the Junta was active in encouraging working-class candidates to stand for Parliament. Two working-men were elected in 1874, another in 1880, and by 1887 there were eleven Members of Parliament representing the workers. They supported the Liberal Party, and accepted competition in industry. After 1889 many workers accepted socialist ideas based on the principles of Karl Marx, the German socialist (1818-83). There emerged also a number of socialist leaders, such as Thomas Mann and Keir Hardie, whose ideas were much more reminiscent of the early English socialists who had been influenced by Robert Owen. They strongly influenced the trade union movement after 1900.

The New Unionism. As early as 1872 Joseph Arch had formed an Agricultural Labourers' Union, but this failed. The first of the successful unions for unskilled workers (The Tea Operatives and General Labourers Union) was organized in 1886 by Ben Tillett, who worked in the London Docks. Shortly afterwards there were several note-worthy strikes. London match girls carried out a sensational and successful strike in 1888, and the Gas Workers and General Labourers' Union formed by Will Thorne in 1889 gained their demand for an eight-hour day without actually striking. The most famous of all the strikes was in the London Docks in 1889, organized by Tillett, Mann, and Burns, to demand ' the docker's tanner.' The orderly methods of the leaders and the revelation of the labour conditions at the docks aroused public sympathy, and financial support was received from all over the world. The success of the dock strike resulted in a huge increase in members of new unions, including the Miners' Federation, the Society of Bricklayers, and the Amalgamated Society of Railway Servants. The new unions paid no sick benefits, and their weekly subscriptions were low, making it possible for poorly paid workers to become members.

TRADE UNIONISM (1900-14)

The years 1900-14 were a period of great prosperity for the country as a whole, but not for the working classes ; real wages fell. There was a rapid rise in trade union membership, and antagonisms arising from fear of the strength of the new unions of unskilled workers arose. This led to new attacks on their legal position.

The Taff Vale Railway Case (1901). The railway company tried to break a strike by using volunteer labour. The Amalgamated Society of Railway Servants persuaded the volunteers to stop work and the Company brought an action for damages. Judgment was given for the Company ; this meant that a trade union could not assist in a strike without fear of being sued by the employers. There was a new agitation to alter the law. In this campaign the unions sought the help of the infant Labour Party. In the 1906 election twenty-six Labour members were returned to Parliament. As a result of their influence in the House of Commons, and of agitation outside, the Liberal Government passed the Trade Disputes Act (1906). This provided that a trade union could not be sued for damages for wrongs (such as calling men out on strike) committed by its members on behalf of the Union. It was a great triumph, for it meant that the trade union funds were safeguarded. The Labour Party had little support from the trade unions until the Taff Vale decision upset them. In 1904 unions instituted a political levy to help the finances of the Party.

The Osborne Case (1909). Osborne was secretary of a local branch of the Amalgamated Society of Railway Servants at Walthamstow. He objected to a compulsory political levy, and he sued his union. The judgment of the House of Lords upheld his objection, maintaining that trade union funds could not be handed over to a political party. Two Acts of Parliament followed : the first, in 1911, authorized the payment of Members of Parliament, and this made it easier for a working man to stand for Parliament. The second, the Trade Union Act of 1913, legalized the political levy, requiring only that the political fund be kept separate from other funds, and that any member should have the right to ' contract out '—that is, to refuse to pay the levy without being deprived of the privileges of trade union membership. By this Act the financial support of the trade unions for the Labour Party was secured.

From 1906 to the outbreak of war in 1914 there was great activity in the trade union movement. Many serious strikes took place, and new strike tactics were suggested, such as sympathetic strikes and lightning strikes. The railway strike of 1907 led to the establishment of conciliation boards of employers and employees. After 1910, through the influence of Tom Mann, who deplored the conflict between the unions representing skilled and unskilled labour, large industrial unions were formed, such as the National Transport Workers' Federation Union, which linked every union covering transport workers, other than railway servants. The National Union of Railwaymen was formed in 1913, and in the same year a ' Triple Alliance ' of the unions of railwaymen, miners, and transport workers was begun. They aimed to present joint demands to all employers at the same time.

GOVERNMENT RELIEF OF DISTRESS

Parliament enacted many reforms in the first half of the twentieth century that helped to improve the condition of the poor.

Poor Law. A Commission set up in 1909 emphasized that poverty was the result more of ill-health than of vice or laziness, and suggested better provision for the needs of the sick, the disabled, and the unemployed.

Old Age Pensions. Non-contributory pensions of 5s. weekly (but subject to a means test) were first granted by the Liberal administration in 1908.

National Health Insurance Act 1911. Lloyd George made compulsory weekly contributions from manual and the less prosperous salaried workers and from their employers to provide a medical service from a panel of doctors, any necessary hospital treatment, and sick pay during absence from work.

National Insurance Act 1911. A scheme of compulsory insurance against unemployment for workers who expected seasonal stoppages—*e.g.*, building and shipbuilding workers. Weekly contributions were again paid by both employer and employee.

Labour Exchanges. First set up in 1909, these were a new means of bringing unemployed workers into contact with employers who had jobs to offer.

MAP 52

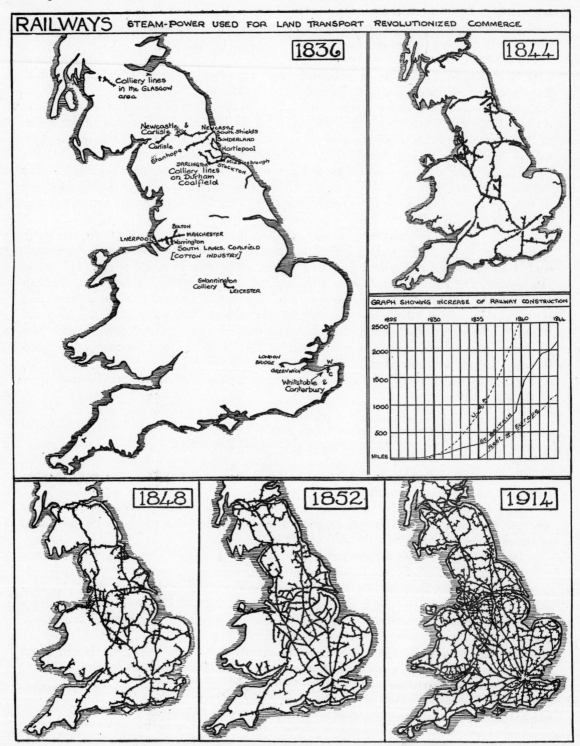

RAILWAYS STEAM-POWER USED FOR LAND TRANSPORT REVOLUTIONIZED COMMERCE

1836

Colliery lines in the GLASGOW area

Newcastle & Carlisle Rly.
NEWCASTLE
South Shields
Carlisle
SUNDERLAND
Stanhope
Hartlepool
DARLINGTON STOCKTON
Middlesbrough
Colliery lines on Durham Coalfield

BOLTON
LIVERPOOL
MANCHESTER
Warrington
South Lancs. Coalfield
[COTTON INDUSTRY]

Swannington Colliery
LEICESTER

LONDON BRIDGE
GREENWICH
W
C
Whitstable & Canterbury

1844

GRAPH SHOWING INCREASE OF RAILWAY CONSTRUCTION

1825   1830   1835   1840   1844
2500
2000
1500
1000
500
MILES

U.S.A.
GT. BRITAIN
REST OF EUROPE

1848   1852   1914

THE GROWTH OF THE RAILWAY NETWORK

30. THE DEVELOPMENT OF BRITISH RAILWAYS IN THE NINETEENTH CENTURY

As in the development of canals and shipping, Britain was a pioneer in the evolution of the railway. In this country :

(i) Railways were built by private companies ; the Government gave no assistance in their construction.

(ii) In their early days they met much opposition ; towns and landowners often kept them as far away as possible. They were charged dearly for their land, and the expense of securing the necessary Act of Parliament was very heavy. They also had to fight the opposition of canal companies, coaching interests, and turnpike trustees.

(iii) Engineering difficulties also added to the cost of construction ; there were few long stretches of straight, easily laid track in Britain.

(iv) Railways were at first regarded as a new type of road, and had to permit all carriers of goods to place their engines and wagons on the lines. It was assumed that competition between carriers would keep the rates low. (N.B. When the canals were constructed the canal companies were not allowed (until 1845) to put their own boats on the waterway, but merely to charge tolls from competing carriers.) When it became clear that private engines were not feasible, and the railway companies had to become the carriers, Parliament laid down strict rules regarding rates and fares.

THE EVOLUTION OF RAILWAYS : THE EXPERIMENTAL PERIOD UNTIL 1840

(a) *Provision of Rails along Roads.* The earliest railways were simply lines of wooden blocks along which horses could drag hopper wagons more easily. Later iron plates were fixed on top of the wooden rails to prevent them wearing quickly, and iron rails became general after 1770. Most of the railways were built on the coalfields, though the first public railway, the Surrey Iron Railway, was constructed to carry corn from Croydon to London.

(b) *Application of Steam Power to Locomotion.* Watt's steam-engine (1765) was not used for steam traction until after 1800. Hedley's *Puffing Billy* (1813) and George Stephenson's model (1814) were the first practical locomotives.[1]

The Stockton and Darlington line, built in 1825, was important in the history of railways. It was built to carry coal from collieries in County Durham to navigable water. It demonstrated that the steam-engine was superior to horse traction, that railways were just as suitable for passenger as for goods traffic, and that, unlike canal companies, railways would have to provide vehicles and means of transport as well as a permanent way. This line was soon followed by the construction of the Canterbury and Whitstable line in Kent and the Bolton and Leigh railway in south Lancashire.

The Liverpool and Manchester Railway was opened in 1830. Its engineer was

---

[1] In 1803 Richard Trevithick ran a steam carriage on the roads of London.

MAP 53

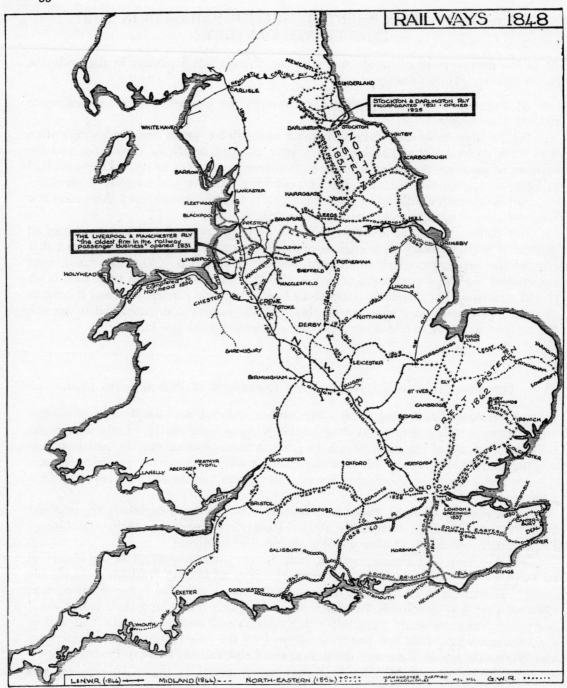

RAILWAYS 1848

STOCKTON & DARLINGTON RLY
INCORPORATED 1821 · OPENED
1825

THE LIVERPOOL & MANCHESTER RLY
"the oldest firm in the railway
passenger business" opened 1831

L&NWR (1844) ←——→   MIDLAND (1844) - - -   NORTH-EASTERN (1854) +°+°+°   MANCHESTER SHEFFIELD   MSL MSL   G.W.R. •••••••
& LINCOLNSHIRE

MAP 54

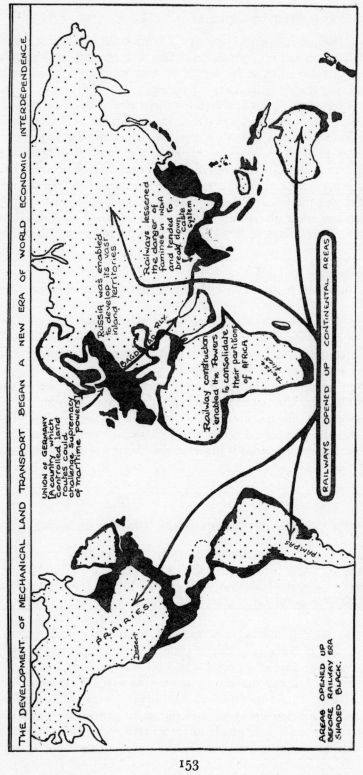

WORLD EFFECTS OF THE DEVELOPMENT OF INLAND TRANSPORT

153

George Stephenson, whose famous locomotive *The Rocket* conclusively demonstrated the superiority of this new means of locomotion. This was the first real passenger railway, and also the first to threaten and be forced to buy out the opposition of canal and waterway interests, the Bridgewater Canal Trustees.

During the years 1836–37 no fewer than thirty-nine Acts were passed authorizing railway construction, but Map 52 shows that most of these railways were short lines. Their close connexion with the coalfields is obvious. Even in 1844 (Map 52) the network of lines (heralded in 1838 by the opening of the London and Birmingham ; the Grand Junction of 1837 ; and the Great Western from London to Bath and Bristol, opened in 1839–41) is closest on the coalfields ; the other lines link together the great cities.

Brunel constructed the Great Western Railway on a broad gauge of 7 ft., and there was a conflict between the railways about the gauges, but in 1846 Parliament decided in favour of the narrower gauge (4 ft. 8½ in.) used by Stephenson (Map 53).

Results of the Coming of the Railways

1. Railways provided a new and effective form of cheap transport for both goods and passengers.

2. They helped to reduce the price of goods as transport was cheaper and goods could be drawn from a wider field.

3. They created a national market for supplies instead of the former local markets. This led to bigger businesses and bigger stores.

4. New towns grew up, such as Crewe and Swindon ; many places, hitherto unimportant, developed while towns untouched by railways decayed.

5. Railways opened up the continental interiors of the world. The iron roads were built first, and the population of farmers followed. England was able to draw her food supplies from regions previously inaccessible (Map 54) (for effects on home agriculture, see p. 161).

The Period of Amalgamation and Consolidation

(a) *Government Control.* Parliament distrusted the railway monopoly, and made attempts to control it. Acts in 1840 and 1842 gave the Board of Trade certain powers ; no new lines were to be opened without notice to the Board, returns about traffic carried and about accidents were to be made ; the Board could not interfere in the actual management.

In 1844 it was decided that all new railways must revise their tolls if dividends of 10 per cent. were paid in three consecutive years. They were also forced to run a train to carry passengers at the rate of a penny a mile at least once a day.

(b) *Amalgamation.* During the 1840's there was a great increase in railway construction, and, in 1845–46, a boom period. In 1843 a total of 1952 miles of line were open ; by 1850, 6621 miles were open, and the main railways systems were complete. The railway companies tended to amalgamate to reduce overhead costs, and to satisfy passengers who disliked changing from one railway system to another. The most important amalgamations were the Midland and the London and North-western (see Map 52). George Hudson, ' the Railway King,' planned many of these amalgamations.

The Railway Clearing House was formed in 1842, and acted as a council to co-ordinate the work of the different lines. It drew up a scheme for classifying goods into

MAP 55

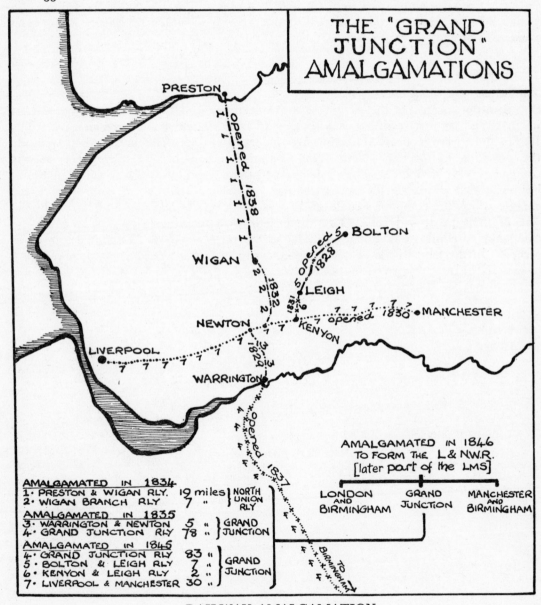

RAILWAY AMALGAMATION

various categories, and also apportioned the revenue derived from goods which had been carried over two or more systems.

(c) *Decline of Canals : Further Measures of Control.* As canals were ceasing to be competitors of the railways, the Government took further measures to control the railway monopoly.

Railway commissioners were appointed to investigate amalgamation schemes, and by an Act of 1854 companies were required to facilitate through traffic from one Company's area to another. They were forbidden to give ' undue preference ' to certain passengers or consignors of goods.

The Railway and Canal Commission

In order to enforce the Act of 1854 the Railway and Canal Commission was set up in 1873. At first regarded as a temporary body, it was made permanent in 1888. Its functions were to hear complaints by traders of undue preference, and to facilitate the provision of through rates. The Commission had powers to prevent railway companies from buying out canals ; it had no power to prevent railway amalgamations, but examined proposals for amalgamation. Further Government control over the charges which the companies could make was given by the Railway and Canal Traffic Acts of 1888, 1891, and 1894. One of the effects of these measures was to cause the companies to eliminate competition as far as the rates and fares chargeable were concerned. In the first decade of the twentieth century wages were increased, and power to increase charges was given by the Railway and Canal Traffic Act of 1913.

RAILWAYS had opened up the great continents of North and South America, Africa, Asia, and Australia, and primary products and foodstuffs could be more easily brought to the ports. The new steam-ships brought these goods to Europe. Railway and steam-ship together made the world one market. At the beginning of the nineteenth century wooden sailing-ships were still in use. By the end of the century iron and steel had replaced wood, and steam-power had outmoded the sail. The iron ship and the steamer developed quite independently.

Iron ships. John Wilkinson (see p. 90) had constructed an iron barge (*The Trial*) in 1787, and in 1817 the first iron ship, known as the *Vulcan*, was built on the Clyde. The development of the new ship was slow. The Post Office refused to allow mails to be carried in them, and, in spite of the fact that the weight of an iron ship was a quarter less than that of a wooden ship of the same size, the Navy would not construct an iron battleship before 1860.

Steam-ships. Early paddle-steamers were built of wood. The *Charlotte Dundas*, constructed by William Symington in 1802 with a Boulton and Watt engine, plied on the Clyde. In 1807 Robert Fulton, again using a Boulton and Watt engine, carried passengers on the *Clermont* from Albany to New York down the Hudson river.

The first successful passenger vessel in this country was Bell's *Comet*, built in 1812. Progress was more rapid after this. In 1813–14 four steamers were built on the Clyde; in 1816, eight; in 1822 the number had reached twenty-two.

In 1818 steamers began to sail between Dover and Calais, and in 1819 the *Savannah* crossed the Atlantic, using steam as auxiliary to sails. Nearly twenty years later (1838) four ships crossed the Atlantic using steam-power alone. Screws were introduced in 1839, and soon after iron ships were constructed, as they were better able to stand the vibration of the screws. Brunel's *Great Britain* (1845) was the first large iron ship and the first large ship to use the screw propellor instead of the paddle-wheel.

Even after 1850 the change-over from sails to steam was astonishingly slow, and English sailing-ships were still being used for the China tea trade as late as 1870. The disadvantage of the sailing-ship was its irregularity, for it depended on the winds. Sailing-ships continued to be used for carrying freight long after iron passenger-liners—which had to adhere to a strict timetable—had been built (Diagram 13).

Steam-ships were not economical until coaling stations had been established on the world's great trading routes. The need to carry fresh water for the boilers also reduced cargo space.[1] The compound engine, introduced in the 1860's, reduced the quantity of coal required, and further great developments followed the change from iron to steel, which made a much lighter ship.

Development of the Mercantile Marine. Between 1830 and 1850 Britain began to feel the competition of American 'clippers,' which were very speedy, and cheaper than the

---

[1] In 1858 Brunel constructed the *Great Eastern* in the hope of overcoming these difficulties. She was nearly 700 feet long, and had space to carry much cargo and many passengers, but was too large to be economic at that time, and had to be used for laying trans-Atlantic cables.

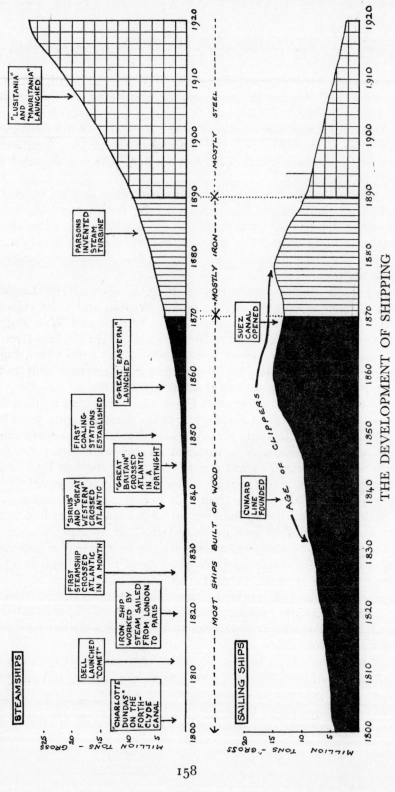

DIAGRAM 13

THE DEVELOPMENT OF SHIPPING

STEAMSHIPS

MILLION TONS - GROSS

"CHARLOTTE DUNDAS" ON THE FORTH-CLYDE CANAL

BELL LAUNCHED "COMET"

IRON SHIP WORKED BY STEAM SAILED FROM LONDON TO PARIS

FIRST STEAMSHIP CROSSED ATLANTIC IN A MONTH

"SIRIUS" AND "GREAT WESTERN" CROSSED ATLANTIC

"GREAT BRITAIN" CROSSED ATLANTIC IN A FORTNIGHT

FIRST COALING-STATIONS ESTABLISHED

"GREAT EASTERN" LAUNCHED

PARSONS INVENTED STEAM TURBINE

"LUSITANIA" AND "MAURITANIA" LAUNCHED

←- MOST SHIPS BUILT OF WOOD - - - - - - -MOSTLY IRON - - - -MOSTLY STEEL- - - - -

SAILING SHIPS

MILLION TONS - GROSS

CUNARD LINE FOUNDED

AGE OF CLIPPERS

SUEZ CANAL OPENED

158

British sailing-ships, that were more lasting but slower. The American Civil War (1861–65) ended this rivalry. Meanwhile British shipowners had been developing regular passenger services by steam-ship. The Cunard Company dates from 1839, the White Star Line from 1870. Side by side with the big liner which sailed on specified routes and at regular times grew up the tramp steamer which sailed from port to port, finding cargo on its journey.

Britain built up an enormous carrying trade in shipping, and by the end of the nineteenth century carried over one-half of the world's cargoes. The reasons for her commercial supremacy include :

(i) the large deposits of coal in Britain not far from the coast (see p. 90) ;
(ii) she possessed various ports and islands throughout the world where coaling stations could be established ;
(iii) her inventors and engineers had been pioneers in the evolution of the steam-ship ;
(iv) a vast empire provided a market for British manufactured goods and an unlimited source of raw materials and foodstuffs ;
(v) the adoption of a free trade policy, removing barriers to the free movement of goods, was an incentive to the shipping industry.

In 1910 the chief ship-owning countries of the world were :

DIAGRAM 14

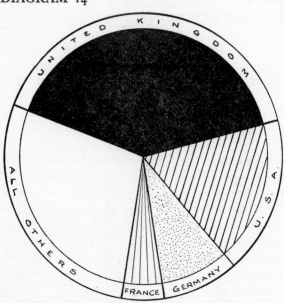

THE CHIEF SHIP-OWNING COUNTRIES
OF THE WORLD

Country	Tons
1. The United Kingdom	10,400,000
2. The U.S.A.	
Foreign service .	500,000
Rivers and Canals .	4,300,000
3. Germany . . .	2,400,000
World Total . .	26,200,000

Foreign competition increased by the end of the century. Many foreign Governments, the German Government especially, gave assistance by granting subsidies to shipping companies. The opening of the Suez Canal shortened the route to the East, and made more shipping-space available. There was considerable cutting of freight rates, which became so unremunerative that the liner companies had to agree to maintain minimum rates.

(1) 1837–73 : THE GOLDEN AGE

BY 1837 the worst of the depression which followed the Napoleonic Wars was over (see p. 128) and a new era of agricultural prosperity began to dawn. The Poor Law Amendment Act (1834) reduced the burden of the rates (see p. 135). The Tithe Commutation Act (1836) helped the farmer by substituting for the delivery of a fixed proportion of his crop the cash payment of a sum which remained constant. New technical improvements helped him to increase output to meet the increasing demands of the town population and make a profit, notwithstanding having to pay higher wages and rents. Farming was profitable, and both tenant farmers and landowners were encouraged to invest more capital in the farms.

(i) *Machinery*. Very little machinery was used in British agriculture before 1840 : corn was cut by scythes and threshed by flails. A reaper had been invented by Bell in 1826, but until the old ridge system of drainage had been superseded, a mechanical reaper could not be successfully used. Robert Ransome's works were started at Ipswich in 1785, but development of agricultural tools and machinery was slow. Between 1840 and 1870, however, many varieties of plough, suitable for different types of soil, were introduced. Jethro Tull's drills, or improvements upon them, became more general. Steam-power was applied to threshing machines, and after 1850 they entered into general use. Iron tools gradually took the place of wooden implements, and iron gates and fences were introduced.

(ii) *Drainage*. The old system of drainage by ridge and furrow was wasteful. Water accumulated in the furrows, and soil from the ridges was washed away. In 1823 James Smith, of Deanston, Perthshire, cut a series of parallel trenches, filled with stones, and so drained his land. This method was adopted in most parts of Britain. Later, clay pipes were substituted for the stones. In 1846 the Treasury encouraged landlords to improve their drainage systems by granting sums of money, repayable by instalments. Farmers on clay lands benefited particularly.

(iii) *Manuring*. Improvements in drainage made manuring more profitable. The value of manure, even of farmyard manure, was not properly appreciated until the middle of the nineteenth century. The use of artificial manures was a direct result of the publication of *Chemistry in its application to Agriculture and Physiology* by the German chemist Liebig in 1840. His ideas were introduced into England by Sir John Lawes and Joseph Gilbert. In 1843 Lawes established a factory at Deptford for producing phosphates. He also began the famous Rothamsted research station, conducting experiments on manuring, rotation of crops, and stock-breeding. He converted ammonia salts which were by-products of gas-making into valuable nitrogenous fertilizers.

In 1835 the first cargo of Peruvian guano arrived in England. From 1840 onward increasing quantities of this valuable phosphatic manure were used by British farmers.

(iv) *Farm Animals*. The work of the early pioneers such as Bakewell was continued, and resulted in improved breeds of cattle and sheep. The consumption of milk, butter, and cheese rose considerably, and imports of oil-cakes made of linseed and cotton-seed —splendid cattle foods—greatly increased.

The Royal Agricultural Society was founded in 1838 to encourage farming on scientific principles. The Society paid rewards for new discoveries, held shows in different parts of the country, and fostered competition. It also published a journal which gave the latest results of agricultural research, and to some extent filled the gap which had been caused when the Board of Agriculture, which had been formed by William Pitt in 1794, was dissolved in 1822.

In spite of the farmers' fears that ruin would follow the repeal of the Corn Laws, there was no catastrophic fall in the price of wheat. This was because :

(i) There was a rising demand for farm products from the growing urban population. The townspeople were better off, and could afford to buy more food. The new railways facilitated the transport of the crops to the towns.

(ii) Many of the corn-exporting countries were engaged in wars, Russia : The Crimean War (1853–56). Germany : war with Denmark (1863), Austria (1866), and France (1870–71). The U.S.A. : The Civil War (1861–65).

They had little surplus to export. Until shipping freights fell (see p. 159) the cost of transport from these Continental competitors was high, and this, as Cobden pointed out, gave an advantage to the home farmer.

(2) 1873–1914 : THE GREAT DEPRESSION AND ADJUSTMENT TO WORLD ECONOMY

The Golden Age of English farming came to an end when railways were constructed across the continental interiors of North America and Australia and steam-ships carried to the Old World the produce of the virgin soils of the New. The farmers of Europe could not compete in price with these cheaply grown crops. In most countries their import was prevented by high tariffs. England alone determined to give the consumer the benefit of the cheapest food, and allowed unrestricted import. Competition was felt successively in corn, wool, meat, and dairy products.

Corn. In 1872–73 for the first time the imports of wheat exceeded home production, and, except for the year 1874–75, they continued to do so. Diagram 21 shows the decrease in the proportion of home-grown to imported food.

After 1880 there was an increasing tendency for farmers to turn over from arable to pasture farming.

Wool. Accompanying the decline in the demand for English wheat was a disastrous fall in the price of English wool, due mainly to the import from Australia and New Zealand of high-class merino wools.

Beef and mutton. Though only a small proportion of our beef supply came from abroad before 1885 (less than 10 per cent.), the price of meat was falling almost continuously. It dropped 20 per cent. between 1871 and 1896. The first cargo of frozen lamb arrived three years after the invention of refrigerated ships, in 1882.

Dairy products. Foreign competition was not felt in the production of hay and straw, or of milk, and only slightly for butter and cheese, until after 1880. In the period 1882–99 mutton imports increased twentyfold, but butter imports only doubled, while cheese imports increased merely by a third.

Foreign competition forced changes on the British farmer :

He turned to the production of perishable commodities which could not easily be imported, especially liquid milk, fresh vegetables, eggs, and fruit, and to compete with

DIAGRAM 15

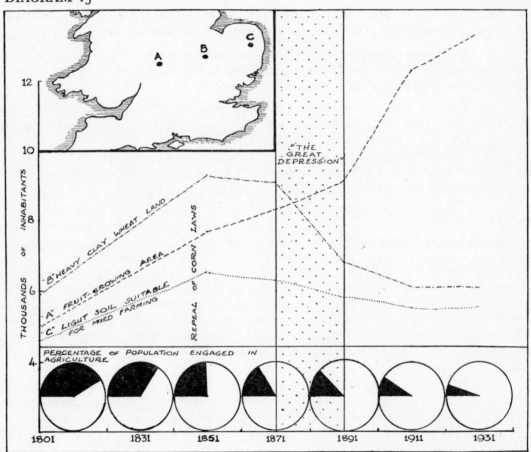

THE EFFECTS OF THE DEPRESSION IN AGRICULTURE

the cheap imported chilled and frozen meat he produced beef and mutton of superior quality. He was helped by the fall in the price of corn and other feeding stuffs. The wealthier population could afford the superior meat, etc.

The period of adjustment to the changed conditions was a long one, and may be said to have lasted until the outbreak of war in 1914. The principal results included :

(i) A decline in arable farming on the heavy soils of the eastern counties, in the

Midlands, and in the western counties (Diagram 15). Between 1880 and 1892 agricultural rents fell by almost a fifth ; by 1900 they had fallen by a half.

(ii) This transition to pasture led to a decline in the number of agricultural workers required (see Diagram 15), some of whom left the countryside for the towns, or emigrated to the colonies and the U.S.A.

(iii) In order to keep men on the land the Government was forced to assist the farming community. Royal Commissions were set up (1879–82 and 1893) to investigate the causes of the depression, and as a result of their recommendations:

(a) Tithe rent charges were transferred from occupiers to owners.

(b) Local authorities received grant-in-aid from the Government which enabled them to reduce their rates on agricultural land.

(c) A Government department—later known as the Board of Agriculture—was set up in 1889 to supervise farming.

(d) The payment of compensation by the landlord for improvements made by a tenant farmer was made compulsory.

(e) An incentive to the agricultural labourer to remain on the land was made by the Smallholdings Acts of 1893 and 1907 which gave County Councils power to acquire farmland and to let it in smallholdings of one or two acres. Between 1908 and 1914 nearly 17,600 acres so acquired provided 14,000 smallholdings. After the War 16,500 ex-Service men were settled on a quarter of a million acres divided into smallholdings.

(iv) A trade union—the Agricultural Labourers' Union—was established by Joseph Arch in 1872. The Union was dissolved in 1884, but as a result of its endeavours some progress was made towards better conditions. The Reform Act of 1884 extended the franchise to the agricultural labourer, and greatly increased his political influence.

E.H.—F

THE GROWTH OF BRITISH INDUSTRY IN THE NINETEENTH CENTURY

THE great technical changes in the eighteenth century described on pp. 84–94 still left industry very much in the handicraft stage. The real Industrial Revolution was not accomplished until mass production (the production of identical articles in large quantities) became a normal feature of industry. This position was not reached until the last quarter of the nineteenth century, when steam-power had been generally adopted and most goods were made in factories.

The use of power-driven machinery developed slowly. The change took place in the cotton industry first in the spinning processes and then in weaving, though by 1830 there were still 240,000 hand-looms as compared with 114,000 power-looms. In the woollen industry power-driven machinery was first used to weave worsteds, though only 5000 power-looms were operating in 1830, and they did not become the normal method of production until 1860. Hand-loom weaving of woollens was quite common in the seventies, and the change in the linen, lace, hosiery, and silk industries was even slower.

The size of businesses was small. Though exceptional firms employed a thousand work-people the average number of workers in cotton factories in 1830 was just over 150, and in woollen mills only 45.

THE REASONS FOR THE SLOW GROWTH OF THE FACTORY SYSTEM

1. There was a dearth of labour, as workers were reluctant to go into factories which were often built away from their own villages. Factory employment put an end to part-time agricultural work. Under the Domestic System all members of the household participated in the work. People were unwilling to break up the unity of family life to take up separate jobs in factories. There was, too, some confusion in the minds of work-people between the new factories and the older work-houses, which were often let out to contracting employers. People would not exchange the freedom of village life for the harsher discipline of the factory.

The shortage of labour was to some extent alleviated by the influx of Irish immigrants in the early nineteenth century. Without the Irish (driven from their country by famine) Lancashire's cotton industry could have expanded but little before 1850.

2. The employers of labour under the Domestic System were reluctant to set up factories. In times of depression it was not *their* buildings and plant which stood idle—the cost of the depression was borne by the work-people. Widely scattered workers were unable to combine against their employers to demand improved conditions. Slowly, however, the advantages of the factory system from the employer's point of view became apparent. He could discipline his staff better, and power-driven machinery reduced the costs of production.

3. An acute shortage of raw materials hindered the expansion of the textile industries. It was not economical to establish a large factory unless a constant and adequate supply

of raw materials could be assured. Eli Whitney's invention of the cotton gin in 1793 solved the chief difficulty in getting more cotton fibre, but it was not until the end of the 1830's that increased supplies of wool were available. They came from Australia, and supplemented the imports from Spain, Saxony, and Silesia.

4. A mechanized industry must have behind it a body of engineers capable of making and servicing machines and tools. This development was very slow.

DEVELOPMENTS IN THE MAJOR INDUSTRIES DURING THE NINETEENTH CENTURY

Textiles. The major inventions had been made in the cotton industry by 1800. The nineteenth century saw improvements—machines became faster and more efficient. Mule-spinning did not become fully automatic until the invention of the self-acting mule in 1825 by Roberts of Manchester. Ring-spinning, a quicker and cheaper method of making yarn, was invented by Thorpe in the United States in 1828. It was not common in Lancashire until after 1880, and even by 1914 barely a quarter of the spindles in Lancashire were ring spindles. The other major advance in the cotton industry in this period, the Northrop automatic loom invented in 1892, also came from America. The weaver could now supervise three or four times as many looms as formerly. The new machines were adopted only slowly in Lancashire, as they were at first unsuited to making the finest cottons.

In the woollen industry the important change was the mechanization of wool-combing. A series of inventions after 1840 perfected a machine which led to the disappearance of the hand comber after 1860. Two new textiles were introduced during the century ; jute, imported from India in increasing quantities after 1830, was manufactured at Dundee, in eastern Scotland, and in 1880 a Frenchman, Chardonnet, produced the first artificial silk, or rayon. A factory for manufacturing viscose rayon yarns was built at Coventry in 1900.

Iron and Steel. John Neilson in 1828 had the idea of heating the blast of air before it entered the furnace. This hot blast process greatly reduced the amount of coal needed, and the cost of pig iron fell. The use of blackband ironstone (which contained enough carbonaceous matter to dispense with preliminary coking) reduced further the consumption of coal. There was an enormous increase in the production of pig iron in Lanarkshire, where this kind of ironstone was found. Map 56.

In the second half of the nineteenth century the principal development was the change-over from wrought iron to steel. This was due to three important inventions which greatly reduced the cost of steel. In 1856 Henry Bessemer evolved the converter method of turning pig iron direct to steel without first changing it into wrought iron. Siemens (a German) and Martin (a Frenchman) achieved the same end by refining the pig iron in an open hearth. This process resulted in a better quality steel than Bessemer's, and by 1913 had almost supplanted it. It was also cheaper in the end, because large quantities of steel scrap could be used (Diagram 16).

These two methods of steel-making were unsuited to phosphoric iron ores. In 1879 Gilchrist and Thomas showed that these could be used if the converter or open hearth were lined with a lime material. France, Belgium, and Germany benefited mostly from

MAP 56

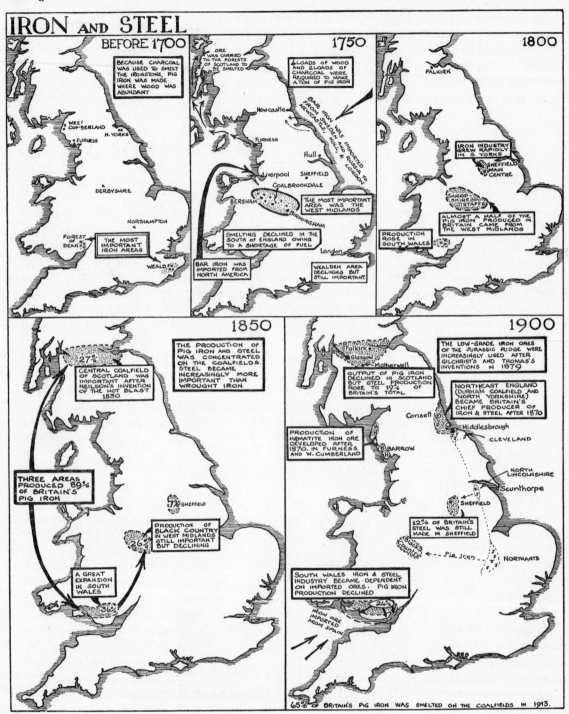

IRON AND STEEL

BEFORE 1700

BECAUSE CHARCOAL WAS USED TO SMELT THE IRONSTONE, PIG IRON WAS MADE WHERE WOOD WAS ABUNDANT

WEST CUMBERLAND
N. YORKS

DERBYSHIRE

NORTHAMPTON

FOREST OF DEAN

THE MOST IMPORTANT IRON AREAS

WEALD

1750

ORE WAS CARRIED TO THE FORESTS OF SCOTLAND TO BE SMELTED

4 LOADS OF WOOD AND 2 LOADS OF CHARCOAL WERE REQUIRED TO MAKE A TON OF PIG IRON

BAR IRON WAS IMPORTED FROM SWEDEN, RUSSIA TO NEWCASTLE, HULL & LONDON

Newcastle

FURNESS

Liverpool

SHEFFIELD

COALBROOKDALE

BERSHAM

BIRMINGHAM

THE MOST IMPORTANT AREA WAS THE WEST MIDLANDS

SMELTING DECLINED IN THE SOUTH OF ENGLAND OWING TO A SHORTAGE OF FUEL

London

BAR IRON WAS IMPORTED FROM NORTH AMERICA

WEALDEN AREA DECLINING BUT STILL IMPORTANT

1800

FALKIRK

IRON INDUSTRY GREW RAPIDLY IN S. YORKS

SHEFFIELD MAIN CENTRE

SHROP-SHIRE STAFFS

ALMOST A HALF OF THE PIG IRON PRODUCED IN BRITAIN CAME FROM THE WEST MIDLANDS

PRODUCTION ROSE IN SOUTH WALES

1850

27%

CENTRAL COALFIELD OF SCOTLAND WAS IMPORTANT AFTER NEILSON'S INVENTION OF THE HOT BLAST 1830

THE PRODUCTION OF PIG IRON AND STEEL WAS CONCENTRATED ON THE COALFIELDS. STEEL BECAME INCREASINGLY MORE IMPORTANT THAN WROUGHT IRON

THREE AREAS PRODUCED 89% OF BRITAIN'S PIG IRON

7% SHEFFIELD

26%

PRODUCTION OF BLACK COUNTRY IN WEST MIDLANDS STILL IMPORTANT BUT DECLINING

A GREAT EXPANSION IN SOUTH WALES

36%

1900

Falkirk
Glasgow
Motherwell

THE LOW-GRADE IRON ORES OF THE JURASSIC RIDGE WERE INCREASINGLY USED AFTER GILCHRIST'S AND THOMAS'S INVENTIONS IN 1879

OUTPUT OF PIG IRON DECLINED IN SCOTLAND BUT STEEL PRODUCTION ROSE TO 19% OF BRITAIN'S TOTAL

NORTHEAST ENGLAND (DURHAM COALFIELD AND NORTH YORKSHIRE) BECAME BRITAIN'S CHIEF PRODUCER OF IRON & STEEL AFTER 1870

Consett

Middlesbrough

CLEVELAND

PRODUCTION OF HAEMATITE IRON ORE DEVELOPED AFTER 1870 IN FURNESS AND W. CUMBERLAND

BARROW

NORTH LINCOLNSHIRE

Scunthorpe

Sheffield

12% OF BRITAIN'S STEEL WAS STILL MADE IN SHEFFIELD

BLACK COUNTRY

PIG IRON

NORTHANTS

SOUTH WALES IRON & STEEL INDUSTRY BECAME DEPENDENT ON IMPORTED ORES. PIG IRON PRODUCTION DECLINED

21%

IRON ORE IMPORTED FROM SPAIN

65% OF BRITAIN'S PIG IRON WAS SMELTED ON THE COALFIELDS IN 1913.

NEW IRON AND STEEL AREAS

this invention, as they held enormous reserves of phosphoric iron ore in Lorraine. In Britain, too, as the older iron deposits of the coal deposits of the coalfields became worked out new iron-fields in the Jurassic scarplands (Cleveland, north Lincolnshire, Northamptonshire) yielding phosphoric ores have been used. For these the basic Gilchrist-Thomas method is suitable.

Coal. The development of our coal resources was a condition of our industrial

DIAGRAM 16

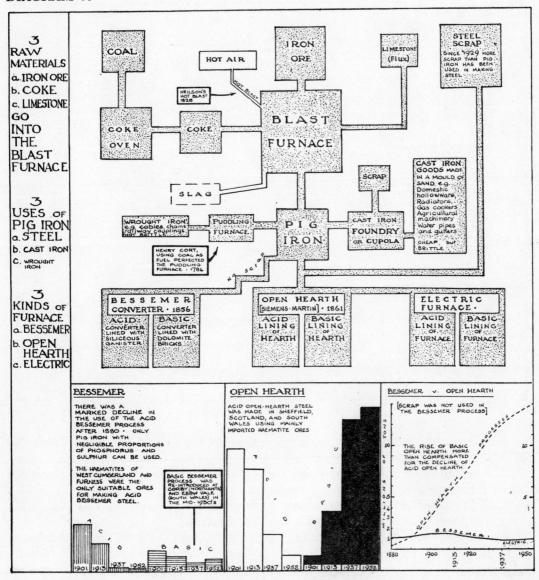

METHODS OF MAKING IRON AND STEEL

expansion. 'Coal commands the Age.' The growth of the coal industry was rendered possible by (i) the invention of the safety lamp by Sir Humphry Davy in 1815 ; (ii) improved methods of extracting coal. (The long-wall system, which aimed at leaving no pillars of support, replaced the bord and pillar system (see p. 79) except in Northumberland and Durham) ; (iii) better methods of winding and haulage ; (iv) more effective methods of ventilation. Fourness of Leeds in 1837 invented an exhaust fan,

DIAGRAM 17

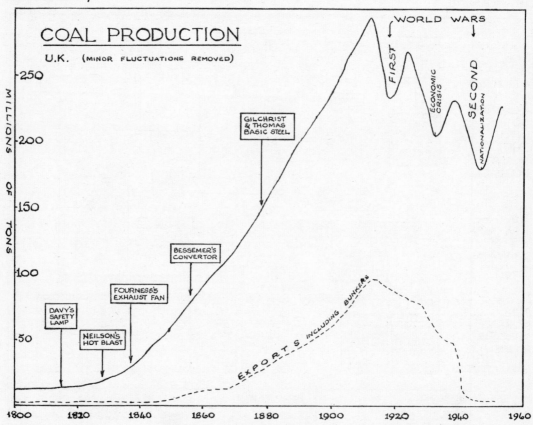

and this device was continually improved so that fresh air could be passed down one shaft and stale air sucked up another.

The demand for coal both at home and abroad increased steadily throughout the century (Diagram 17). This demand could only be met by working deeper pits, which was bound to raise the cost of production. The rise in price was for a long time offset by improved mechanical methods and better organization.

Engineering. The engineering industry is mainly concerned with the production of machines, vehicles, implements, and machine tools. The development of all industry and transport is dependent upon progress in engineering. The early machinery used in the cotton industry was generally made by its user. The first steam-engines were never true to specification owing to the poor workmanship of engineering parts (see pp. 92–93). The evolution of the mechanical engineer—that is, of the professional maker of machines—dates from about 1800, and was assisted by the development of machine tools, or tools for making machines, and particularly by the work of Henry Maudslay, chief foreman from 1789 to 1796 to the inventor Joseph Bramah. Bramah had invented a new type of lock, but was unable to make the parts with sufficient exactness until he obtained the services of Maudslay. When in 1797 Maudslay set up in business for himself he devised a number of machine tools, and in particular the slide rest which enabled machine parts to be made to specification. Roberts (see p. 165), Nasmyth, and Clements, the inventor of a planing machine, were his employees.

Machinery made by hand depended for its accuracy upon the dexterity and the sense of sight of the maker. The development of the machine tool brought about an improvement in the quality and an increase in the quantity of machinery made in the country as well as a reduction in its price. Joseph Whitworth devised a standard thread for screws (1841) which was adopted throughout the world.

Although British engineers had made progress in the invention of new machines by the middle of the nineteenth century, in the United States production engineering was proceeding more rapidly than in Britain. Mass production methods were introduced, and devices employed to work machinery automatically. The introduction of the sewing-machine (1846) and the mechanical reaper (1834) showed the importance of American influence. Exports of engineering products from Britain increased rapidly from 1870 to 1914, though German and American competition grew even more quickly, until by 1919 the exports of the three countries were equal in value.

Changes in the Structure and Organization of Industry in the Nineteenth Century

Until the nineteenth century most businesses were owned and controlled by one man or by a partnership. There were few companies. When more capital was needed another partner was introduced, or loans secured by mortgaging the firm's land and buildings. Profits were often ploughed back into the business. Some firms worked on credit obtained from the merchants who supplied their raw materials or to whom their finished products were sold. The limited financial resources of the businesses prevented expansion, and the Bubble Act of 1720 forbade partnerships of more than six persons.

Joint-stock companies had existed since Tudor times (see p. 57); they could only be incorporated by Royal Charter or special Act of Parliament. Companies of shareholders with limited liability were permitted by an Act of 1856, but industrialists were at first slow to take advantage of the provisions. Limited liability companies were distrusted. From 1885–1914 the number of limited liability joint-stock companies increased, though many were small firms.

Limited liability greatly facilitated the progress of combination. Firms amalgamated with one another in order to restrict competition, especially when a world-wide fall in prices began after 1870. Trusts were formed in the U.S.A., and cartels in Germany. There were many combinations among the iron and steel firms of Britain before the

Great War of 1914–18. Most of them were ' vertical combinations ' made to secure control of the raw materials the firms required as well as the outlets for their manufactured goods. Thus a steel-producing firm would acquire iron-ore mines, limestone quarries, coal-pits, and coke-ovens and would also invest in ship-building, armaments, or other engineering products. Examples are Armstrong-Whitworth's (1891), John Brown (1899), Vickers (1897). Horizontal combination, the amalgamation of firms all doing the same type of work, also took place, as with Stewart and Lloyds (1902). Horizontal combinations were important in the textile industry, as in J. and P. Coats (between 1890 and 1896), the English Sewing Cotton Industry (1897), the Bradford Dyers' Association 1899, and the Fine Cotton Spinners' and Doublers' Association (1898). Combinations also appeared in the soap, wallpaper, tobacco, cement, whisky, and chemical industries.

DEVELOPMENT OF TELEGRAPHIC COMMUNICATION IN THE NINETEENTH CENTURY

Telegraphs. Early in the nineteenth century an American, Samuel Morse, had invented a method of sending messages by electrical impulses. He also invented the code, named after him, of long and short signals. The electric telegraph was first extensively used by the early railways (after 1837) as a method of signalling. Cables were laid across the Channel (1851) and to America (successfully in 1866).

Alexander Graham Bell's invention of the telephone in 1876 enabled the human voice to be electrically transmitted. Its use spread quickly; London's telephone exchange system dates from 1879.

More remarkable still was Marconi's discovery in 1895 of a method of sending messages without wires. Progress at first was comparatively slow. In 1900 signals were sent from the Lizard to the Isle of Wight (200 miles), and in 1907 the first trans-Atlantic wireless communication was made from western Ireland to Newfoundland. Wireless telephony developed in 1914, and after the First World War, in 1920, regular broadcasting of sound radio was begun by the B.B.C. Baird in 1926 transmitted pictures without wires and the B.B.C. began its television services in 1936.

By the middle of the twentieth century it became abundantly clear that wireless waves and the aeroplane had made the world much smaller than it had ever been; the barriers of distance have been destroyed.

34. BANKING SINCE 1793

Banking during the French Wars (1793–1815). The outbreak of war imposed a great strain on the banking system. The Government borrowed money for war purposes, industrialists borrowed to build factories ; people wished to draw out more money than the banks held, and many banks defaulted. In 1797 the ' run on the banks ' was so

DIAGRAM 18

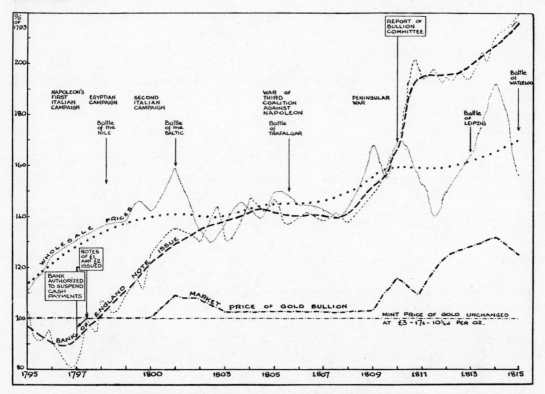

EFFECTS OF THE BANK RESTRICTION ACT

serious, and the reserves of the Bank of England so depleted, that Parliament passed the Bank Restriction Act, authorizing the Bank of England to suspend cash payments. This meant that the Bank could increase its issue of paper notes without having to exchange cash for them on demand.

The Bullion Committee (1810). The danger of issuing inconvertible paper notes is that too many might be issued, so that their value would depreciate. At first the Bank regulated the issue successfully, but by 1810 an over-issue of paper notes caused a fall in value (Diagram 18). Parliament appointed the Bullion Committee to investigate the Bank's policy, and in 1810 the Committee recommended the resumption of cash

MAP 57

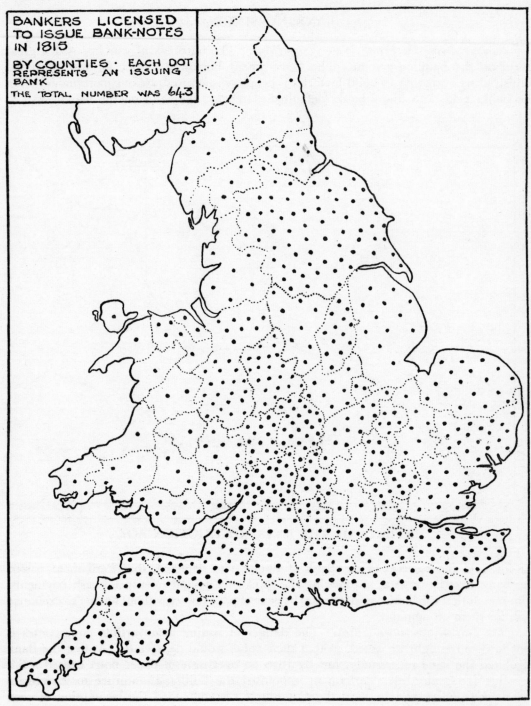

BANKERS LICENSED
TO ISSUE BANK-NOTES
IN 1815

BY COUNTIES · EACH DOT
REPRESENTS AN ISSUING
BANK

THE TOTAL NUMBER WAS 643

payments. Because of the Government's need for money to continue the war, and because of the drain on the gold reserves to pay for imported corn, this could not be done. When peace came there was further pressure, and a new Committee was appointed in 1819. This also recommended the resumption of cash payments, which was carried out in 1821.

The Development of Joint-stock Banking. In the years following 1822 successive reductions in the rate of interest paid on the National Debt attracted considerable investment in businesses at home and abroad where the financial return was greater. The collapse of many unsound firms, including some new banks, caused a financial crisis in 1825–26, for the Bank of England failed to act quickly enough to avert panic. The Government, forced to inquire into the working of banking system of the country, considered the chief cause of the crisis to be the over-issue of notes of small denomination, and by an Act of 1826 forbade the issue of notes below £5 in value. (£1 notes were not issued again until 1914.) This Act also permitted joint-stock banks to be established 65 miles from London, and to have the right to issue notes (see Map 58). In 1832 joint-stock banks without note-issuing rights (deposit banks) were allowed in London. The first of these new banks was the London and Westminster, established in 1834. There was little co-operation in the early days between the Bank of England and these new banks.

The Bank Charter Act (1844)

The years 1836–39 were a period of depression, and many bank failures occurred. Following land speculation in America and the failure of an Irish bank, gold was drawn from the Bank of England's reserves. A poor corn harvest and the need to import corn caused a further drain on the gold reserves. It was this prolonged financial crisis of 1836–39 which eventually led to the Bank Charter Act of 1844, designed to put British banking on a sound footing.

Some people held that bankers should be free to issue as many notes as they wished so long as they could pay cash for them on demand ; others maintained that the amount of notes issued should be determined by the gold held by the bank. The latter view was accepted by Peel's Government, which passed the Bank Charter Act in 1844. Its provisions included :

(i) The Issue Department of the Bank of England was to be kept separate from the Banking Department—that is to say, note-issuing should be kept distinct from ordinary banking business.

(ii) The amount of paper money which the Bank could issue against securities— the fiduciary issue—was fixed at £14,000,000. The rest of the notes issued by the Bank had to be backed by gold.

(iii) No new bank was to be given the right to issue notes ; existing banks were to lose the right of issue if they had not already exercised it, or if they amalgamated or changed into a joint-stock bank. Two-thirds of the note issue thus given up were to be added to the fiduciary issue of the Bank of England.

(iv) The Bank of England had a duty to buy and sell gold at a fixed rate.

(v) The Bank had to publish a weekly return so that its financial position should be known to the public.

MAP 58

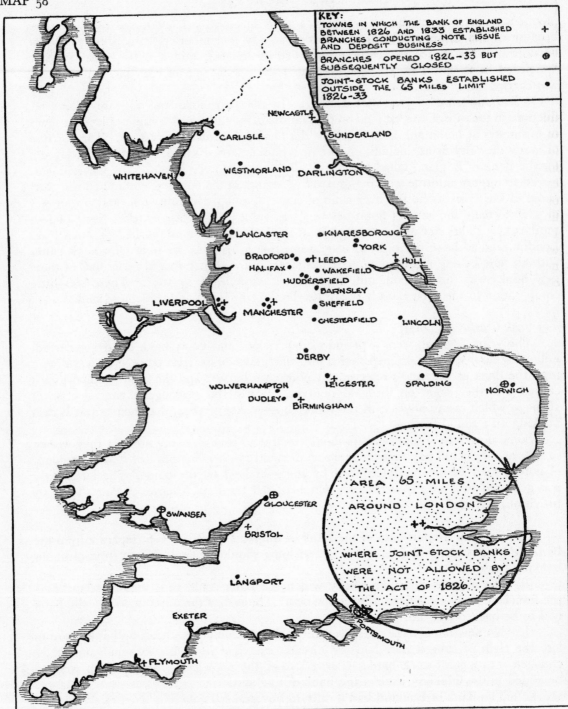

NEW BANKS OPENED (1826–33)

Financial Crises after the Bank Charter Act (1844). Though provision had been made in the Act of 1844 to give the Bank of England an eventual monopoly of the note-issue of England and Wales, this could not, by itself, give the Bank control over other banks, or the amount of credit they issued by overdraft or the cheque system. Indeed, control was not possible until :

(i) the market rate of interest followed the Bank rate. At that time changes in the market rate were followed by changes in the Bank rate ;
(ii) the commercial banks kept substantial reserves with the Bank of England, which could use them for advances in times of crisis.

Not until several severe financial crises had occurred did the Bank of England become an effective ' Central Bank,' concerned more with the safety of the country's banking system than its private profit.

The Crisis of 1847. Bad corn harvests in 1845 and 1846, and particularly the failure of the potato crop in Ireland, necessitated large imports of corn, and led to a drain on the Bank's gold reserves. Speculation in corn resulted in high prices, and when supplies again became plentiful prices fell steeply, and many corn merchants went bankrupt. About the same time the railway mania at home and abroad led to excessive investment in railway shares and businesses, some of doubtful stability, connected with railways.

The Bank of England for a time kept its rate of interest lower than the market rate, thus encouraging speculation by providing cheap money, and did nothing to discourage the outward flow of gold. When in October 1847 the crisis was at its height, and the Bank's reserves had begun to fall, the Government notified the Bank that if it were necessary to increase the fiduciary issue beyond the amount permitted by the Act of 1844 a Bill of Indemnity would be passed. Though this proved unnecessary, confidence was restored.

The Crisis of 1857. This was the first ' world crisis,' affecting America as well as England and the countries of Europe. It followed a boom in the U.S.A. which had been caused by a rapid increase in gold-production and an enormous railway construction (21,000 miles were built in eight years). A large number of new banks, many of them unsound, had been opened. The failure of many of these American banks and the fall in the value of railway securities (many of them held by British investors) brought the crisis to England, and gave rise to heavy demands on the Bank of England's reserves. It was necessary to suspend the Act of 1844 and issue notes beyond the amount which could be backed by gold.

The Crisis of 1866. This was a domestic crisis due to the failure of a reputable banking-house, Overend, Gurney, & Co., which did a large business discounting bills of exchange, not all of which represented sales of goods. The firm was also concerned in other unsound financial schemes. Its failure upset the money market, but the Bank of England continued to advance money, though at 10 per cent. It did not become necessary to break the Act of 1844. The crisis showed that there was some distrust of British banking, for, though the rate of interest in France was but 4 per cent., little gold was sent to England.

The Crisis of 1873. Primarily an American depression, this crisis was not serious in

England. During the years 1868-72, 25,000 miles of railway had been laid in the U.S.A. and trade had boomed. Germany too, using the French indemnity (see p. 190), had launched many industrial ventures, not all of which were sound. Panic in America when the boom broke spread to England, but the Bank countered the effect by raising its rate of discount to 9 per cent. There was no general crisis, and the Bank's reserves remained high.

The Crisis of 1890. Baring's was a reputable banking-house which had underwritten the issue of shares in many South American concerns. They got into difficulties when some shares they were issuing were not taken up by the general public. In this crisis the Bank of England acted energetically, exercising the functions of a Central Bank which is responsible for the economic welfare of the whole country. Securing the co-operation of the joint-stock banks which were found willing to help, the Bank established a Guarantee Fund to make good any losses which might be incurred in advancing money to Baring's.

35. PUBLIC FINANCE

In medieval times there was no division between the King's private and his public revenues. He was expected 'to live of his own'—that is to say, on the receipts from his Crown lands, feudal dues, the profits of justice, and the 'ancient customs' levied on the export of wool and skins, and subsidies granted with the 'common counsel of the realm.' The Saladin tithe (1188), imposed to finance Richard I's Crusade, was the first of a series of fixed percentage charges on people's movables and land. These were known as tenths, fifteenths, and subsidies. Lacking adequate administrative machinery to collect these taxes, the King was forced to leave each local community to collect a fixed amount from the people in the neighbourhood. Some of these taxes were very unpopular. The Poll Tax of 1380, as we have seen on p. 50, led to a rebellion. The ordinary revenues of the King were hardly ever sufficient to meet expenses, and he was forced to borrow money frequently (from the Jews until the time of their expulsion by Edward I).

The Tudor kings had even greater difficulties, for not only were the tenths, fifteenths, and subsidies which had become fixed in amount less valuable as the level of prices rose but the export of wool had seriously declined (see p. 44), and this cut off an important source of revenue. They supplemented their income by demanding benevolences, or forced loans. Large sums were gained by despoiling the monasteries and gilds and by debasing the coinage, yet, nevertheless, they were forced to sell some of the Crown lands, and also to borrow extensively from the merchants of Antwerp.

Yet the continuous flow of silver from the New World to Europe, greatly increasing the quantity of money in circulation, resulted in increased prices. Queen Elizabeth found it impossible to continue without further revenues, and sought the aid of Parliament to raise additional taxes.

In Stuart times the difficulties became more acute. The early Stuarts continued the illegal practices of the Tudor monarchs, and this was one of the chief causes of the constitutional struggle between King and Parliament leading to the Civil War. New sources of taxation were found in the seventeenth century :

(i) Excise duties, which were taxes on home-produced articles of consumption such as ale, salt, and soap.

(ii) Window taxes and hearth taxes were levied on the number of windows or hearths in a person's house.

(iii) Land tax. In 1692 the whole of the land in the country was revalued and a tax of 1s. in the £ was imposed.

(iv) The Stuart kings also borrowed in anticipation of revenues, issuing 'tallies' and 'orders of repayment' which bore interest and were negotiable instruments, discounted with the goldsmiths.

(v) Elizabeth and James I granted patents of monopoly to companies and individuals.

(vi) Loans were also raised by the Crown upon the security of particular taxes.

The sanction of Parliament was necessary for both the loan and the tax. This method, used spasmodically by Charles II, became a regular practice under William III. The outstanding instance is the foundation of the Bank of England in 1694. The Bank advanced £1,200,000 to the Government and received an annuity of £100,000 (representing interest at 8 per cent. and £4000 for management expenses). The annuity was charged on duties on Tonnage and on Excise.

DIAGRAM 19

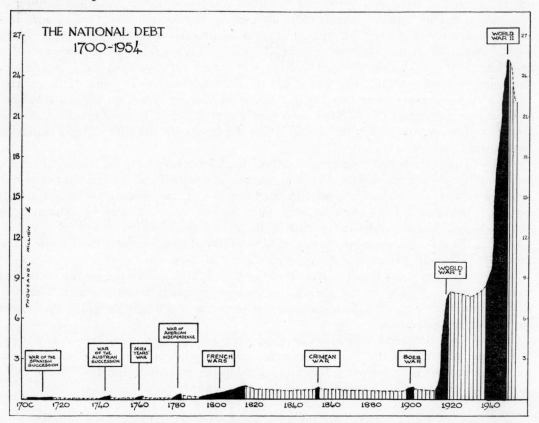

Walpole. Throughout the eighteenth century indirect taxation continued to be important. Walpole abolished nearly all export duties, completing a policy begun in the seventeenth century. He also reduced some high import duties to discourage smuggling. He made an attempt to improve the collection of revenue by transferring the work of collecting the Customs duties to the Excise service, but he failed as regards two of the most important, tobacco and wine.

Pitt. To meet current expenditure in war Pitt was forced to look for new sources of revenue. In this respect his most notable achievement was the introduction of the Income Tax in 1798. Each person had to declare his income from all sources as a lump sum, and a levy of 10 per cent. was made on this declared sum. There was much evasion and fraud, and changes were made by Addington in 1803, by which taxes were levied at source and income was declared in five different categories—that is, on land ownership, land occupation, investment, business profits, salaries, under Schedules A, B, C, D, and E. The income tax was not the major source of State revenue during the Napoleonic Wars, Customs and Excise taxes being much more important. The unpopularity of the income tax led to its withdrawal in 1816.

Nineteenth Century. The free trade reforms carried out at the beginning of the century by reducing and abolishing Customs duties resulted in a loss of revenue. Fortunately, this was a period of peace, and there was little economic and social reform legislation which demanded large expenditure.

In 1842 Sir Robert Peel's budget restored income tax at 7*d.* in the £ to correct Budget deficits which had appeared in the late thirties and to make possible proposed reductions in the tariff (see p. 131). It continued until 1845. Gladstone renewed the tax in 1853 to pay for the Crimean War. Though he had promised to withdraw it later, in order to put through the fiscal reforms in 1860, the tax was retained. Nevertheless, it was not considered to be a permanent part of our fiscal machinery until the end of the century.

Once the income tax was accepted, changes in its structure took place. In 1907 a differentiation between earned and unearned income was made, higher rates of tax being charged on the latter. After 1909 still more tax was charged on persons with larger incomes.

Income tax, death duties—first introduced in its modern form in 1889—and the Land Tax were the main direct taxes after 1842, but up to 1900 produced less than half the country's total revenue. The remainder came from indirect taxes, Customs and Excise on tobacco, wines and spirits, tea, and sugar.

After 1900 successive Chancellors of the Exchequer used income tax as a means of redistributing the wealth of the country by financing schemes of social reform, such as National Insurance. This practice has been considerably extended since 1918. The social services have necessitated growing expenditure, and represent a larger percentage of the national income. Between the two world wars J. M. Keynes analysed economic depressions in terms of an excess of saving over investment, and his teaching suggested that public expenditure was a method of fighting depression. If private individuals did not spend enough of their earnings public authorities should compensate by spending more.

The National Debt

The practice of raising loans upon the security of particular taxes brought into being the National Debt, for though it was agreed in 1694 that the loan from the Bank of England should be repaid, the sum which was borrowed and other loans from other persons and corporations (as from the New East India Company in 1698, and from the South Sea Company in 1711) were never repaid. They became a permanent liability of the State, known as the Funded Debt. (Funding denotes the conversion of a short-term debt into a long-term one.) The Unfunded or Floating Debt consists of those borrowings which the State intends to repay.

After the disastrous South Sea Bubble (1720) the Government ceased to borrow

DIAGRAM 20

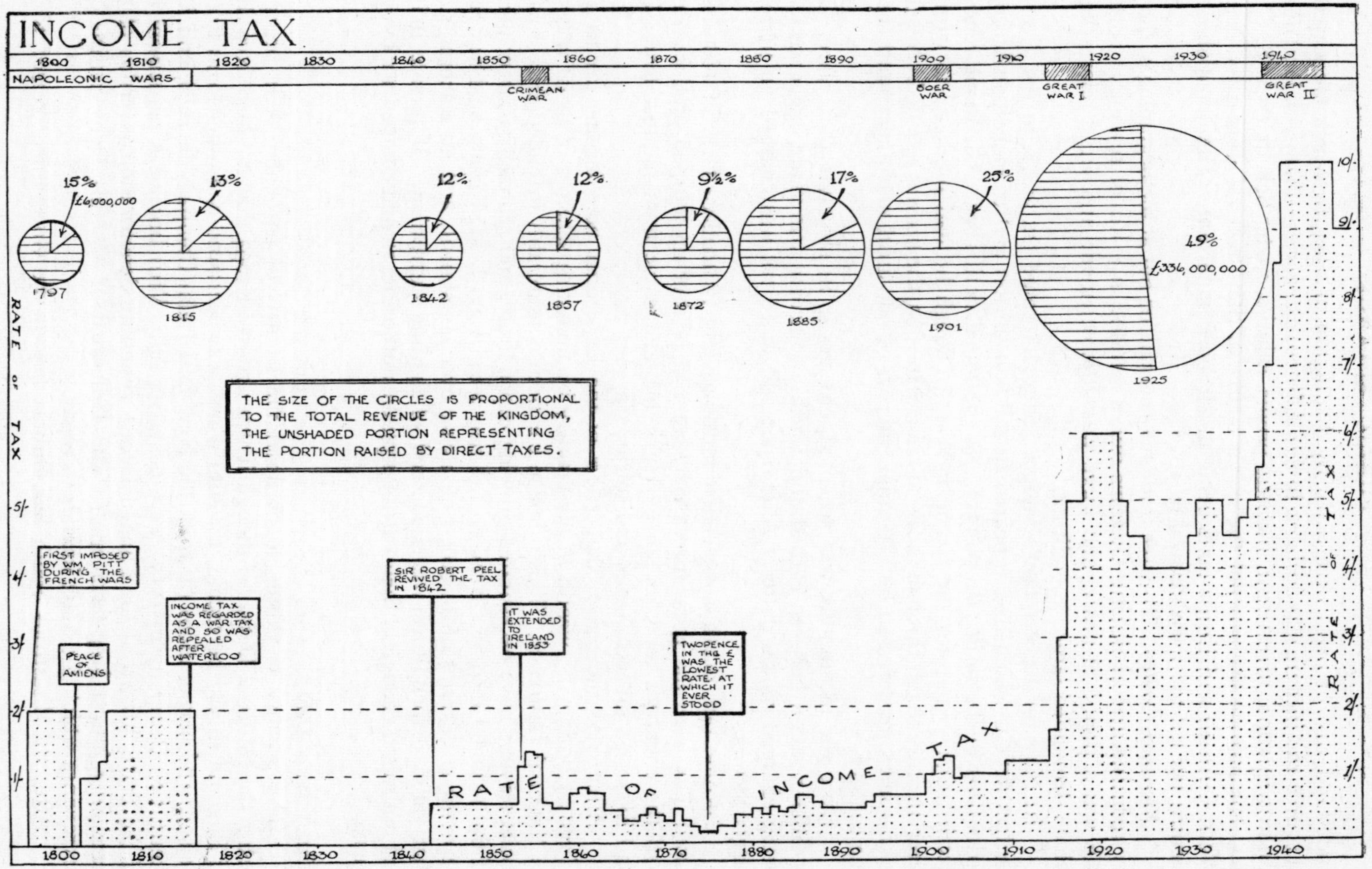
INCOME TAX
1800
1810
1820
1830
1840
1850
1860
1870
1880
1890
1900
1910
1920
1930
1940
NAPOLEONIC WARS
CRIMEAN WAR
BOER WAR
GREAT WAR I
GREAT WAR II
15%
£6,000,000
1797
13%
1815
12%
1842
12%
1857
9½%
1872
17%
1885
25%
1901
49%
£336,000,000
1925
THE SIZE OF THE CIRCLES IS PROPORTIONAL TO THE TOTAL REVENUE OF THE KINGDOM, THE UNSHADED PORTION REPRESENTING THE PORTION RAISED BY DIRECT TAXES.
RATE OF TAX
FIRST IMPOSED BY WM. PITT DURING THE FRENCH WARS
PEACE OF AMIENS
INCOME TAX WAS REGARDED AS A WAR TAX AND SO WAS REPEALED AFTER WATERLOO
SIR ROBERT PEEL REVIVED THE TAX IN 1842
IT WAS EXTENDED TO IRELAND IN 1853
TWOPENCE IN THE £ WAS THE LOWEST RATE AT WHICH IT EVER STOOD
RATE OF INCOME TAX
1/
2/
3/
4/
5/
6/
7/
8/
9/
10/

from privileged companies and raised the money which was required from the general public. From the beginning of the eighteenth century the floating debt chiefly took the form of exchequer bills—negotiable securities, bearing interest, and being payable on demand.

Wars led to borrowing on an ever-increasing scale, and both the funded and unfunded debt grew throughout the eighteenth century. Walpole and his successors made efforts to reduce the National Debt and the rate of interest paid on it. For many years he avoided wars, and was able to create a Sinking Fund (which reached nearly £13,000,000 by 1828) with the object of paying off the debt. Interest rates were driven down from 6 per cent. to 5 per cent. and later to 4 per cent., and in 1751 to 3 per cent. The consolidated issue of annuities in 1751 became known as Consols, and lasted until 1888, when they were converted into $2\frac{3}{4}$ per cent., and in 1903 to $2\frac{1}{2}$ per cent., where they remain to-day. Consols are the best-known example of the funded debt. Pitt's new Sinking Fund, established in 1786, was built up from budget surpluses which were to be paid to Commissioners who acquired Government stock from the public and cancelled it. The scheme failed because it was impossible to provide a surplus throughout the Revolutionary and Napoleonic Wars. Pitt, however, borrowed at a high rate of interest to maintain his fund. The Fund was not abandoned until 1829.

At the end of the Napoleonic Wars there was a large deficit between revenue from taxation and expenditure causing the National Debt to rise to £834,000,000. Borrowing was necessary because public opinion forced Parliament to repeal the Income Tax (see above) which produced £14,000,000 annually as well as war malt duty producing approximately £3,000,000 annually. During the nineteenth century small budget surpluses were applied to the redemption of the National Debt. The absence of costly wars and the attitude of the State against too heavy public expenditure helped to reduce the Debt, though there were temporary rises during the Crimean and Boer Wars.

Then came the First World War and excessive expenditure. Instead of financing expenditure by the issue of Consols, the Government issued loans at varying rates of interest, all relatively high, which were to be redeemed at a fixed date—for instance, 5% War Loan, repayable 1929–47. It drew on the savings of the small man by issuing Savings Certificates, and also raised loans from foreign Governments, such as the U.S.A. Large amounts were borrowed by Treasury Bills (invented by Bagehot in 1877), for these were particularly useful for banks to invest in their surplus funds. At the end of the War the Floating Debt included £1,000,000,000 Treasury Bills.

The National Debt, 1919–39. The methods used during the War to borrow money— high rates of interest and rights to transfer to more favourable issues—proved expensive, and the entanglements caused by war finance lasted until 1932, when a considerable amount of 5% War Loan was converted to $3\frac{1}{2}$%. The conversion led to a gradual fall in interest rates on other securities. By a new technique of debt management the Treasury was able to drive down bill discount rates to under 1 per cent. In 1920 the rate had been 6 per cent. On the outbreak of the Second World War the discount rate had risen just above 1 per cent. ; the Government was in a much better position for borrowing than in 1914.

36. THE GROWTH OF BRITISH FOREIGN TRADE IN THE NINETEENTH CENTURY

At the beginning of the nineteenth century foreign trade was of minor importance in the lives of most British people, who were still interested mainly in farming. Most of

DIAGRAM 21

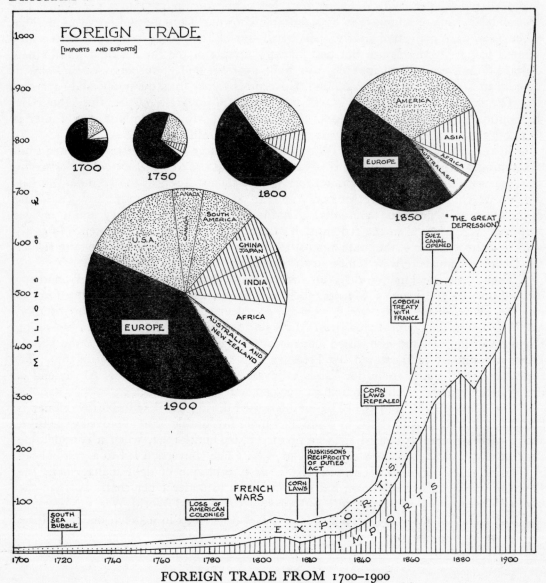

FOREIGN TRADE FROM 1700–1900

DIAGRAM 22

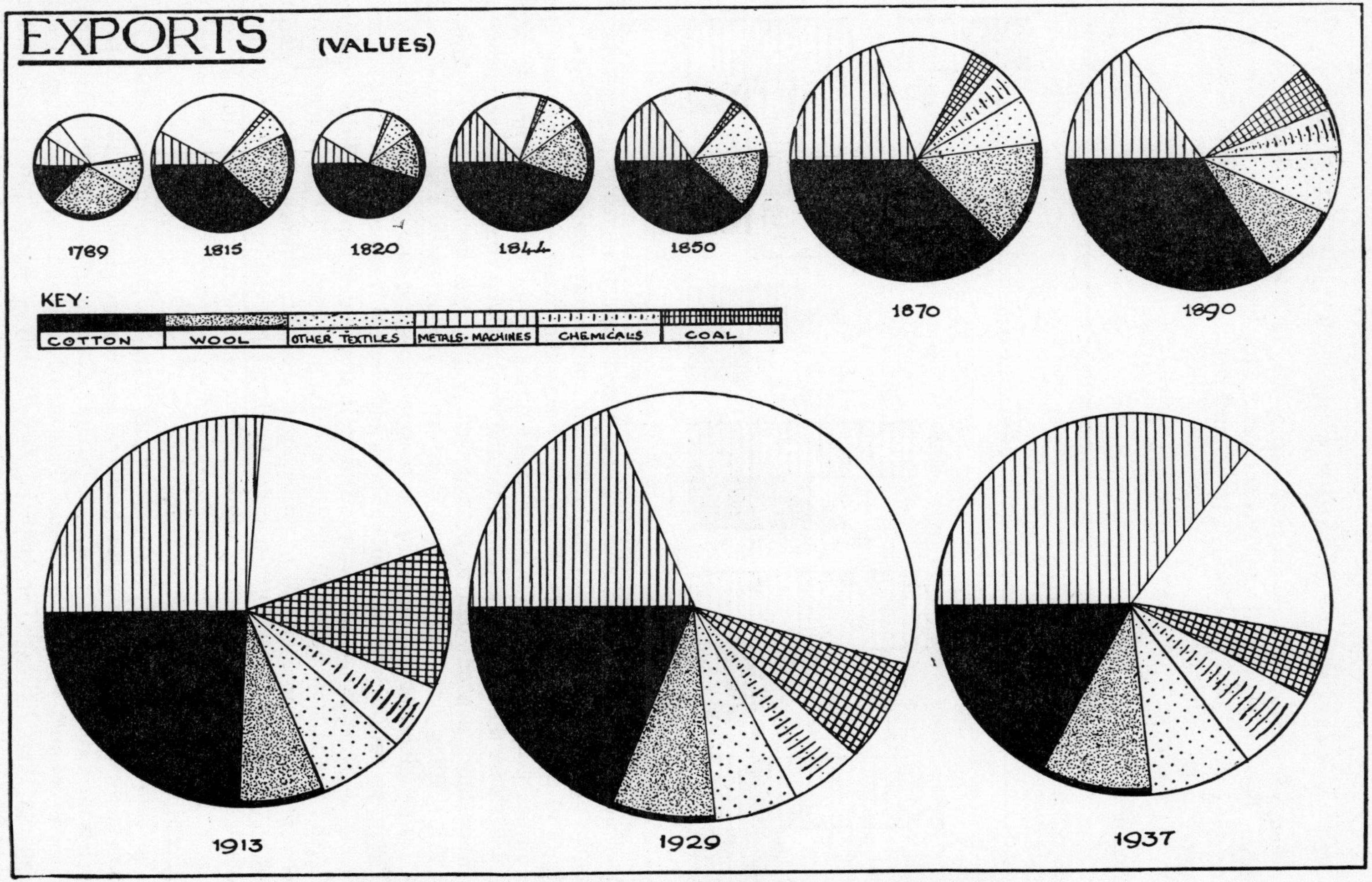

EXPORTS (VALUES)

1789 1815 1820 1844 1850 1870 1890

KEY:
COTTON | WOOL | OTHER TEXTILES | METALS-MACHINES | CHEMICALS | COAL

1913 1929 1937

EXPORTS 1789—1937—THE CHIEF COMMODITIES

their wants were satisfied by home-produced goods, such as wheat, barley, wool, and ironware. Foreign trade was mostly concerned with luxuries. By 1913 Britain was earning much of her living by foreign trade, and was the world's greatest exporter and importer.

DIAGRAM 23

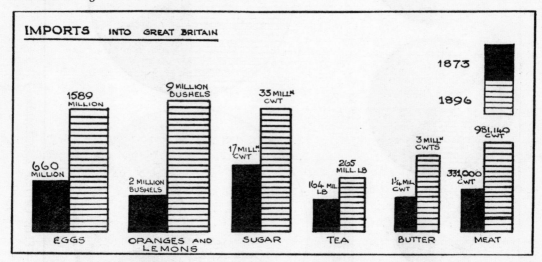

During the century the volume of imports and exports increased sixteenfold, and the staples of trade became bulky raw materials and factory-made manufactures. The difference in the character of the trade was due to the change-over in the occupations of the British people from farming to manufacturing : this created the need to import raw materials for the factories and food for the workers who could no longer grow their own, while finished goods had to be exported to pay for the imports. Diagram 22 shows that textiles continued to be the chief export throughout the nineteenth century, but in 1913 engineering and metal products were becoming equally important.

The industrialization of the United States and western Europe had by 1913 advanced sufficiently to create dangerous rivals to Britain in the field of exports. British exporters were forced to seek new outlets in neutral and Empire markets for their manufactures. The competition led to a revival in protectionist thought. France, Germany, and the United States had all increased their tariffs by the end of the century. In 1903 Joseph Chamberlain started his vigorous campaign for tariff reform. A new attitude to our colonies developed, and a demand for imperial preference which was fostered by Chamberlain as Colonial Secretary 1895–1903.

The Colonial Stocks Act (1900) gave trustee status to Dominion Government loans, and thus facilitated investment in the Empire. Loans were granted by the Government to develop the Crown Colonies. In 1902 Britain refused to import sugar from countries which gave bounties to sugar-growers. This greatly assisted the production of cane-sugar in the West Indies. The Imperial Department of Agriculture (1898) and the School of Tropical Medicine (1899) were established at the end of the century.

37. THE CHANGING ECONOMIC CONDITIONS OF NINETEENTH-CENTURY ENGLAND

THE Industrial Revolution unleashed giant forces which first worked themselves out in Britain. The economic history of the nineteenth century is a record of the vast material progress of the British people and the extension of their influence throughout the world. Other nations, with greater natural resources, developing later, challenged Britain's predominance after 1870, though not until the First World War was the inevitability of her relative decline realized.

(1) *1800–37*

Britain at the beginning of the century was already the manufacturer and shop-keeper for Europe. The failure of Napoleon's Berlin and Milan Decrees to keep British goods out of Europe shows how indispensable they had in fact become. Trade, however, was stagnant during the French wars, and recovered very slowly in 1815. The dislocation of the wars and of the peace which followed was intensified, as we have seen in Chapter 26, by difficulties which were caused by the changes of the Industrial and Agrarian revolutions. It was not until 1837 that the effects of the Napoleonic Wars had worked themselves out.

(2) *1837–48*

The ten years after 1837 prepared industry and trade for the period of ' golden prosperity' which was to follow. The use of the new inventions and the new factory system had by this time resulted in an enormous increase in production ; railways, too, were built, and solved the major problem of inland transport. Tariffs and Navigation Acts which had hindered the exchange of goods were removed ; free trade was established. The Bank Charter Act (1844) put banking on its feet, and the first important Factory and Mines Acts and the earliest Public Health legislation date from this period.

(3) *1848–73*

Britain became the workshop of the world. As the network of railways and steam-ship lines spread across the continents and oceans, Britain was provided with wider markets for her manufactures and further sources of supply for food and raw materials. She had a long start over her competitors, being organized for world trade before other nations were organized for a national economy. Continental wars and the Civil War in America prevented effective competition. The policy of free trade suited the times, and business was also helped by the discovery of gold in California and Australia. The evolution of the joint-stock company facilitated the acquisition of the large capitals required by big businesses. A great increase in productivity (Diagram 24) accompanied a rise in the standard of living. Real wages rose by a fifth, and all classes of society were prosperous, for both industry and agriculture flourished. In spite of the general prosperity there were times of slump in 1857, and 1866 (see p. 175), due to financial crises, and a cotton famine in Lancashire during the American Civil War, 1861–65.

(4) *1873–96*

These years are generally known as the ' Great Depression.' There was in fact no general depression, except in agriculture, but rather a fall in prices and profits.

From 1873–79, as Diagram 25 shows, there was a slump. The value of exports

185

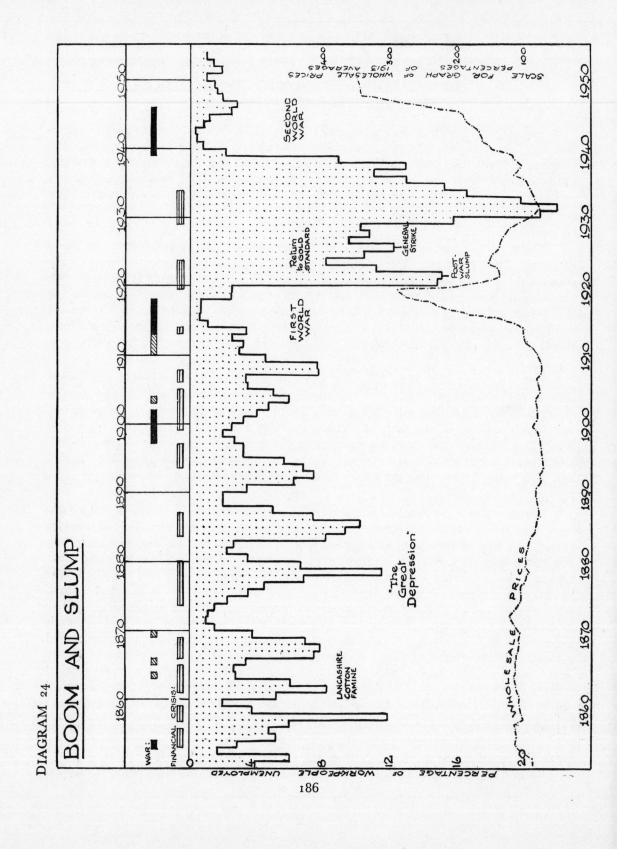

DIAGRAM 24

BOOM AND SLUMP

fell sharply, but wholesale prices had fallen by 25 per cent., and the quantities of goods were little different.

Trade and industry improved during the next three years 1879–82. Both exports and imports rose, while wholesale prices remained steady. The five years 1882–86 were another period of slump. British exports again fell and unemployment increased (Diagram 25). Wholesale prices fell sharply by nearly one-fifth. The years 1886–90 saw another period of recovery. Exports and imports rose while prices remained steady. The next slump followed in 1890 and lasted until 1896, though there was some recovery in 1894.

During the twenty-three years there was alternating boom and depression. Prices fell almost continuously throughout the period; this fall in prices was world-wide. Yet all the time the standard of living was rising. Money wages rose by about 6 per cent., but because of the fall in prices the money could buy 36 per cent. more. The consumption of commodities which had not previously been the staple foods of working people notably increased (Diagram 26).

DIAGRAM 25

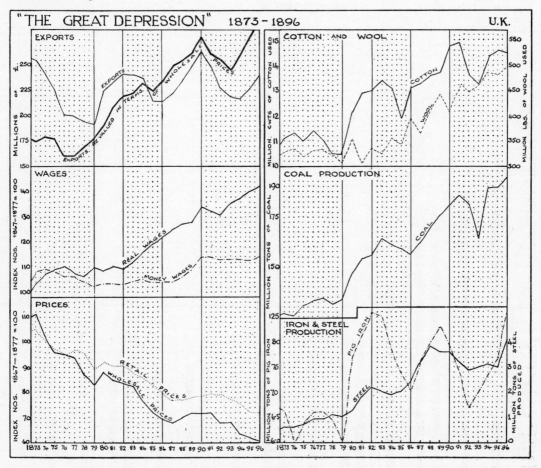

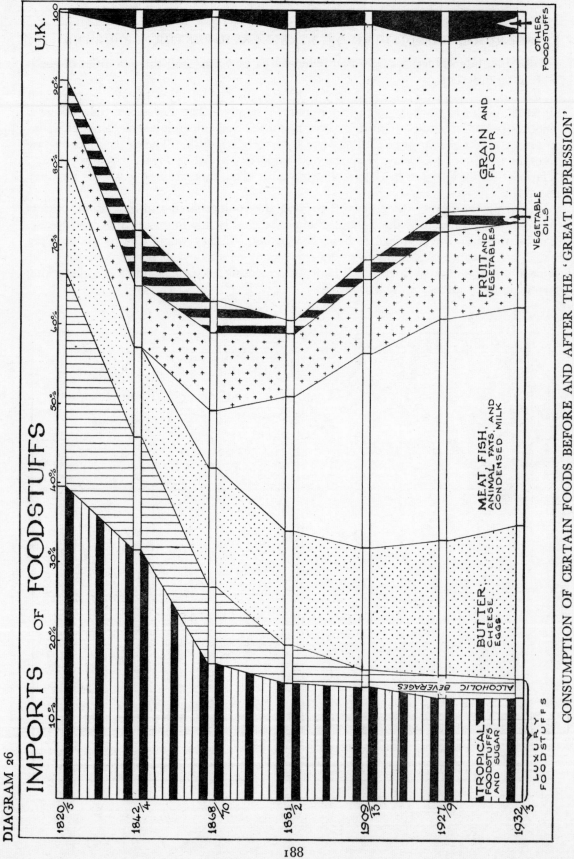

DIAGRAM 26

IMPORTS OF FOODSTUFFS

U.K.

OTHER FOODSTUFFS

GRAIN AND FLOUR

VEGETABLE OILS

FRUIT AND VEGETABLES

MEAT, FISH, ANIMAL FATS, AND CONDENSED MILK

BUTTER, CHEESE, EGGS

ALCOHOLIC BEVERAGES

TROPICAL FOODSTUFFS AND SUGAR

LUXURY FOODSTUFFS

1820/5   1842/4   1868/70   1881/2   1909/13   1927/9   1932/3

CONSUMPTION OF CERTAIN FOODS BEFORE AND AFTER THE 'GREAT DEPRESSION'

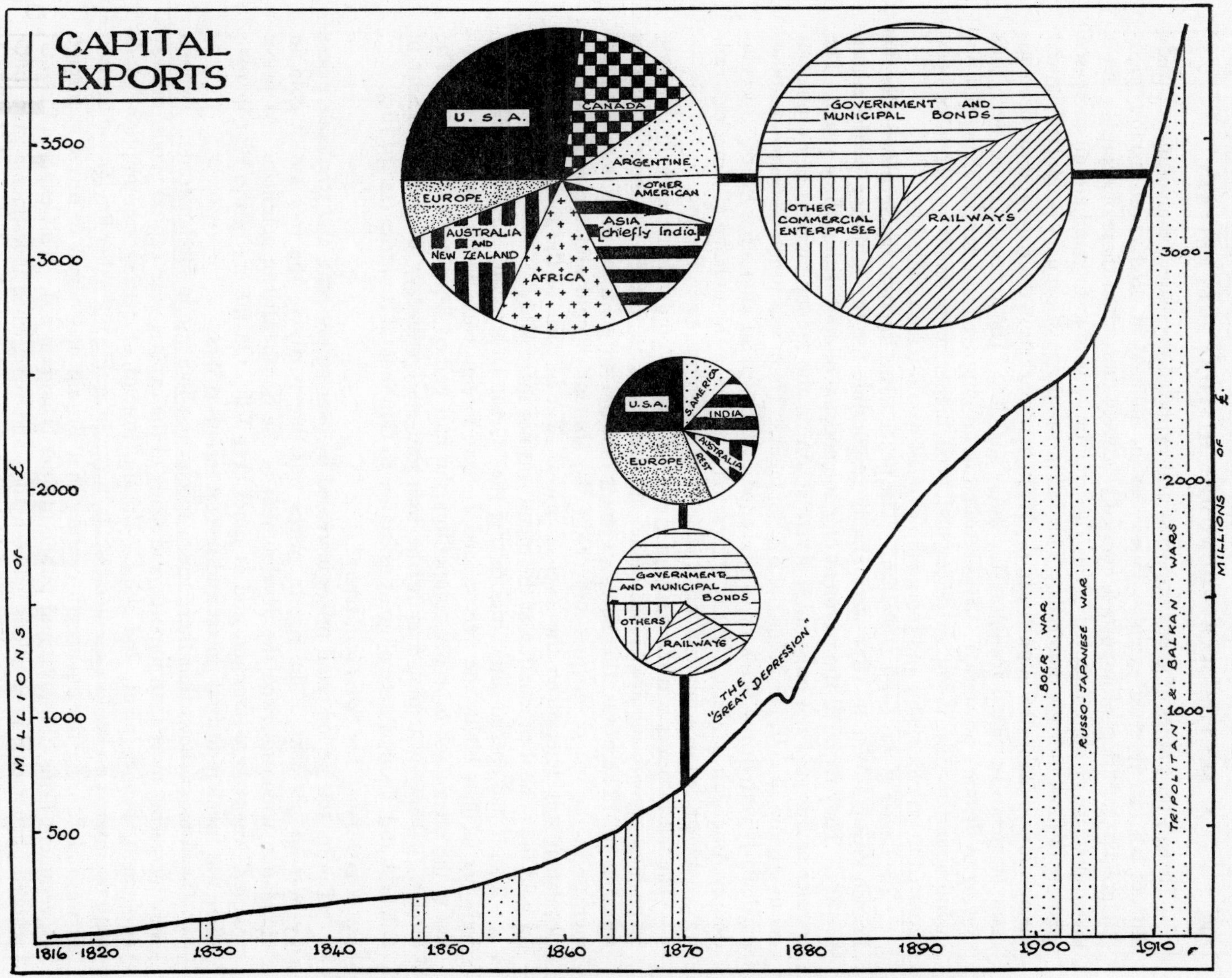

DIAGRAM 27

CAPITAL EXPORTS

CAPITAL EXPORTS DURING THE NINETEENTH CENTURY

189

Though the values of goods imported and exported decreased, the volume of trade did not fall to any great extent. There was an increase in production of most goods (Diagram 25). Prices of imports decreased relatively more than those of exports ; for a given quantity of manufactured goods this country was able to purchase an increased quantity of food and raw materials. This fall in the prices of primary products followed the opening up of the new countries in the West, new markets in the East, and the development of means of cheap transport for bulky articles. The terms of trade were thus moving to Britain's advantage. This resulted in an improved standard of living but not in full employment ; if import prices had been higher more goods would have been exported to pay for them, and more employment would have resulted.

The Causes of the ' Great Depression.' The peace terms imposed by Germany after the Franco-Prussian War in 1871 were chiefly responsible for the initiating of the slump in 1873. They required the payment of £200,000,000 of gold within three years. The transfer of this gold not only put a severe strain on the money markets of Europe but led to a boom in German industrial development. There was much German spending, particularly with British firms, on capital goods, which fell off after a few years. Speculation by American banks in railway shares 1865-72, when the mileage of American railways doubled, led to a financial crisis which had repercussions in Europe.

The fall in prices was the result of greatly increased productivity, and this increase in business activity required more money in circulation to finance the more numerous transactions. There was, therefore, a greater demand for gold, for in spite of the great increase in the use of cheques and credit the amount of gold and the rapidity of its circulation still determined the level of prices. Yet in spite of the increased demand for gold the annual production of the metal was not increasing.

Britain had special difficulties during the ' Great Depression,' 1873-96. Not only were her farmers hit by the free import of cheap foreign corn, but in industry she was losing the advantage over her competitors she had gained from her early start. The foreign challenge was first seen in the iron and steel industry, for the inventions of Gilchrist and Thomas were of great assistance to Continental countries (see p. 165).

(5) *1896-1913—' The Period of Recovery '*

During this period retail prices increased by over 25 per cent. and wholesale prices by over 40 per cent. The rise in prices was due partly to the increase of gold in circulation which followed the development of the South African goldfield. As prices rose real wages were stagnant, and at times even fell. On the eve of the War in 1914 there was much industrial unrest and several serious strikes.

Diagram 27 shows that there was a spectacular increase in foreign trade. Exports were increasing more than imports, and many of the exports were capital goods, railway equipment, factory plant, and ships. Britain, instead of getting consumption goods with the interest on her foreign investments, was reinvesting in further foreign enterprises. It was only during the nineteenth century that Britain had begun to invest in foreign Government loans, railways, and public utilities (Diagram 27). This export of capital reached phenomenal proportions between 1904 and 1913, when investments were made in many parts of the Empire. Before this most of the exports of capital goods had gone to the countries of Europe, the U.S.A., and states of South America. Diagram 27 shows the territorial distribution of British overseas investments in 1913.

38. POPULATION IN ENGLAND AND WALES (1850–1950)

THE population of England and Wales grew from about eighteen millions in 1851 to nearly forty-six millions in 1961.

Birth Rate

Both the marriage rate and the birth rate remained high during the period 1850–80, but while after 1880 the marriage rate continued to be high, the birth rate commenced its steady decline. It is true that women tended to marry later in life (see Diagram 28), but it is probable that the main cause of the decline in the birth rate was the spread of

DIAGRAM 28

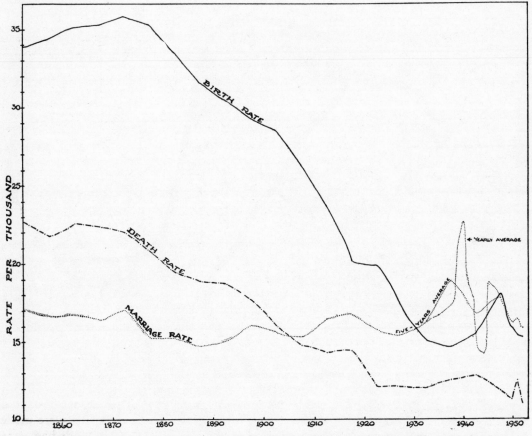

COMPARISON OF BIRTH, DEATH, AND MARRIAGE RATES (1851–1951)

191

MAP 59

POPULATION 1901

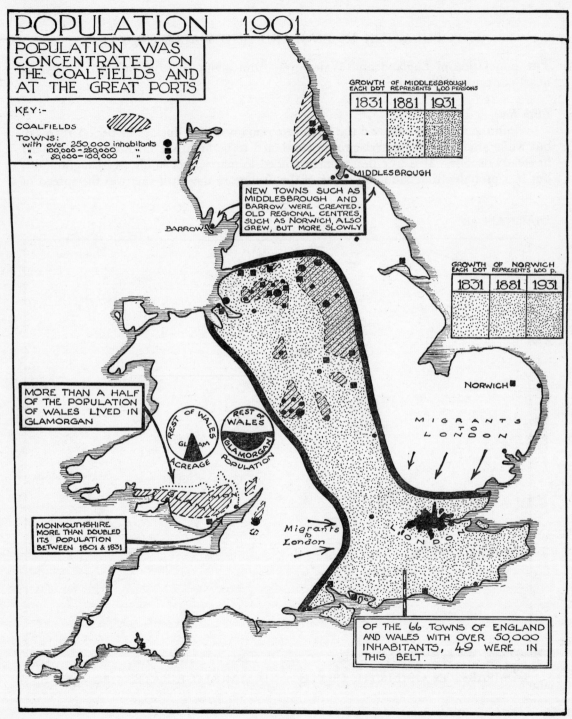

POPULATION WAS CONCENTRATED ON THE COALFIELDS AND AT THE GREAT PORTS

KEY:-

COALFIELDS

TOWNS:
with over 250,000 inhabitants ●
" 100,000 - 250,000 " ■
" 50,000 - 100,000 "

GROWTH OF MIDDLESBROUGH
EACH DOT REPRESENTS 1,00 PERSONS

1831	1881	1931

MIDDLESBROUGH

NEW TOWNS SUCH AS MIDDLESBROUGH AND BARROW WERE CREATED. OLD REGIONAL CENTRES, SUCH AS NORWICH, ALSO GREW, BUT MORE SLOWLY

BARROW

GROWTH OF NORWICH
EACH DOT REPRESENTS 1,00 P.

1831	1881	1931

MORE THAN A HALF OF THE POPULATION OF WALES LIVED IN GLAMORGAN

REST OF WALES
GLAM
ACREAGE

REST OF WALES
GLAMORGAN
POPULATION

NORWICH

MIGRANTS TO LONDON

MONMOUTHSHIRE MORE THAN DOUBLED ITS POPULATION BETWEEN 1801 & 1831

Migrants to London

LONDON

OF THE 66 TOWNS OF ENGLAND AND WALES WITH OVER 50,000 INHABITANTS, 49 WERE IN THIS BELT.

medical knowledge leading to birth control. There was also the deliberate preference for smaller families, due to :

(i) The expense of raising a family. Under the domestic system the family worked as a unit, and the wages paid by the employer were intended to keep the family. In the early nineteenth century children were put into the new factories by their parents, and the wages were brought home to supplement the parents' income. Public opinion, factory legislation, and the Education Act of 1870 raised the age at which young people could go to work, until by the end of the century children were an expense rather than a source of income.

(ii) The improvements in housing accommodation, sanitation, and education made parents feel that there was a minimum standard required for each child, and that to bring additional children into the world might mean deprivation for the existing family. The smaller the family the better start in life the children would receive.

DIAGRAM 29

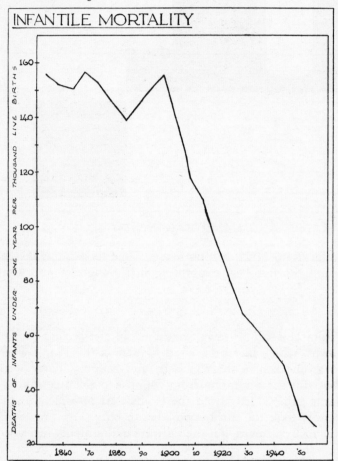

INFANTILE MORTALITY

The Death Rate

The death rate, which had begun to rise after 1820, continued high until about 1870. The high rate was due almost entirely to unhealthy conditions in the towns. The improvement after 1870 was due to the steady advance of medical knowledge and better public health services. The increase in the quality of food available to the community (see p. 188) resulted in a better-nourished population able to resist disease. It was not until the twentieth century, however, that the rate of infant mortality began its spectacular fall (Diagram 29).

Immigration and Emigration

The opening up of the American and Australian continents in the latter half of the century led to increased numbers of emigrants, most of whom were young, unmarried men. Diagram 30 shows that during the years of 1850-1930 there was a loss of population

DIAGRAM 30

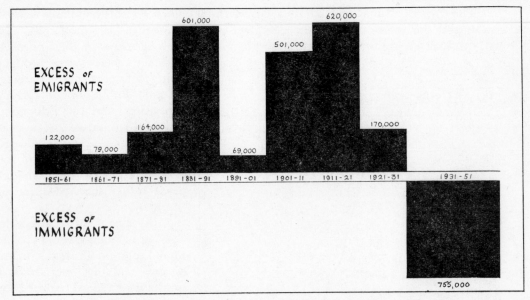

EXCESS OF EMIGRANTS AND IMMIGRANTS (1851–1951)

by excess of emigration over immigration. Irishmen no longer came to settle in Britain in large numbers (see p. 120), and the numbers emigrating in the eighties and after 1904 were large.

Redistribution of Population

The migration of workers from country to town continued in the second half of the century. The drift to the towns, which had been at its highest in the 1840's when it included many Irish people, was checked in the 1880's by emigration. There were fewer emigrants in the 1890's, but still the migration from country to town continued. After 1900 an increase of emigrants came chiefly from the towns. At no time was the countryside depopulated ; the towns took the surplus population only. As previously (p. 120), people usually went to the nearest towns, but the railways undoubtedly increased long-distance migration.

PART VI: THE FIRST WORLD WAR (1914-18)

39. THE WAR ECONOMY

BRITAIN, not having experienced a major war for a hundred years, was faced with the unfamiliar task of harnessing the productive resources of the country for a war effort. For the first two years the general attitude of both Government and industry was ' business as usual,' and little was done to interfere with the mechanism of the free market.

Government control of industry was introduced very slowly and not according to any preconceived plan. As early as 1914 the railway system was taken from the control of the private companies and placed under a Railway Executive (consisting of the general managers of the companies) which could give priority to military traffic.

Lloyd George as Minister of Munitions (1915) began a policy of more direct control of industry, directing labour and allocating raw materials, subordinating civilian interests to the war effort. By the last year of the War the Government had direct control of all railways and shipping, indirect control over farming and industry; it purchased 90 per cent. of all imports, marketed 80 per cent. of all the food consumed in Britain, and controlled the prices of most commodities.

CAPITAL

From January 1915 a company could not issue share capital by inviting the public to subscribe for new shares without Treasury sanction. After 1916 the export of capital was forbidden. A licence for building work was required early in the War.

AGRICULTURE

In 1916 War Agricultural Executive Committees were set up in each county. These committees, backed up by the Board of Agriculture's Food Production Department (1917), initiated a vigorous policy of increasing the arable acreage of Britain. Farmers were encouraged to plough up pasture in order to grow wheat by the guarantee of a minimum price, while landlords were prevented from raising the farmer's rent. Wages Boards fixed legal enforceable minimum wages for farm workers (Corn Production Act, 1917).

SHIPPING

Diagram 32 shows the enormous shipping losses during the War. Unless they were required for the transport of troops, shipowners were free to use their vessels where they pleased (freight rates rose considerably), but from 1915 the Government had to take over ships in order to bring food and raw materials to Britain. A Ministry of Shipping was established in 1916, and early in the following year when the submarine campaign was at its height all ships were requisitioned for the North Atlantic run.

E.H.—G   195

DIAGRAM 31

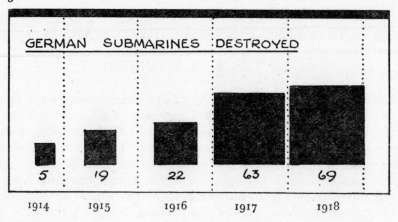

GERMAN SUBMARINES DESTROYED

5 — 1914
19 — 1915
22 — 1916
63 — 1917
69 — 1918

DIAGRAM 32

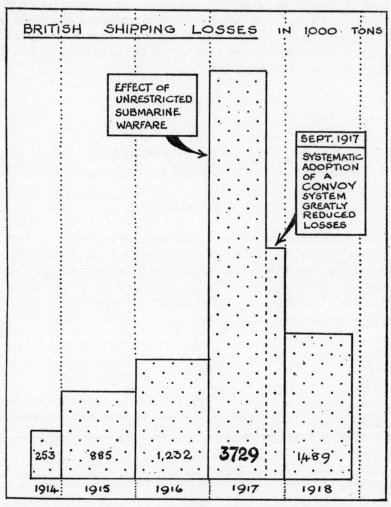

BRITISH SHIPPING LOSSES IN 1,000 TONS

EFFECT OF UNRESTRICTED SUBMARINE WARFARE

SEPT. 1917
SYSTEMATIC ADOPTION OF A CONVOY SYSTEM GREATLY REDUCED LOSSES

253 — 1914
885 — 1915
1,232 — 1916
3729 — 1917
1489 — 1918

LABOUR

Men volunteered for the services with enthusiasm in 1914, but after 1916 the heavy casualties made the introduction of conscription necessary. (The armed forces rose from half a million men in 1914 to four and a half millions in 1918.) Frequently skilled men joined the forces voluntarily or as conscripts, and there was a grave shortage of skilled men in the arms factories. This problem was solved by the co-operation of the trade unions, who allowed unskilled men to do jobs traditionally reserved for skilled men (dilution of labour). Strikes were lessened by the unions agreeing to submit disputes to arbitration. Towards the end of the War industrial unrest increased, and the Government was forced to meet demands for higher wages. Employees in munitions factories were prohibited from striking. After 1917 skilled men, working in certain key occupations, were not called to the armed forces. The unrest was due to the rising price and scarcity of food, caused mainly by shipping losses. It was found necessary to control the prices of the principal foods and late in the War to ration the quantities purchasable first of sugar and later of fats, bacon, and meat, jam, cheese, and tea. A Ministry of Food was created in 1917.

PUBLIC FINANCE

The Government increased taxes during the War, but its revenues were insufficient to cover the vast sums expended (see Diagram 33). The rate of income tax was raised and an Excess Profits Duty introduced to meet complaints about profiteering; this duty eventually yielded about a quarter of the tax revenue. The McKenna duties (1915) at a rate of 33⅓ per cent. on luxury imports—e.g., motor-cars, motor-cycles, watches, musical instruments—were originally designed to save shipping space and to economize foreign currency, but became the basis of a new protective tariff system.

Government borrowing included three large long-term War Loans at a high rate of interest,[1] and after 1916 a National Savings Movement attracted small savings from poorer people.

But the large deficit still uncovered was met by short-term borrowings by Treasury Bills or advances from the Bank of England. Banks and financial houses used Treasury Bills as a means of lending their surplus money for short periods to the Government, which invited tenders for them, accepting those which called for the lowest rate of interest. This method of raising money led to inflation. The borrowed funds were paid out to manufacturers who had done contracts for the Government. Some of it they paid out as wages; some went back to the banks and eventually formed the backing of even more loans both to the public and to the State. The large amount of money in circulation caused prices to rise (inflation). See Diagram 24.

[1] The interest offered did not exceed 5 per cent., but at that time 2½ per cent. was normal for Government issues—e.g., Consols.

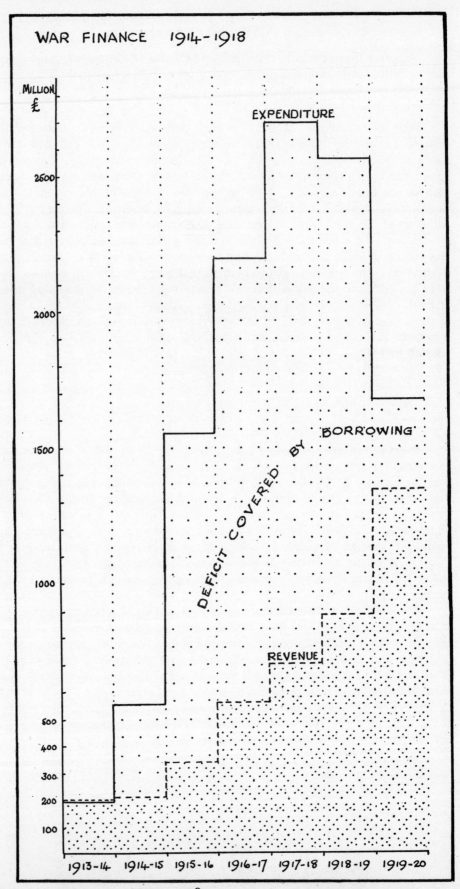

Supplies from abroad, principally from the U.S.A., were paid for largely by the sale of British overseas investments, which totalled nearly £4,000,000,000 and were being increased by almost £200,000,000 yearly. In 1917 the Treasury was given power to acquire compulsorily from British citizens their holdings of these foreign securities. A third of the American investments disappeared during the War. After the U.S.A. declared war on Germany, however, purchases of food and munitions were covered by loans from the U.S.A. Government.

DIAGRAM 34

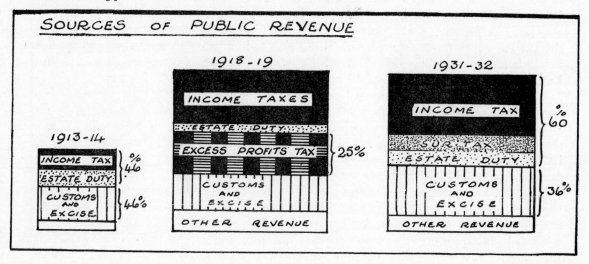

BANKING DURING THE WAR

The outbreak of war in 1914 might have led to panic in the financial circles of London but for the immediate raising of the Bank rate (as the charge was higher there were fewer borrowers), the extension of the Bank Holiday (no borrowing at all !), and the closing of the Stock Exchange. A Currency and Bank Notes Act was passed by which the Bank of England was allowed to exceed its fiduciary issue with the authority of the Treasury. 'Treasury Notes' of £1 and 10s. were issued without complete gold cover. Though theoretically these notes were convertible into gold on demand, in practice it was impossible—too many difficulties were placed in the way. No further gold sovereigns and half-sovereigns were issued, and the public gradually became accustomed to paper money. The export and melting down of gold ceased.

40. ECONOMIC EFFECTS OF THE WAR

NEARLY three-quarters of a million men of the British forces were killed, and about 1,700,000 men were wounded. This large number of deaths of the fittest men between twenty and forty-five and of marriageable age was the most serious of Britain's war losses ; its full effects cannot be calculated. The most severe capital losses were ships.

(1) For two years after the War there was a boom in trade, as manufacturers tried to satisfy the demand for goods of which the world had been starved for four years. Prices were high, and the labour force was kept fully employed. See Diagram 24.

(2) The prosperity was short-lived. Competition grew from countries, especially the U.S.A., which during the War had been able to build up new industries and capture Britain's former markets. Many South American and Asian countries unable to buy English cottons during the War had begun to make their own.

(3) The countries of Western Europe (France, Germany, and Britain) which had dominated European and world trade in 1913 (see Diagram 35) were challenged by the U.S.A. Never again were they to be so important economically or politically. These three countries with less than half Europe's population dominated its manufacturing industry, producing 93 per cent. of its coal (weight) and 72 per cent. (value) of its manufactures. Hydro-electric power had not yet been significantly developed.

(4) Both employers and workpeople were much better organized in 1919 than before the War. During the period of hostilities many trade-union leaders actively supported the Government, in some cases losing power to shop stewards whose influence over the workers in factories grew. Employers and workmen were loath to lose the artificially high profits and wages they enjoyed during and immediately after the War. Peace eventually brought a reduction in both, and industrial unrest ensued.

(5) The National Debt rose from £650,000,000 to nearly £8,000,000,000 (see Diagram 19), with a corresponding increase in the burden of the annual interest payments from £24,000,000 to £332,000,000. In addition war pensions at the outset cost nearly £100,000,000 annually.

(6) The reparation demands of the victorious allies helped to spread economic dislocation.

(7) There was a net sale of over 10 per cent. of Britain's long-term foreign assets (p. 199). Some—e.g., those in Russia—were confiscated.

DIAGRAM 35

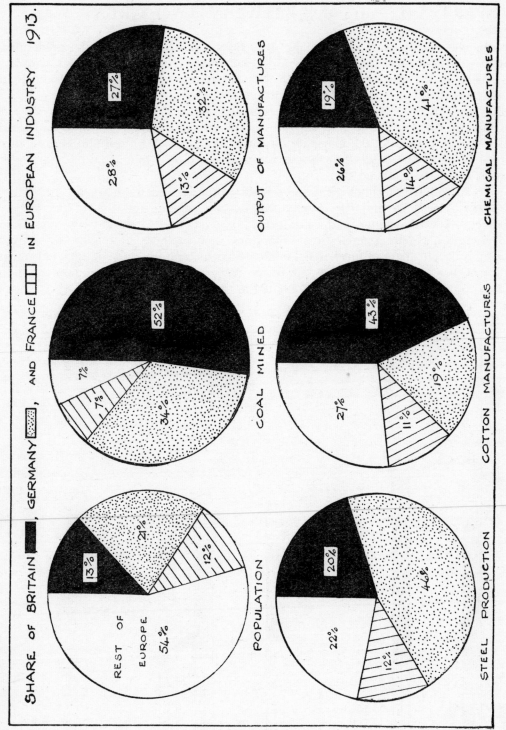

SHARE OF BRITAIN ■, GERMANY ▦, AND FRANCE ▢ IN EUROPEAN INDUSTRY 1913.

POPULATION

REST OF EUROPE 54%
13%
21%
12%

COAL MINED

52%
7%
7%
34%

OUTPUT OF MANUFACTURES

27%
28%
13%
32%

STEEL PRODUCTION

20%
22%
12%
46%

COTTON MANUFACTURES

43%
27%
11%
19%

CHEMICAL MANUFACTURES

19%
26%
14%
41%

PART VII: 1919-39: BETWEEN TWO GREAT WARS

DURING the twenty years between the wars Britain failed to recover the predominant position she had once held in the world's economic affairs. In spite of a temporary depression in the thirties (see Diagram 36) the volume of goods manufactured in the world increased, but an increasing proportion was being made in Russia and the U.S.A., India, and Japan. Most agricultural countries found it more difficult to sell their produce in Western Europe, where the rate of growth of the population had slowed down (partly because of the mortality of young men in the War and also because of the spread of birth-control); they began to foster their own manufactures, particularly textiles and small metal goods.

In all countries technological and scientific progress became marked; new sources of power—electricity and the internal combustion engine—speeded up the technical changes. A vast increase in the number of products and processes—e.g., alloy steels, ball bearings, canning, domestic refrigerators, new methods of oil-refining—resulted from this development of mechanical engineering, metallurgy, and industrial chemistry. Many of these products were of standardized design and suitable for the new techniques of mass production which largely originated in the U.S.A.

DIAGRAM 36

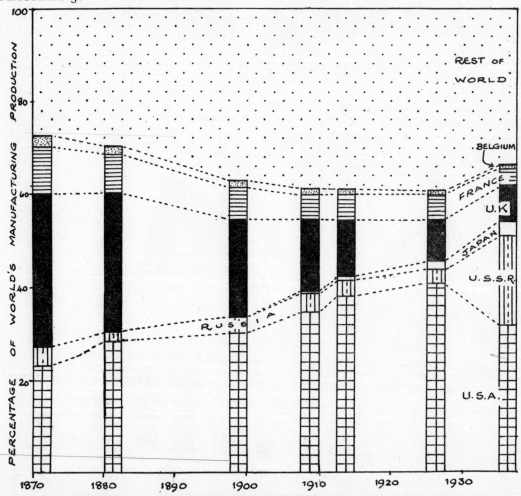

The use of H.E.P. and oil as sources of power enabled factories to be built outside the coalfields, which since the Industrial Revolution of the eighteenth century had been the main locations of industry. Britain, whose economy was based on coal, had lost one of her main advantages over her competitors as a manufacturing country, and the demand for her coal from overseas, both for factories and ships, diminished.

International trade stagnated during the period, particularly during the depression (see p. 227), and Britain's share in it declined. While new agricultural techniques had greatly increased the supply of primary products—*e.g.*, wheat, wool, coffee—the demand for them lessened, and consequently their prices fell sharply. Britain needed to export fewer manufactured goods in order to satisfy her need of these imported foods and raw materials. New types of manufactures, machinery, chemicals, durable household equipment, became increasingly the staples of world commerce, and the older products— cotton textiles and coal—declined relatively in importance.

The War had upset the financial systems of the countries of Europe ; they had abandoned the gold standard, and their currencies were inflated. Though by 1929 most countries had nominally returned to a gold standard, confidence was low, and ' hot ' money was transferred from one country to another on the first sign of financial weakness. When Britain abandoned the gold standard in 1931 it ceased to be the universal financial goal ; most Governments began to protect their trade balances by restrictive quotas and tariffs.

DIAGRAM 37

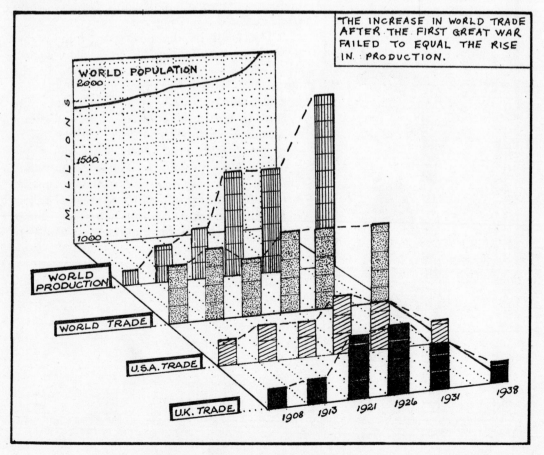

THE INCREASE IN WORLD TRADE AFTER THE FIRST GREAT WAR FAILED TO EQUAL THE RISE IN PRODUCTION.

DIAGRAM 38

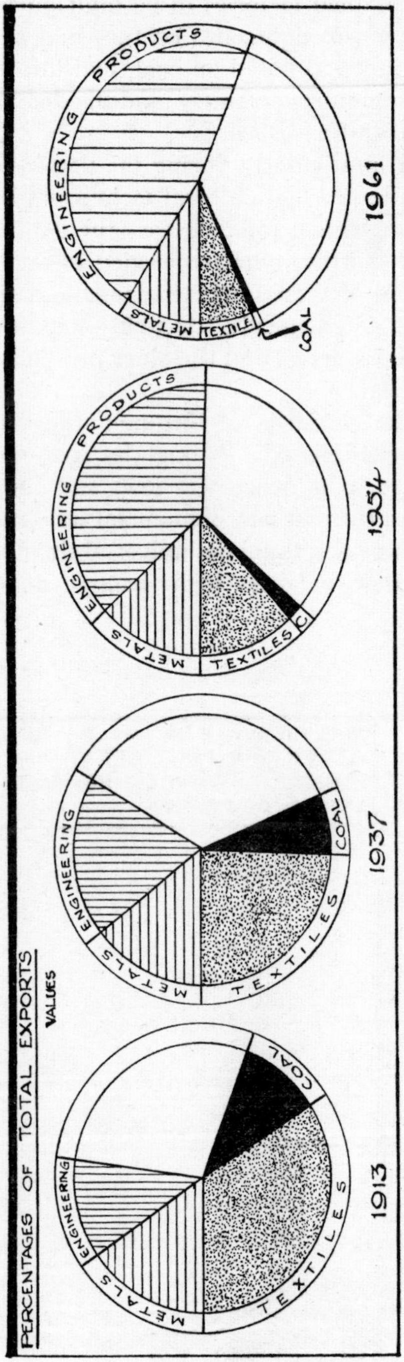

PERCENTAGES OF TOTAL EXPORTS

VALUES

1961 — ENGINEERING PRODUCTS / METALS / TEXTILE / COAL

1954 — ENGINEERING PRODUCTS / METALS / TEXTILES / C.

1937 — ENGINEERING / METALS / TEXTILES / COAL

1913 — COAL / TEXTILES / ENGINEERING / METALS

41. BRITISH INDUSTRY (1919–39)

THE post-War boom in production broke when four million men, demobilized from the armed services, reinforced the labour supply and replenished the acute shortage of consumer goods. Prices reached a maximum in 1920 and then fell rapidly (Diagram 24). The slump which followed the post-War boom was most apparent in the old staple industries—coal-mining, shipbuilding, and cotton manufacture—and resulted in heavy unemployment. The new industries —*e.g.*, motor vehicles, rayon, electrical goods— suffered less, and because of their comparative success there was an increase in the total industrial production of the country, a rise in the output per man, and a higher real income per head of the population. Notwithstanding this increase in production Britain's share of world trade declined (see Diagram 37).

The crisis of the post-War slump came between 1929 and 1933 (the Great Depression), when there was a still greater decline in the demand for primary products and a collapse of business and international trade. Though the decline in the production of Britain was not so severe as in other countries, the collapse of the export trade, particularly of the old staple products, was very serious. The world gradually climbed out of the depression after 1933, and British industrial production rose steadily except in the shipbuilding and cotton industries. There was a great boom in building, especially of houses.

DIAGRAM 39

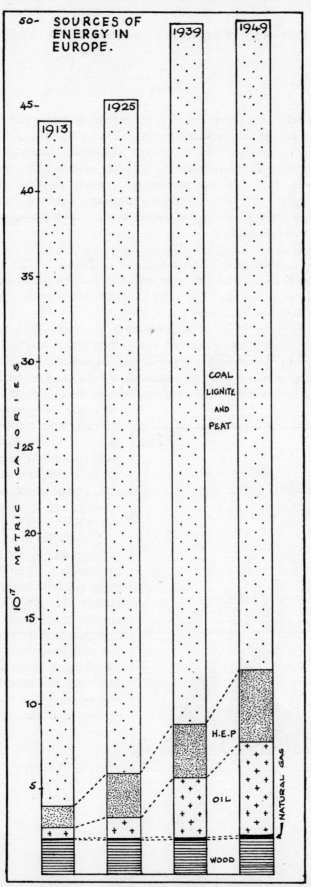

SOURCES OF
ENERGY IN
EUROPE.

COAL
LIGNITE
AND
PEAT

H.E.P

OIL

NATURAL GAS

WOOD

In order to compare
H.E.P. and coal the
diagram shows the
quantity of coal
needed in these years
to make the amount
of electricity produced
by H.E.P.

COAL

Instead of the world's consumption of coal increasing each year by 4 per cent. as it did in the years before 1914 there was a general slowing up in demand after the War. Improvements in boiler techniques led to a more economical use of coal. Other fuels became increasingly competitive—petroleum, the price of which became steadily lower, and natural gas, while electricity was produced by water power and the burning of lignite. Motors, using oil for their internal-combustion engines, competed with the steam-engines of the railways, which still used coal. Oil-burning and motor ships replaced the coal-burning steamships.

Meanwhile more coal was being mined not only in the U.S.A. and Germany, but also in countries formerly dependent on British coal—e.g., France. The coastal coalfields, South Wales, Northumberland, and Durham, and the Scottish fields, suffered most from the inevitable decline in demand. The only considerable increased demand for coal came from the newly built electricity power stations.

The British coal industry failed to adapt itself to the post-War situation. Between the years 1913 and 1934 Belgium increased her output per man-shift by 39 per cent., the Ruhr by 77 per cent., Holland by 105 per cent., but Britain only by 7 per cent. The progress in these countries was due to mechanization. As early as 1924, 70 per cent. of American coal was cut by machine. The chief weakness of the British coal industry was the

DIAGRAM 40

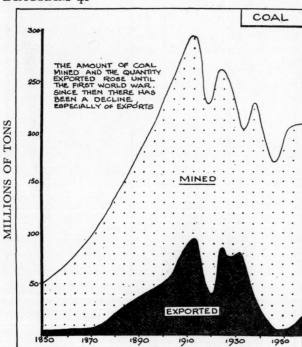

existence of numerous competing mines (1936 : 1000 companies, 2000 mines). A few were large and had modern equipment, but many were old and their best seams were worked out. It was uneconomic to introduce coal-cutting machinery into small mines with only thin seams of coal.

The chief need was to promote amalgamations in order to reduce overheads. The Coal Mines Act 1930 established a Commission to further this aim, but it could not enforce such a policy. This Act also provided for the control of output and prices in each mining area. The Sankey Commission (1919) and the Samuel Commission (1925) recommended the nationalization of mining royalties, and the former the nationalization of the mines. These recommendations were not carried out in this period.

SHIPBUILDING

During the First World War Britain lost 8,000,000 tons of mercantile shipping, yet her total fleet in 1919 was only about 14 per cent. less than in 1913 (see Diagram 61). The world's fleet, however, was slightly greater than in 1913, Britain's share having fallen from 39 per cent. to 33 per cent. (see Diagram 60). U.S.A. had now become a great maritime and shipbuilding nation.

The decline of international trade in the middle twenties depressed the shipping industry, as shipowners had ample capacity. After 1926 demand arose for a new type of vessel, the motor ship, which was rapidly satisfied. By 1930 the proportion of motor-propelled ships launched exceeded that of steamships. Britain lagged behind her competitors in constructing this new type of ship.

DIAGRAM 41

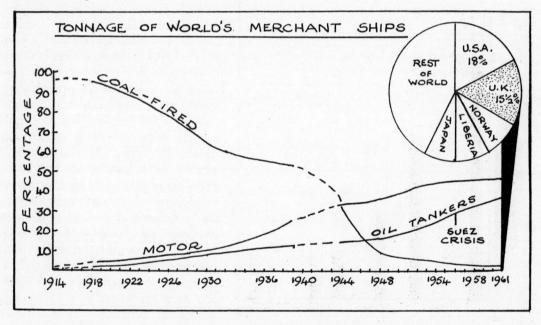

The world depression seriously injured the shipbuilding industry in all countries. In Britain, however, shipbuilders, unaided by Government assistance as were their foreign competitors, were slow to recover until orders for ships of war were received in the late thirties.[1] In 1930 the shipbuilding firms decided to eliminate the inferior yards, and about a third of the total building capacity was brought out and scrapped (National Shipbuilders' Security Ltd.).

[1] Britain gave very small subsidies under an Act of 1936. Favourable loans were made by the Government to facilitate the construction of the *Queen Mary* and *Queen Elizabeth*.

COTTON

Of all British industries cotton showed the most phenomenal decline after 1918. There was a serious fall in the quantity of cotton yarns and cloth entering international trade, and Britain, hitherto the chief exporting country, suffered most. This severe fall in exports from Lancashire was due chiefly to a decline in the demand for coarse cotton goods from India, China, and Japan, the Balkan countries, and the Near East, which were beginning to produce their own cloth. The market at home and in Western Europe, mainly for fine cottons, was maintained. Japan was increasingly exporting to Afro-Asian countries which had once been markets for Britain. Competition from the manufacturers of synthetic fibres—*e.g.*, rayon—also grew.

DIAGRAM 42

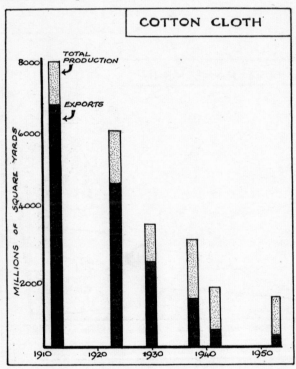

It was difficult for the cotton millowners to realize that the industry was never to regain its pre-eminence. Improved organization would have mitigated the painful effects of the decline, but the millowners were unwilling to support new ideas when old methods had proved so successful in the past; the workpeople were equally averse to change. The traditional remedy for a depression due to a drop in demand was short-time working. When it became apparent that markets had been permanently lost steps were gradually taken to eliminate surplus capacity by scrapping the oldest machinery, closing down out-of-date factories, and amalgamating businesses. In the nineteen-twenties a number of combines were formed—*e.g.*, the Lancashire Cotton Corporation, which in 1929 took over factories that together had 10,000,000 spindles for spinning yarn and 30,000 looms for weaving cloth. The decline in the cotton industry was not arrested before the outbreak of the Second World War.

IRON AND STEEL

In the century which followed the invention of the Bessemer and Siemens-Martin processes the world's production of steel rose from 300,000 tons in 1866 to 275,000,000 tons in 1960. Britain had been the leading producer, but even before 1914 (see Diagram 43) she had been surpassed by the U.S.A. and Germany, whose resources of iron ore were much greater. The demand for wrought iron and acid steel declined as steel replaced iron and cheaply produced basic steel replaced the acid steels in which Britain had specialized (see Diagram 16).

As we have seen, Britain's iron and steel industries had developed in the eighteenth and nineteenth centuries on her coalfields. The iron ore from the coal measures was not

DIAGRAM 43

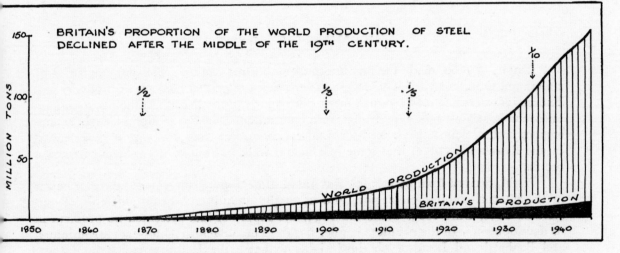

suitable for the new processes, and iron ore and pig-iron were increasingly imported from Spain and Sweden. It therefore became advantageous to site new steel plants on the coast—e.g., at Middlesbrough, Margam, Cardiff.[1]

Though no longer the leading producer of steel, Britain was in the van of technological progress. In 1882 Hadfield began the commercial development of alloy steel, using manganese and later silicon to toughen and harden the metal. Stainless (chromium) steel was developed by Brearley in 1913, and greater use was made of alloys—e.g., nickel and vanadium—to produce light steels capable of resisting rust and containing stresses caused by high steam pressures and temperatures. Such special steels were increasingly demanded for motor-cars, aeroplanes, and machine tools. They are best made in electric furnaces, and between the wars the production of these was doubled.

[1] The plan to develop an inland site at Ebbw Vale in 1938 for an integrated steel works (coke ovens, blast furnaces, converters, continuous strip mill, and, later, tinplate plant) was a political one determined by the need to combat unemployment.

After the perfection of the Gilchrist-Thomas process (see p. 165) new plant was built to develop the phosphoric ore of the Jurassic scarplands which, though of inferior quality, was easy to quarry. The Scunthorpe works in north Lincolnshire, established in the late nineteenth century, developed in the inter-war period, while new plant was built at Corby, in Northamptonshire, in 1932.

The output of the steel plants was greatly stimulated during the War, but after 1921 production fell rapidly. In the Great Depression production fell to two-thirds of the 1913 output. Recovery after 1933 was not due to a rise in exports, but to increasing demands for steel from the engineering and motor-car industries, which used a large part of the strip steel produced in the new integrated plants, and also to the imposition in 1932 of a $33\frac{1}{3}$ per cent. import duty on a wide range of steel products. The imposition of a quota in 1935 further restricted imports. These measures ensured that the British iron and steel industry was free from foreign competition, and the steel firms agreed to form the British Iron and Steel Federation (1934) to encourage schemes of reorganization and development.

THE MOTOR-CAR INDUSTRY

Lenoir, in 1860, made the first internal-combustion engine. This was improved by a German, Otto, in 1876. These were gas engines using either coal gas or producer gas. The engines were first used by small firms, particularly in the English Midlands, to replace uneconomic steam-engines, and they were later adapted for locomotion. (Early steam-engines had, of course, been used for road carriages, but their development was halted by the Regulation (1831) that some one should walk in front of the vehicle carrying a red flag.)

Petrol, derived from petroleum, was found to be a more convenient source of power in the internal-combustion engine, and as ample quantities became available (Pennsylvania 1859, Ohio 1885, California 1895) the supply of fuel presented no problem in its development. In the eighties Daimler began to manufacture motor-cars in Germany, and Panhard and Levassor obtained rights to make the Daimler engine in France. About this time the pneumatic tyre (Dunlop) and electrical devices for igniting the petrol were invented. Alloy steels which reduced the weight of the engine were utilized.

Not surprisingly, though the first motor-cars were made in Western Europe, they were first mass produced in the U.S.A. For her size she was relatively poorly supplied with railways, but many of her people could afford a motor-car. In 1908 Ford of Detroit built a cheap standardized car. In England the manufacture of motor-cars was first taken up by bicycle manufacturers in the Midlands (at Coventry, Birmingham, and Wolverhampton) in order to keep their workers busy in the ' off ' season. In 1912 Britain built only 25,000 private and commercial vehicles compared with U.S.A's half million. In that year more motor-cycles (38,000) than cars were being made ; this was half the number made in America. Not until 1915 was a cheap standardized car built in Britain by Morris of Oxford.

At the end of the War the U.S.A. were producing more than two million cars every year, a number far greater than the rest of the world put together. In 1929 American exports were twice the whole of Britain's production, though Britain had become the largest producer and exporter of motor-cycles.

The Great Depression brought a decline in production throughout the world, but Britain was less affected than U.S.A. The number of cars built in Britain continued to rise, though less rapidly, from 5 per cent. of U.S.A. production in 1929 to 18 per cent. in 1938. Britain was also well ahead of all Continental competitors. Her exports of cars was about twice that of 1929, though still small when compared with those of U.S.A. The trade in motor-cycles from Britain, however, stagnated in the thirties, and by 1937 exports had fallen to about two-fifths of the 1929 number. Many Continental countries had developed their own motor-cycle industry.

The motor industry had grown since 1915 with the protection of a high tariff. The British road tax and insurance system favoured an engine of small horse-power, but this type of car, less robust on poor roads than the big American car, was less acceptable in the export market. Little was done to reduce the large number of models or to amalgamate the many small firms which produced them, though the key to success in the mass market, as the Americans had shown, was a cheap, standardized mass-produced machine.

The comparative prosperity of the Midlands and the South of England during the inter-war years owed much to the continuous growth of the industries.

DIAGRAM 44

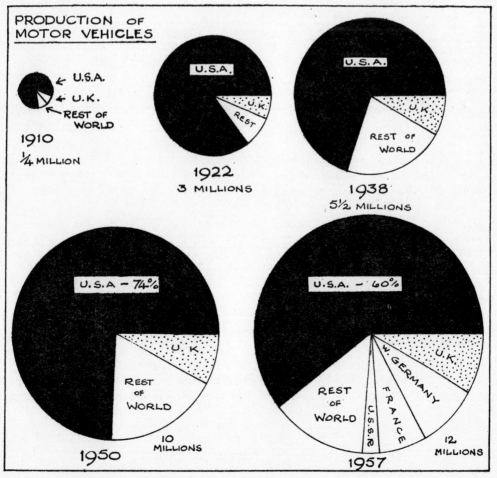

CHEMICALS

The production of certain basic chemicals—*e.g.*, caustic soda and sulphuric acid—have become the prerequisite of a country's industrial development to-day ; although barely two centuries old, the chemical industry is a cornerstone on which the whole of modern Britain's manufacturing industries rest.

(1) *Heavy chemicals.* Many small firms developed in the nineteenth century on the saltfield of Cheshire and in the mid-Mersey valley to produce soda by the Leblanc process (1790), which used salt and sulphuric acid. In the course of making sulphuric acid, hydrochloric and nitric acids were produced ; at first large quantities of chlorine and sulphur fumes were allowed to escape and poison the atmosphere round the works. When this was prevented by the Alkali Act 1863 the soda firms were forced to recover the waste products—*e.g.*, chlorine, which was made into bleaching powder, and later sulphur. Thus the manufacture of one chemical led to that of another.

In 1890 fifty of these acid and alkali firms amalgamated to form *United Alkali, Ltd.*, in order better to compete with *Brunner, Mond, and Co.*, who had in 1873 begun to manufacture soda by the new ammonia-soda process. Mond also developed a new process for extracting pure nickel.

(2) *Explosives.* The outbreak of war in 1914 found the chemical manufacturers unprepared for *mass* production of explosives. Technical co-operation between many small units during the War led to their amalgamation in 1918 to form *Nobel Industries, Ltd.* By reason of its manufacture of ammunition this firm had many connexions with the non-ferrous metal industry.

(3) *Dyestuffs.* The War also stimulated Britain's production of dyes, which had become almost a German monopoly, although the original discovery of aniline had been made by the English chemist Perkin in 1856. Amalgamations of firms in the textile areas of Lancashire and Yorkshire and at Grangemouth, in Scotland, led to the formation in 1918 of the *British Dyestuffs Corporation, Ltd.*

The amalgamation of these four large and many smaller firms in 1926 concentrated the production of Britain's chemicals in a vast combine—*Imperial Chemical Industries, Ltd.*

Another giant combine arose in the soap industry, where the Sunlight soap firm merged with other firms interested in vegetable oils—*e.g.*, Cattle Cake Mills and the Margarine Union—to form *Unilever, Ltd.* (1929), with factories in fifty different countries.

Other chemical products, notably artificial silks known as rayons, and synthetic nitrates for fertilizers, were energetically developed during the inter-war years.

THE BUILDING INDUSTRY

Over a quarter of Britain's building workers were unemployed in 1932. From 1933 onward, however, stimulated by lower rates of interest which reduced the repayment charges, the number of houses built for sale, largely through Building Societies,

DIAGRAM 45

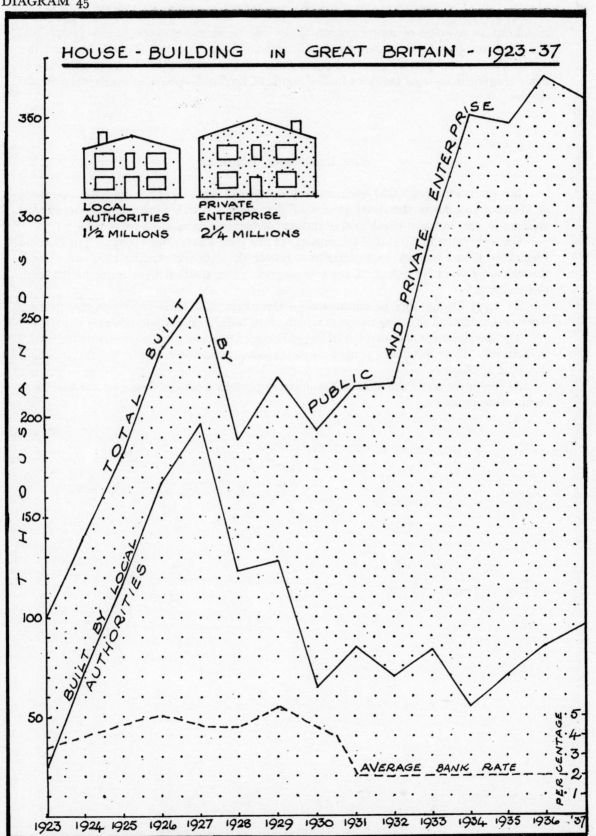

HOUSE - BUILDING IN GREAT BRITAIN - 1923-37

LOCAL AUTHORITIES 1½ MILLIONS

PRIVATE ENTERPRISE 2¼ MILLIONS

TOTAL BUILT BY PUBLIC AND PRIVATE ENTERPRISE

BUILT BY LOCAL AUTHORITIES

AVERAGE BANK RATE

THOUSANDS

PERCENTAGE

rose from an average of under 70,000 (1923–28) to almost 300,000 yearly (1934–38). See Diagram 45. Over 4,500,000 dwellings were built in Great Britain between the wars. About one-quarter received some form of State subsidy. A great quantity of other construction—e.g., factories in the South of England—was also undertaken in the thirties.

The Electrical Industry

Britain before 1920 was backward as compared with America and the countries of Western Europe in the development of electricity. There were not only numerous voltages in use, but also many power stations of varying sizes, some very small.

Changes came as a result of the findings of the Weir Committee (1925). The Central Electricity Board was set up to distribute power through the existing companies' lines throughout Britain by means of a national grid. The smallest generating plants were closed down.

By 1939 the number of consumers of electricity had risen from 730,000 to over 9,000,000. Most of the new factories which were built used electric power.

The development of cheap electricity gave rise to new electrical engineering industries in Britain. Their products ranged from massive generators and dynamos to small domestic appliances.

At the outbreak of the War about 400,000 persons were employed by the electrical engineering industry.

42. BRITISH FARMING

THE policy of guaranteeing minimum prices for the chief farm products and minimum wages for farm workers was continued after the War. For two years farmers were prosperous, but after 1920 agricultural prices slumped—*e.g.*,

	1920	1922
Wheat, per quarter	86s. 4d.	40s. 9d.
Oats, per quarter.	45s. 7d.	26s. 6d.

The Government was not prepared to support prices to the extent which was now necessary, and repealed the post-War Acts which had given it powers to control prices, wages, and farming policy. From 1921 until the early thirties a general attitude of *laissez-faire* was adopted. Arable land tended to revert to pasture ; as the acreage under the plough and the labour force required to work it declined, the number of beef and dairy cattle increased (see Diagram 46).

Despite this, the period between the wars was one of great technical advance in agricultural methods. Farming became increasingly mechanized. Horse teams were replaced by tractors (see Diagram 47), using oil as fuel. Enormous combine-harvesters which cut the ripe corn, threshed out the seeds, and filled sacks with the grain were introduced into Britain in 1928. New milking machines were used. Fertilizers, weed-killers, pest controls, were increasingly employed. These new methods ensured higher output per acre and per man. Yet only one arable crop, sugar beet, increased its acreage, and this resulted from a measure of protection in 1922 and a subsidy given to producers in 1924 (Map 60). An Act of 1924 reintroduced State control of agricultural wages. In 1928 agricultural land and buildings were relieved of local rate burdens.

After 1931 the Government's attitude towards farming changed. Many measures were passed to encourage agriculture with the dual object of decreasing Britain's dependence on foreign food (cp. Adam Smith, 1776 : *The Wealth of Nations*, " Opulence is of less importance than national security ") and protecting the British farmer against the collapse of world prices of farm products, though still giving some preferential treatment to Empire products.

(i) Subsidies were given to growers of wheat (1932), barley and oats (1937), and rearers of cattle (1934 and 1937).

(ii) Grants were also given to help to pay the cost of draining and liming land.

(iii) Marketing Boards were instituted by the Agricultural Marketing Acts from 1931 onward with extensive powers to buy, sell, process the commodity if necessary, and to determine the amount to be produced and the price to be paid. The schemes were compulsory when two-thirds of the main producers approved of them. Boards were set up for marketing hops, potatoes, milk, and bacon and pork. By this means competition in the home market was eliminated.

(iv) Methods of restricting the import of foreign agricultural products such as Danish bacon were adopted, including maximum quotas (1932) and tariffs.

DIAGRAM 46

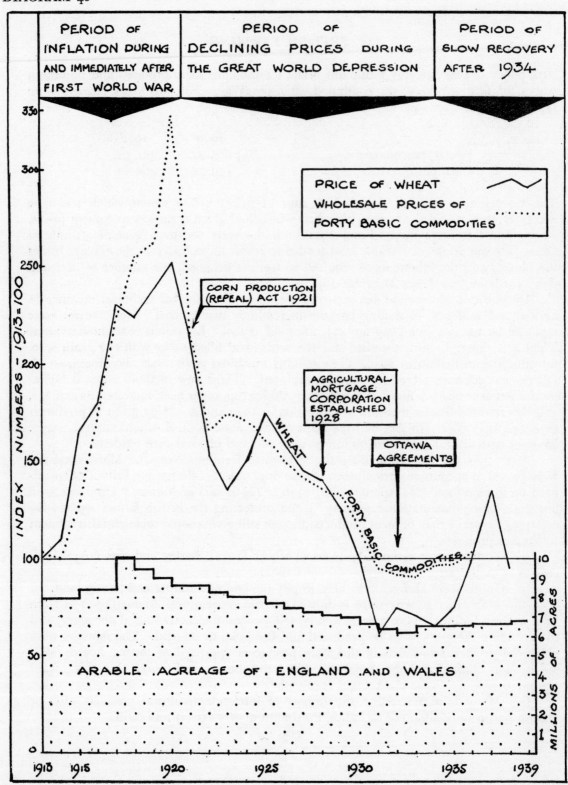

216

(v) Colleges of agriculture were established to promote more scientific methods of farming.

(vi) The Ministry of Agriculture gave help by providing expert advice, spreading knowledge by pamphlets.

DIAGRAM 47

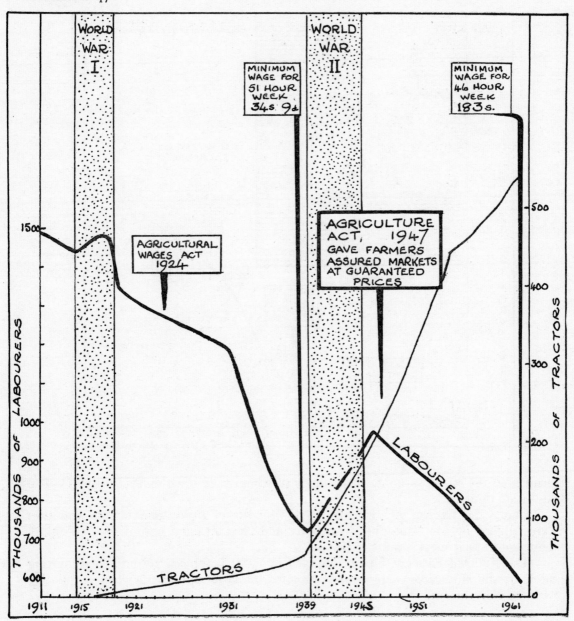

(vii) Agricultural Wages Boards improved the farm labourers' pay and conditions, and thereby helped to arrest the drift from the land.

The number of farmers who owned their land rose between the Wars especially after 1925. The Agricultural Mortgage Corporation (1928) granted loans to purchase

MAP 60

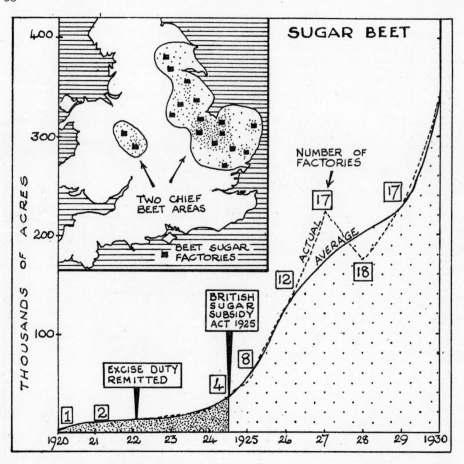

farms from the estates of landowners, many of whom were often obliged to sell land to pay estate duties.

Under the Ottawa Agreements (1932) imports of meat from foreign countries were reduced by over one-third. Australia and New Zealand agreed to a voluntary reduction in their meat exports to Britain.

The National Farmers' Union (founded in 1907) became a powerful body during the War, and afterwards energetically promoted the farmers' interests when negotiating with the Government.

43. TRANSPORT

RAILWAYS

At the end of hostilities it became apparent that :

(i) The railways were old and in many ways out of date ; their rolling stock had deteriorated, and much of the permanent way required extensive overhaul.

(ii) They no longer held a monopoly of transport, but instead had to face the rising competition of a new method of transport—the road motor which was not subject to strict legal control of its rates and fares.

MAP 61

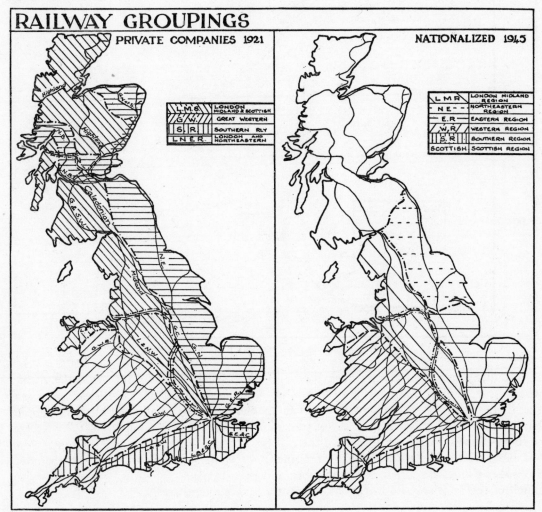

By the Railways Act of 1921 the companies were divided into four groups (see Map 61), taking the titles of Great Western, Southern, London and North-Eastern, and London, Midland, and Scottish. A Railway Rates Tribunal took over that part of the work of the Railway Commission which concerned charges. These were to be so fixed that the railways could earn a 'standard revenue' based on their net earnings in 1913. In fact no company ever earned its standard revenue.

DIAGRAM 48

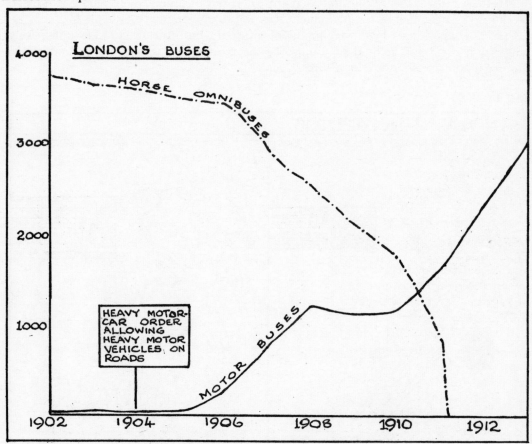

LONDON'S BUSES : HORSE v. MOTOR

Railway rates had always been based on the principle of charging what the traffic would bear. Bulky commodities of low value—*e.g.*, stone and coal, paid lower rates per ton than expensive manufactures such as machinery and woollen cloth. The road haulier concerned only with the *cost* of transport was best able to compete in the carriage of these valuable commodities where the railway charges were high. The railways were left more and more with the least remunerative traffic. Much of the short-distance passenger traffic was lost to the motor-bus and private car ; the railways were left with much of the relatively unprofitable commuter and seasonal traffic.

Road Transport

Owing to the greatly increasing number of motor vehicles on the roads of Britain (see p. 210) the highway authorities were forced to undertake major improvements. Many roads were widened, and dangerous bends eliminated. New 'arterial' roads were constructed in places where it was difficult to improve old roads. The country's roads were classified according to their width and importance, the main trunk roads becoming the direct responsibility of the Ministry of Transport (established 1919).

The transport of passengers by motor omnibus became so profitable that a large number of these vehicles, often working at breakneck speeds, competed for the available traffic. This, together with some alarm at the effect of their competition on the railways, led to the passing of the Road Traffic Act of 1930, which provided that only vehicles licensed by three district commissioners could ply on stated routes. The Road and Rail Traffic Act 1933 established a similar licensing system for goods lorries.

MAP 62

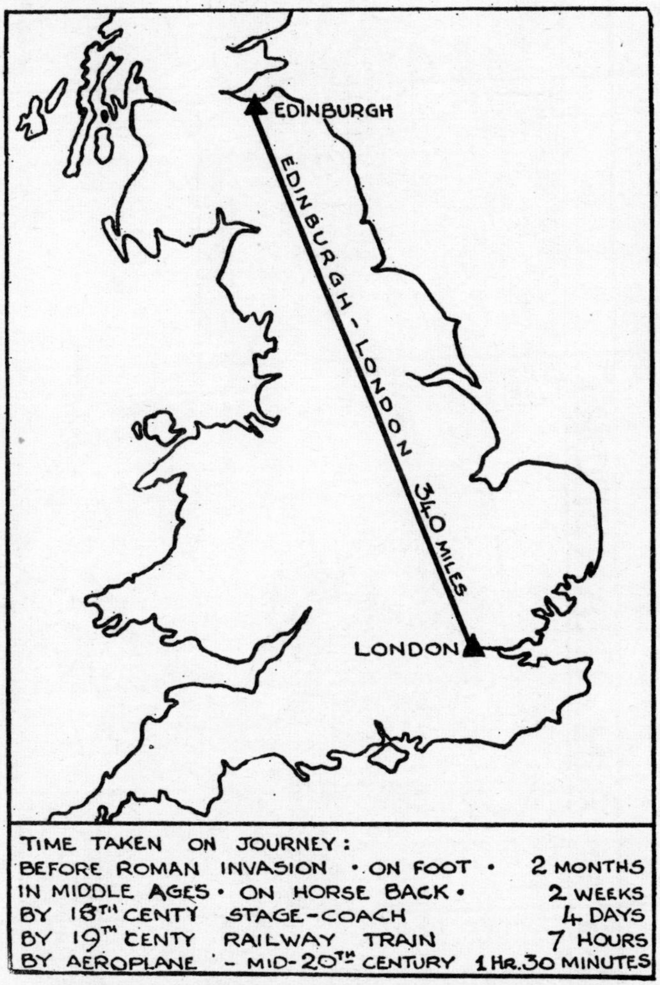
EDINBURGH
EDINBURGH - LONDON
340 MILES
LONDON
TIME TAKEN ON JOURNEY:
BEFORE ROMAN INVASION • ON FOOT • 2 MONTHS
IN MIDDLE AGES • ON HORSE BACK • 2 WEEKS
BY 18TH CENTY STAGE-COACH 4 DAYS
BY 19TH CENTY RAILWAY TRAIN 7 HOURS
BY AEROPLANE - MID-20TH CENTURY 1 HR.30 MINUTES

COMPARISONS OF THE TIME TAKEN ON A JOURNEY FROM LONDON TO EDINBURGH

Sea Transport

During the twentieth century the size and speed of steamships continued to increase. Tramp steamers of up to 8000 tons, built to run at speeds over ten knots, were launched. Monster liners, over 80,000 tons, were built between 1935 and 1940 (*Normandie*, *Queen Mary*, *Queen Elizabeth*), and the Atlantic was crossed at $31\frac{1}{2}$ knots.

MAP 63

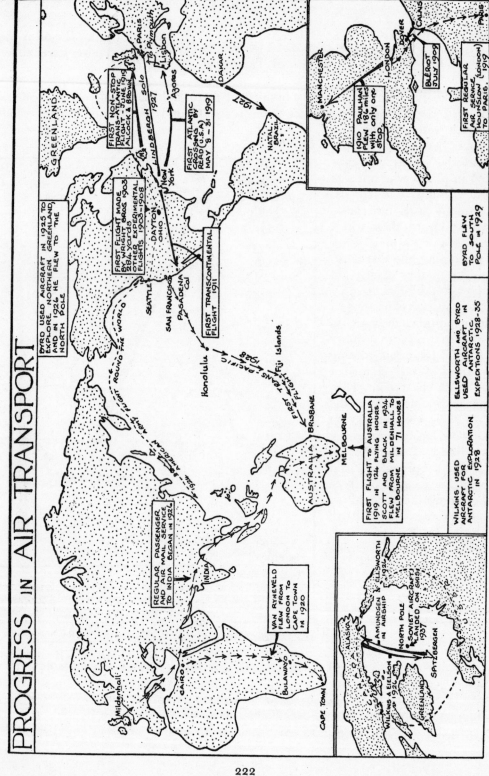

PROGRESS IN AIR TRANSPORT

BYRD USED AIRCRAFT IN 1925 TO EXPLORE NORTHERN GREENLAND, AND IN 1926 HE FLEW TO THE NORTH POLE

GREENLAND

FIRST NON-STOP TRANS-ATLANTIC FLIGHT JUNE 1919 ALCOCK & BROWN

PARIS

To PLYMOUTH

LISBON

LINDBERGH 1927 Solo

Ajores

New York

FIRST ATLANTIC CROSSING BY READ (U.S.A) MAY 8 - 31 1919

DAKAR

NATAL BRAZIL

1927

FIRST FLIGHT MADE BY WRIGHT BROS 1903 OTHER EXPERIMENTAL FLIGHTS 1903-1908

DAYTON OHIO

SEATTLE

SAN FRANCISCO

PASADENA Cal.

FIRST TRANSCONTINENTAL FLIGHT 1911

FLIGHT ROUND THE WORLD

HONOLULU

FIRST TRANS PACIFIC FLIGHT 1928

Fiji Islands.

BRISBANE

AUSTRALIA

MELBOURNE

FIRST FLIGHT to AUSTRALIA 1919 IN 124 FLYING HOURS. SCOTT AND BLACK IN 1934 FLEW FROM MILDENHALL TO MELBOURNE IN 71 HOURS

MANCHESTER

LONDON

DOVER

CALAIS

PARIS

1910 PAULHAN FLEW 186 MILES WITH ONLY ONE STOP.

BLÉRIOT JULY 1909

FIRST REGULAR AIR SERVICE HOUNSLOW (LONDON) TO PARIS. 1919

INDIA

REGULAR PASSENGER AND AIR MAIL SERVICE TO INDIA BEGAN IN 1926

Mildenhall

CAIRO

BULAWAYO

CAPE TOWN

VAN RYNEVELD FLEW FROM LONDON TO CAPE TOWN IN 1920

ALASKA

AMUNDSEN & ELLSWORTH 1926 IN AIRSHIP

NORTH POLE

SOVIET AIRCRAFT LANDED ON ICE 1937

WILKINS & EIELSON 1928

GREENLAND

SPITZBERGEN

WILKINS USED AIRCRAFT FOR ANTARCTIC EXPLORATION IN 1928

ELLSWORTH and BYRD USED AIRCRAFT IN ANTARCTIC IN EXPEDITIONS 1928-35

BYRD FLEW TO SOUTH POLE IN 1929

PROGRESS IN AIR TRANSPORT : MEMORABLE EARLY FLIGHTS

Oil to an increasing extent replaced coal as fuel, for, though dearer, the oil is more easily taken on board, occupies less space, and the oil-driven ship requires fewer stokers.

AIR TRANSPORT

The most striking feature of all twentieth-century advance in transport has been the development of the aeroplane. Although the Wright Brothers made their first biplane flight in 1903, little advance was made in aeronautics until Blériot crossed the Channel in 1909, and aviation was still in its infancy in 1914. Nevertheless, aircraft played no small part in the naval and military operations of the First World War, which stimulated technical advance towards greater range, speed, and reliability to a remarkable degree.

The earlier biplanes were superseded by monoplanes; new metals were used, such as duralumin, an alloy of aluminium which was discovered in 1906, and proved to be a strong yet light metal suitable for aircraft construction.

In 1919 Alcock and Brown made the first non-stop flight across the Atlantic; this was the first of a series of record-breaking and memorable long-distance flights (see Map 63). At the same time there was a sensational increase in the speed of flight. Blériot in 1909 crossed the Channel at a speed of ten miles an hour. In 1939 a Messerschmitt 109 set up a record of 469 miles per hour.

Like ocean transport, air transport is subject to severe international competition. The Government, therefore, concerned with national defence, was anxious to develop aviation, and in 1924 subsidized Imperial Airways, Ltd., an amalgamation of all the British air transport companies. It was not, however, until 1926 that Imperial Airways extended its services outside Europe. Internal air traffic only developed in the thirties.

DIAGRAM 49

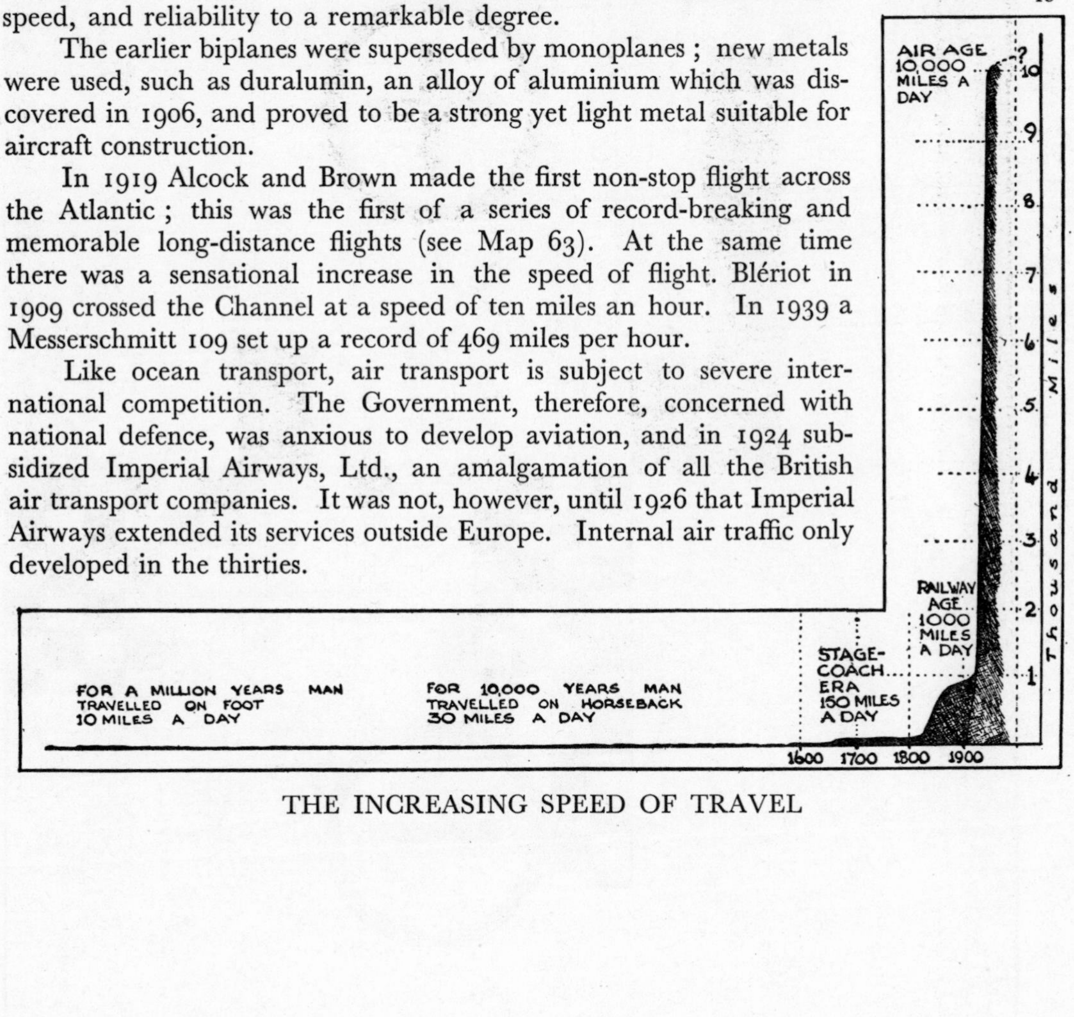

AIR AGE
10,000
MILES A
DAY

RAILWAY
AGE
1000
MILES
A DAY

STAGE-
COACH
ERA
150 MILES
A DAY

FOR A MILLION YEARS MAN
TRAVELLED ON FOOT
10 MILES A DAY

FOR 10,000 YEARS MAN
TRAVELLED ON HORSEBACK
30 MILES A DAY

1600   1700   1800   1900

Thousand Miles

THE INCREASING SPEED OF TRAVEL

DIAGRAM 50

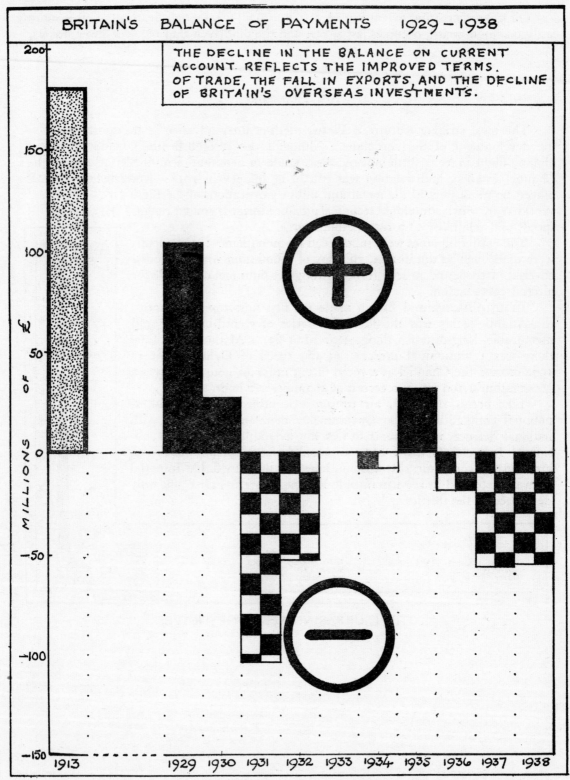

BRITAIN'S BALANCE OF PAYMENTS 1929-1938

THE DECLINE IN THE BALANCE ON CURRENT ACCOUNT REFLECTS THE IMPROVED TERMS OF TRADE, THE FALL IN EXPORTS, AND THE DECLINE OF BRITAIN'S OVERSEAS INVESTMENTS.

44. MONETARY AND FISCAL POLICY

A. The Gold Standard

Before the War the undisputed centre of the world's banking and finance was London, where trading debts of all nations could be settled and their currencies exchanged for gold. During the War, as we have seen, gold sovereigns were withdrawn from circulation. The aim of the Government at the peace of 1918 was to return to pre-War financial arrangements, and this was partly achieved by 1919. It was still necessary to protect the country's gold reserves, and in 1919 the export of gold was prohibited : Britain was now in law and fact off the gold standard. The Government accepted the main recommendations of the Cunliffe Committee on currency and foreign exchanges, which were that :

(i) The size of the note issue not covered by gold (the fiduciary issue) should be progressively reduced.

(ii) The gold standard should be restored as soon as possible and at the pre-War parity.

From the end of 1919 a limit was set to the fiduciary issue by requiring that the actual maximum issue in each year should become the legal maximum for the following year.

A return to the gold standard was much more difficult. In 1925 the attempt was made to return to the pre-War position of an exchange rate of 4·86 dollars to the pound sterling. Many economists (notably J. M. Keynes) thought this rate overvalued sterling, and that by now the pound was worth only 90 per cent. of what it had been as compared with the American dollar. Partly because of this Britain's prices were relatively high in comparison with those of America, and her merchants found difficulty in selling their products in other countries against U.S.A. competition. Once Britain had returned to the standard it had to be protected. In order to keep a large gold reserve in London it was found necessary to offer high rates of interest, a serious handicap to British manufacturers when they wanted to borrow money to build new plants.

World Economic Crisis 1929–32

Since the end of the War impoverished Europe had relied heavily on American loans. During 1929 a speculation boom in America made it more profitable for Americans to lend their money at home than in Europe. American loans to Europe practically ceased. The most devastating economic crisis in post-War history was precipitated when the American speculation boom broke, this at a time when the prices of primary products were low. The crisis soon spread to Europe. Bank failures in Austria and Germany had quick repercussions in Britain. Foreigners who had kept money on deposit in London because of the high rates of interest became anxious : £200,000,000 in gold was withdrawn between July and September 1931. At the same time British

DIAGRAM 51

ANNUAL AVERAGES OF NEW INVESTMENT ISSUES IN LONDON

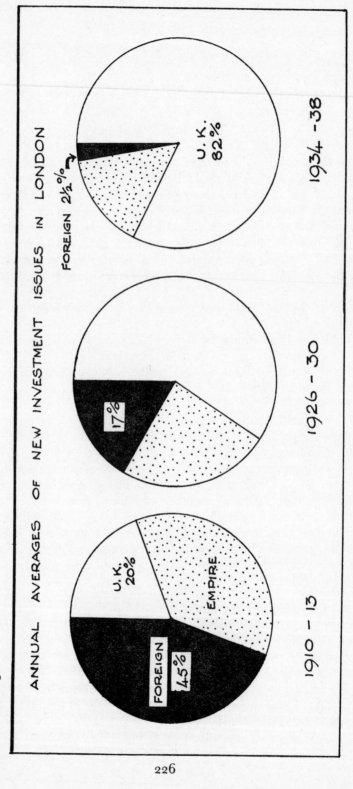

financiers were unable to recover the money they had lent to Europeans. Thus Britain was once again forced from the gold standard. The value of the £ sterling dropped from 4·86 to 3·4 U.S.A. dollars. The new exchange rate helped, at least temporarily, British exports. The Bank rate was lowered to 2 per cent., at which rate it remained during the thirties, reducing the burden of interest on the National Debt and encouraging activity in those industries—e.g., housing—within which capital charges were heavy.

B. The Balance of Payments

The financial crisis was accompanied by deep concern about Britain's trading position ; the need to redress the balance of trade became a decisive argument in favour of abandoning her traditional free-trade policy.

Foreign trade, the exchange of goods for goods, rarely balances. The difference between imports and exports is the balance of trade, an excess of the latter being considered favourable. The balance of payments includes, besides the visible goods, 'invisible' items, payments for services such as shipping freights and insurance charges paid to foreigners, holiday expenditure abroad, and, most important of all, interest due on past capital investments abroad or on short-term loans.

During the twenty years following the War, Britain's ability to compete in the export markets of the world declined, particularly, as we have seen (p. 208), in the old staple industries. The trade surplus which she had hitherto enjoyed gradually declined and eventually disappeared (see Diagram 52). She was unable to supply all domestic and foreign demands for capital. In 1913 some 45 per cent. of the new issues of stocks and shares in London were for foreign concerns. In the thirties the percentage was negligible. Official regulations, a consequence of the unfavourable balance of payments, created difficulties, but in any case there was a diminishing field for profitable international investment.

Meanwhile the terms of trade moved steadily against the suppliers of primary products—food and raw materials—in favour of countries such as Britain which were predominantly exporters of manufactured goods (see Diagram 52). The volume of trade in primary products will increase if the terms of trade move against them. When they are cheap fewer manufactures need to be exported to pay for them. The flow of emigrants from Europe had brought increased manpower and investment capital to the 'newer' countries. Scientific agriculture had increased the output of farm products, railways had been built to carry them to the coast, and shipping services had been improved—e.g., refrigeration, to facilitate their transport. As the supply increased the prices of primary products tended to fall, a trend which continued to 1939. For a given amount of manufactures Britain could buy increasing quantities of food and raw materials. Though cheap food raised the standard of the people as a whole, the decreasing demand for exports caused heavy unemployment, and the stagnation in world trade led to a serious loss of income from shipping, banking, and insurance services. Britain during the thirties was faced with the problem of how to increase employment and keep a favourable balance of trade, a problem that was to become more familiar in the fifties.

E.H.—H

DIAGRAM 52

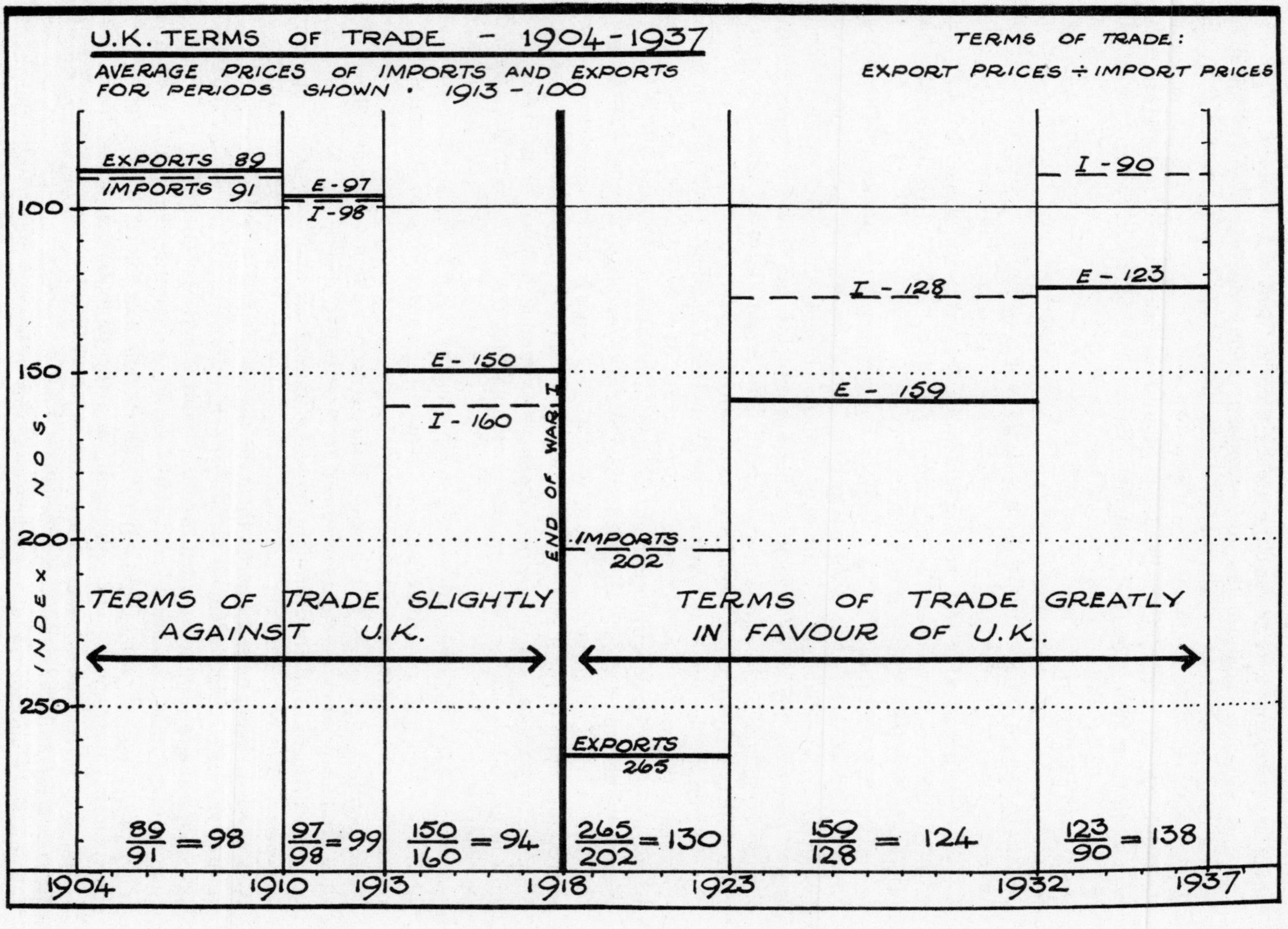

U.K. TERMS OF TRADE — 1904–1937

AVERAGE PRICES OF IMPORTS AND EXPORTS
FOR PERIODS SHOWN • 1913 = 100

TERMS OF TRADE:
EXPORT PRICES ÷ IMPORT PRICES

INDEX NO.S.

EXPORTS 89 / IMPORTS 91

E-97 / I-98

E-150 / I-160

END OF WAR I

IMPORTS 202

EXPORTS 265

I-128

E-159

I-90

E-123

TERMS OF TRADE SLIGHTLY AGAINST U.K.

TERMS OF TRADE GREATLY IN FAVOUR OF U.K.

$\frac{89}{91} = 98$

$\frac{97}{98} = 99$

$\frac{150}{160} = 94$

$\frac{265}{202} = 130$

$\frac{152}{128} = 124$

$\frac{123}{90} = 138$

100   150   200   250

1904   1910   1913   1918   1923   1932   1937

C. The End of Free Trade

After the War Britain became increasingly protectionist in her trade policy. An Act of 1921 safeguarded certain industries which were ' developing '—*e.g.*, wireless valves, precision instruments, ignition magnetos, and certain chemicals. The McKenna Duties (see p. 197) were renewed in 1925, though there was no longer any need to save shipping space. When the slump began in 1929 inroads had already been made into her free-trade system, though Britain remained the one great importing country into which foreign producers of primary products could still unload their surpluses.

In 1931 free-trade policy was abandoned and a general tariff was introduced : all foreign imports, unless specifically exempted, were subject to a 10 per cent. tariff ; most manufactures were charged 20 per cent. and luxuries 33⅓ per cent. Empire goods were exempted from tax or charged at preferential rates according to agreements reached at Ottawa in 1932. Even the highest duties charged on luxuries, however, were small compared with those demanded by most other countries. A quota system was also used to benefit home and Empire producers : the tax on iron and steel products varied with the quantities imported. An Import Duties Advisory Committee was set up to recommend modifications to the general 10 per cent. tariff.

The favoured Empire producers expanded their trade ; their exports to Britain rose from 29 per cent. in 1930 to 40 per cent. in 1938. A number of bilateral commercial treaties were negotiated to secure preferential treatment for certain commodities—*e.g.*, with Scandinavian countries for coal, with Poland and the U.S.A. for textiles.

THE population of England and Wales continued to increase during the inter-War years, but at a declining rate. Though people lived longer and infant mortality declined further, most families were smaller ; two children were the average as compared with the four, five, and more in the Victorian family. The main reasons for the declining birth rate have been discussed on p. 193. In addition it should be noted that there were new ways of spending money (radios, motor-cars), new opportunities for getting on, and a desire to ' keep up with the Joneses.' In their efforts to reach a higher standard of comfort some parents considered children a handicap, and they strictly limited the size of their families. The lack of political security abroad, the constant threat of war in the thirties, and the economic depression led some couples to believe that it was unwise to have children, who would have to face too bleak a future.

DIAGRAM 53

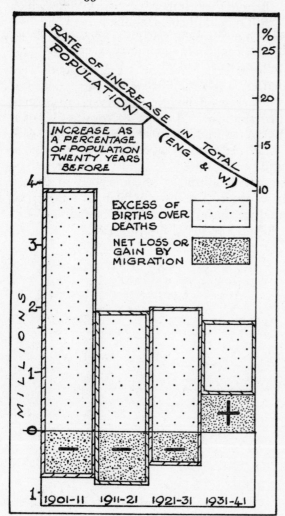

IMMIGRATION AND EMIGRATION

Diagram 53 shows that the number of people leaving Britain exceeded the number of immigrants until 1931, when the influx of people to the United Kingdom was greater, accounting for 30 per cent. of the total increase in Britain's population. The size of the rectangles in the diagram is proportional to the excess of births over deaths, the portion above the datum line representing the actual increase when the net loss or gain by migration is allowed for. From 1931 to 1941 the number of immigrants exceeded the number of emigrants and helped to counteract the effect of a severe drop in the natural increase in population. Many people who had left the country previously and failed to make good abroad because of the depression returned ; workers from

Ireland continued to come for employment, and the number of immigrants was also swollen by political and racial refugees from Europe.

CHANGES IN OCCUPATIONS AND THE LOCATION OF INDUSTRY

The decline of the old staple manufactures and the rise of new industries led not only to changes of occupation, but also to new centres of industry in the Midlands and South-east of England. During the inter-war years a considerable number of workers —although probably not enough—migrated from the depressed areas in the Scottish Lowlands, South Wales, and the North of England to the newer industrial areas. They came both with and without financial aid from the Government. An attempt was made to make the older areas more attractive to industry and by the Special Areas Act 1934 and subsequent legislation financial help was granted. Factories engaged in diversified light industries were attracted to Government Trading Estates—e.g. Hillington, Treforest, and the Team Valley (Gateshead). The development of road transport tended to reduce the attraction of industrial sites near the railway arteries. Many new factories were built along the new arterial roads (p. 214).

46. TRADE UNIONISM BETWEEN THE WARS

THE trade unions emerged from the War considerably increased in membership and influence. Diagram 12 shows that the number of members doubled between 1914 and 1920, reaching a peak of 8,300,000. By 1933, however, because of the Great Depression, the number had fallen to 4,400,000, after which there was a recovery to reach a total of over six millions when the Second World War broke out. There were fewer people working in the old staple industries where unionism had been strong, and in the new industries trade-union loyalty was slower to develop. There was, however, a spread of unionism among white-collared workers. By 1937, because of the amalgamation of small unions, half the trade unionists in the country were to be found in twelve giant unions—*e.g.*, the Transport and General Workers Union, with over a million members. The prestige of the General Council of the Trade Union Congress was continuously increasing.

Similar organizations were formed by the employers—*e.g.*, the Federation of British Industries (1916), the National Union of Manufacturers (1917),[1] and the British Employers' Confederation [2] (1919). The Whitley Committee, one of many committees established to consider post-War reconstruction, recommended the establishment of Joint Industrial Councils in those industries where trade-union and employer organization was adequate, as a result of which there was a move towards replacing local settlements with national wage agreements. The Whitley Council also suggested the establishment of a voluntary arbitration court, a recommendation which was embodied in the Industrial Courts Act 1919.

INDUSTRIAL UNREST BETWEEN THE WARS

The standard of living had increased somewhat during the War, and the workers offered determined resistance to all attempts to reduce their wages. Great unrest prevailed, and strikes were frequent. There were over a thousand in the years 1919–20, two of the most important of which concerned the miners and the railwaymen. The mine-owners were determined to get away from national agreements and back to local settlements on wages ; they were equally determined to reduce wages. There was a bitter strike in 1920. A period of declining wages, with coal prices falling lower as competition from the restored Ruhr mines developed, led to the owners' demands for further wage reductions and the restoration of the eight-hour day. The miners demanded higher wages, a seven-hour day, and the nationalization of the mines. The Government set up the Sankey Commission in 1919, which accepted the idea of nationalization in the coal industry (see p. 206), and suggested some immediate improvement in hours of labour

[1] This developed from the earlier British Manufacturers' Association (1915).
[2] This developed from the earlier National Confederation of Employers' Organizations (1918).

and wages. In 1921 the miners renewed their attempts to secure nationalization, and the railwaymen and transport workers threatened sympathetic strikes in support of the miners' demands. All this unrest led finally to a general strike in 1926, when, in support of the miners whose wages had been cut, workers in the iron and steel, printing, building trades, electricity and gas supply, and transport industries came out on strike. The Government dealt with the situation firmly, and middle-class opinion opposed the strikers. Volunteers came to the aid of the Government, and after a week the trade-union leaders were forced to order their members back to work.

The results of the General Strike were :

(i) A weakening of the financial strength of the unions, for the strike had been a strain on their resources.

(ii) The Government regarded the strike as a challenge to its authority, and in 1927 the Trade Disputes and Trade Unions Act was passed. This measure considerably restricted the power of the unions : (a) it made illegal sympathetic strikes and those intended to intimidate the Government, (b) it made it almost impossible for unions of civil servants to remain affiliated to the Trade Union Congress, (c) it hampered the finances of the Labour Party by requiring that trade unionists must ' contract in ' for the payment of the political levy.

(iii) The miners gained nothing ; their strike lasted seven months, and when the Union funds were exhausted they were forced to return to work at even lower wages. Trade unions became more accommodating in their relations with employers, and disputes after 1926 were on the whole insignificant.

DIAGRAM
54

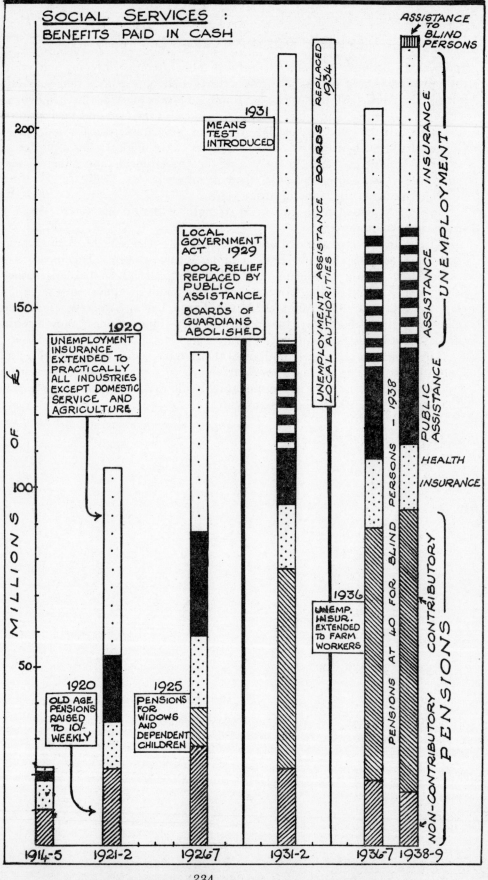

SOCIAL SERVICES :
BENEFITS PAID IN CASH

ASSISTANCE
TO
BLIND
PERSONS

1931
MEANS
TEST
INTRODUCED

REPLACED 1934

LOCAL
GOVERNMENT
ACT 1929

POOR RELIEF
REPLACED BY
PUBLIC
ASSISTANCE

BOARDS OF
GUARDIANS
ABOLISHED

1920
UNEMPLOYMENT
INSURANCE
EXTENDED TO
PRACTICALLY
ALL INDUSTRIES
EXCEPT DOMESTIC
SERVICE AND
AGRICULTURE

UNEMPLOYMENT ASSISTANCE BOARDS
LOCAL AUTHORITIES

PUBLIC ASSISTANCE — UNEMPLOYMENT

ASSISTANCE — INSURANCE

HEALTH
INSURANCE

1936
UNEMP.
INSUR.
EXTENDED
TO FARM
WORKERS

PENSIONS AT 40 FOR BLIND PERSONS - 1938

CONTRIBUTORY

NON-CONTRIBUTORY — PENSIONS

1920
OLD AGE
PENSIONS
RAISED
TO 10/-
WEEKLY

1925
PENSIONS
FOR
WIDOWS
AND
DEPENDENT
CHILDREN

MILLIONS OF £

200

150

100

50

1914-5   1921-2   1926-7   1931-2   1936-7 1938-9

47. THE STANDARD OF LIVING

DURING the twenty-five years 1914–39 the total national income and the average real income per head of population increased considerably. The average money earnings about doubled, but the cost of living rose by only 55 per cent. The average employed worker was thus better off in 1939 than he had been in 1914. The average, however, conceals great variations ; earnings in the staple industries were depressed.

The improvement in wages was accompanied by a general reduction of the standard working week. A 48-hour week (a substantial reduction of the pre-War week) became normal in the twenties. In the late thirties there was in some industries not only a reduction in the weekly hours from 48 to 45, but also a rapid extension of paid annual holidays, a privilege previously given only to the salaried worker.

In spite of these beneficial changes the most remarkable feature of the period was the very high level of unemployment. On an average one insured person in every seven was out of work during the whole period from 1921 (when records were first kept) [1] to 1938. Only in 1927 did the figure drop to one in ten, and during 1931 and 1932 one man was out of a job for every four who were working. The new industries were not immune, but the highest rates of unemployment were found in the old staple industries ; in June 1932, when the average number in the United Kingdom was 22 per cent., approximately 60 per cent. of the shipbuilders, 40 per cent. of the coalminers, and 45 per cent. of the iron and steel workers were unemployed. These figures and those in Diagram 55 relate to insured workers. There were numbers unemployed who were not covered by the Unemployment Insurance Acts.

RELIEF OF THE POOR

The main provisions of the reports of the Poor Law Commission of 1909 remained shelved until after the First World War, and the administration of the Poor Law was still in the hands of Boards of Guardians as established nearly a century before (see p. 137). Not only did they offer poor relief, but their workhouses were the last resort of the destitute, the sick and infirm, the mentally deficient, as well as of many children. Meanwhile county and county borough councils had built up specialized medical and welfare services, and the workhouses were often duplicating these services. The public became increasingly insistent that this was not only uneconomic and wasteful, but also morally unjustifiable : destitution was not a crime, and the unemployed man was not necessarily lazy. The Local Government Act 1929 abolished the Boards of Guardians, transferring their powers and functions, including the running of the workhouses, to the county and county borough authorities.

[1] Trade Unions kept some records before 1921.

An Act of 1920 extended unemployment insurance to practically all industries except agriculture and domestic service. It was not intended to give unemployment benefits for extended periods—fifteen weeks was considered the limit. Almost immediately afterwards, however, heavy unemployment occurred and the Government was forced to supplement the unemployed men's pay when their 'standard' benefit was exhausted. To cut down the cost of these extended benefits a means test (administered by the local authorities, though payments were made out of funds provided by the Treasury) was instituted in 1931. The test invoked bitter hostility from the unemployed and from the local authorities who paid out the 'dole.' The Unemployment Insurance Act of 1934 reconstructed the scheme on an actuarial basis relating the number of weeks of benefit to the amount of the contributions paid. Able-bodied men who had exhausted their benefits received assistance from a new Unemployment Assistance Board which took over from the local authorities the administration of the means test.

MAP 64

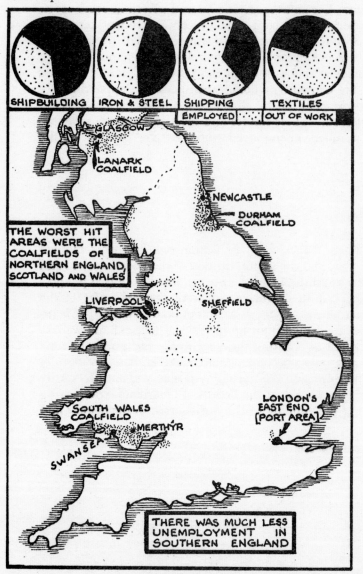

DIAGRAM 55

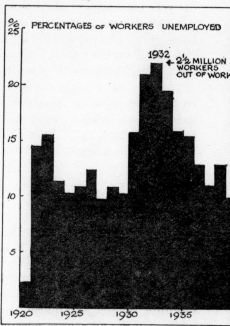

Map 64 shows the chief areas of unemployment between the Wars

PART VIII: THE SECOND WORLD WAR

48. ECONOMIC PLANNING AND GOVERNMENT POLICY

HAVING learned from the experience of the First World War, the Government, upon the outbreak of the Second, planned from the start to make the fullest use of the nation's resources of men and materials. New Ministries were created (of Food, Shipping, Supply, Economic Warfare, Aircraft Production) and extensive powers to control industry were assumed—*e.g.*, power to requisition a ship and to decide its cargo and destination. Lulled by a false sense of security in the uneventful first months of the War, however, the steps taken were not sufficiently energetic; a million men were still unemployed in April 1940. The disaster at Dunkirk (May 1940) led to a state of emergency. Men and materials could be directed to essential trades from which the workers were not conscripted to the forces. The most vital industries—*e.g.*, railways—were directly controlled. The iron and steel and shipbuilding industries (which had suffered during the inter-War depression) began to boom. Non-essential trades were hampered in obtaining raw materials as well as by the conscription of their labour force. The import of luxury goods was restricted, though at the beginning of the War their export was encouraged to earn money to pay for goods and raw-material imports. Workers at home had to make them—*e.g.*, nylon stockings for Americans—yet were unable to buy them for their own use.

Help was given to the farmers in the form of grants for ploughing up old pastures, more guaranteed prices for farm products, and more food subsidies, and the area under the plough increased from 12,000,000 acres to 18,000,000 acres. The use of machinery and fertilizers spread rapidly, and the output per acre rose spectacularly (see Diagram 67).

Labour troubles were less frequent than during the First War, partly as a result of the appointment of a prominent trade-union leader (Ernest Bevin) as Minister of Labour and National Service, and partly because of the payment of higher wages and improved conditions in factories, canteens, and welfare provisions. A National Arbitration Tribunal (1940) settled wage disputes; its decisions were enforceable.

Many articles were rationed to ensure fair shares for all: certain foods—*e.g.*, sugar, butter, bread, milk, meat—and clothes, coal, and petrol. After 1941 'utility' wares were introduced—*e.g.*, clothes, furniture, pottery—in which a reasonable price was charged and a minimum standard of quality ensured by the elimination of non-essential decoration. Because of the policy of food-rationing, food subsidies, and utility products there was little rise in the cost of living after the first year of war, during which the pound depreciated in terms of the dollar.

DIAGRAM 56

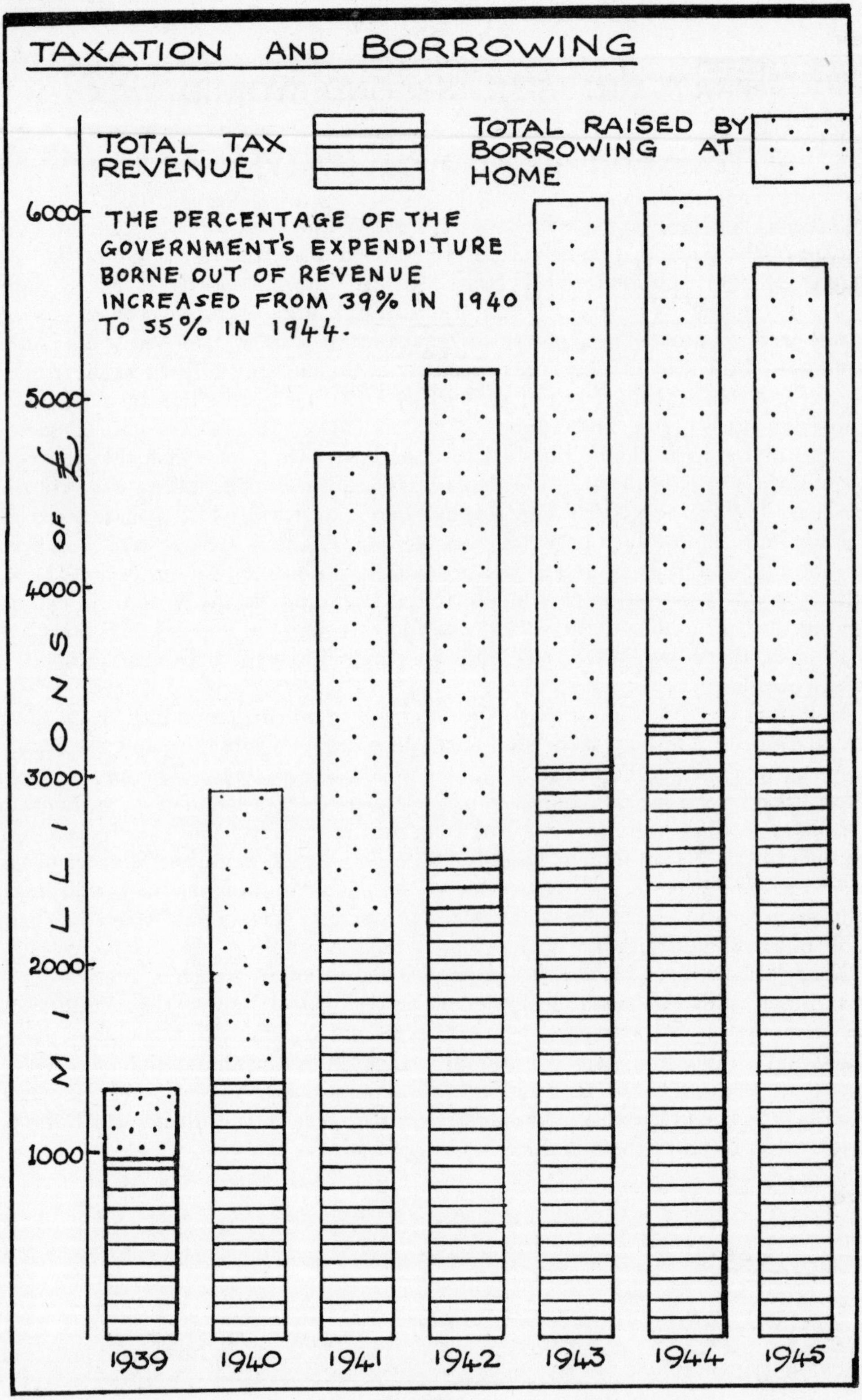

TAXATION AND BORROWING

TOTAL TAX REVENUE

TOTAL RAISED BY BORROWING AT HOME

THE PERCENTAGE OF THE
GOVERNMENT'S EXPENDITURE
BORNE OUT OF REVENUE
INCREASED FROM 39% IN 1940
TO 55% IN 1944.

6000

5000

4000

3000

2000

1000

MILLIONS OF £

1939 1940 1941 1942 1943 1944 1945

DIAGRAM 57

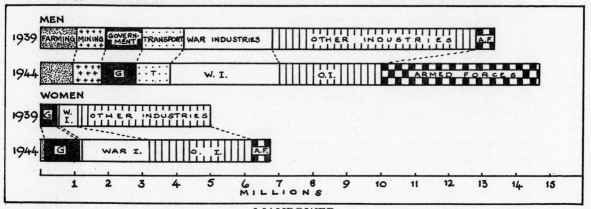

MANPOWER

DIAGRAM 58

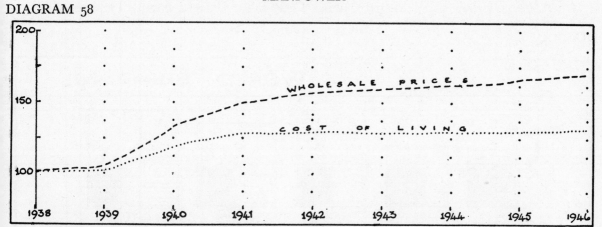

THE COST OF LIVING WAS KEPT DOWN BY GOVERNMENT SUBSIDIES

DIAGRAM 59

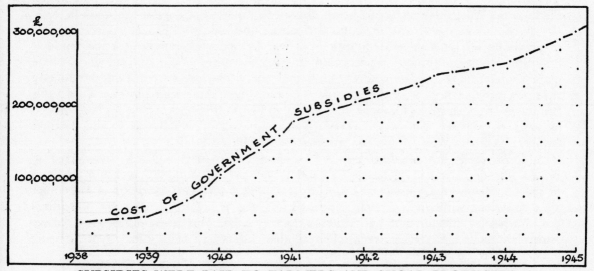

SUBSIDIES WERE PAID TO FARMERS AND SUGAR PRODUCERS

GOVERNMENT FINANCE

The heavy cost of the War had to be met by :

(*a*) *Increased Taxation.* Diagram 20 shows that reliance was placed on direct rather than indirect taxation. From 1940 the standard rate of income tax was raised to 8*s.* 6*d.* in the pound (in 1941 to 10*s.* in the pound), and the Excess Profits Duty increased to 100 per cent. in 1940 from 60 per cent. (1939). A Purchase Tax was introduced in October 1940 to reduce spending.

(*b*) *Borrowing at Home.* Expenses could not be wholly met by current revenue, and a National Savings Campaign was organized to encourage loans to the State. These took many forms—*e.g.*, National Savings Certificates, Defence Bonds, Treasury Bills,

DIAGRAM 60

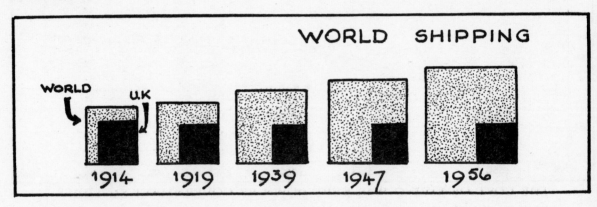

Tax Reserve Certificates. The rates of interest paid were usually lower than in the First World War, different terms being offered to different sectors of the market.

(*c*) *Sale of Foreign Assets.* Britain's agriculture and industrial capacity was incapable of providing all the food and munitions of war her people needed, and she found it impossible to maintain her exports and invisible earnings of foreign currency. The main supplier (U.S.A.) demanded ' cash and carry ' terms—*i.e.*, Britain should pay cash and provide her own ships to take the goods from American shores. To do this Britain was obliged to sell foreign assets : in 1939 British investors owned £4,000,000,000 of overseas property, railways, factories, etc., over half of which was in the Empire. By the end of the War £1,200,000,000 had been sold.

(*d*) *Borrowing Abroad—Lend-Lease.* In September 1940 the U.S.A. transferred to Britain fifty destroyers in exchange for the lease of certain valuable naval and air bases in the Carribean area. Following the Japanese attack on Pearl Harbour in December 1941 American willingness to help increased. A new policy of ' lend-lease ' was introduced whereby Britain and her allies—France, China, Russia—continued to receive American goods and services even when all their assets had been sold, payment being deferred until after the War. This new policy enabled Britain to dovetail her industrial production with that of America. Goods and services were supplied by Britain to U.S.A. on the same terms, constituting 'lend-lease' in reverse.

(e) *Borrowing Abroad—Sterling Balances.* The sterling area consisted of countries in the British Commonwealth (except Canada), but included Egypt and Iraq, which settled their trade debts in sterling. Many of these countries and also some outside the sterling area—*e.g.*, in South America—were able to allow Britain extended credit during the War, not expecting to be repaid immediately for goods and services supplied to Britain, for example, during the campaign against Japan, in the defence of India and the Middle East. When the War ended over £3,400,000,000 was owing, only a third of which was for goods actually sent to Britain. These were the Sterling Balances.

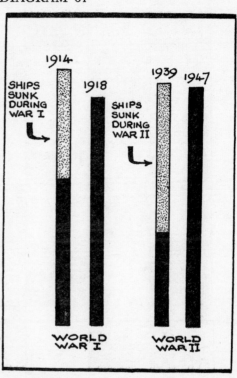

DIAGRAM 61

As a result of the deficit on lend-lease and the sterling balances Britain emerged from the Second World War with fewer assets to earn income and, instead, an external debt on which interest was payable amounting to £73,000,000. Even though some of this was cancelled it was clear that in order to survive Britain had to increase her exports to something like 75 or 80 per cent. above the pre-War volume.

WAR LOSSES

The number of military casualties was less than in the First World War (killed : 373,372, as compared with 1,089,900), but the number of civilians killed rose from 1100 to over 60,000. From 1940 to 1945 some four million houses were damaged, of which half a million were rendered completely uninhabitable. Shipping losses were very heavy (see Diagram 61). The loss of these ships reduced Britain's capacity to earn 'invisible' income when the War was over. Meanwhile U.S.A's proportion of the world's shipping had risen from less than one-seventh to over one-half.

DIAGRAM 62

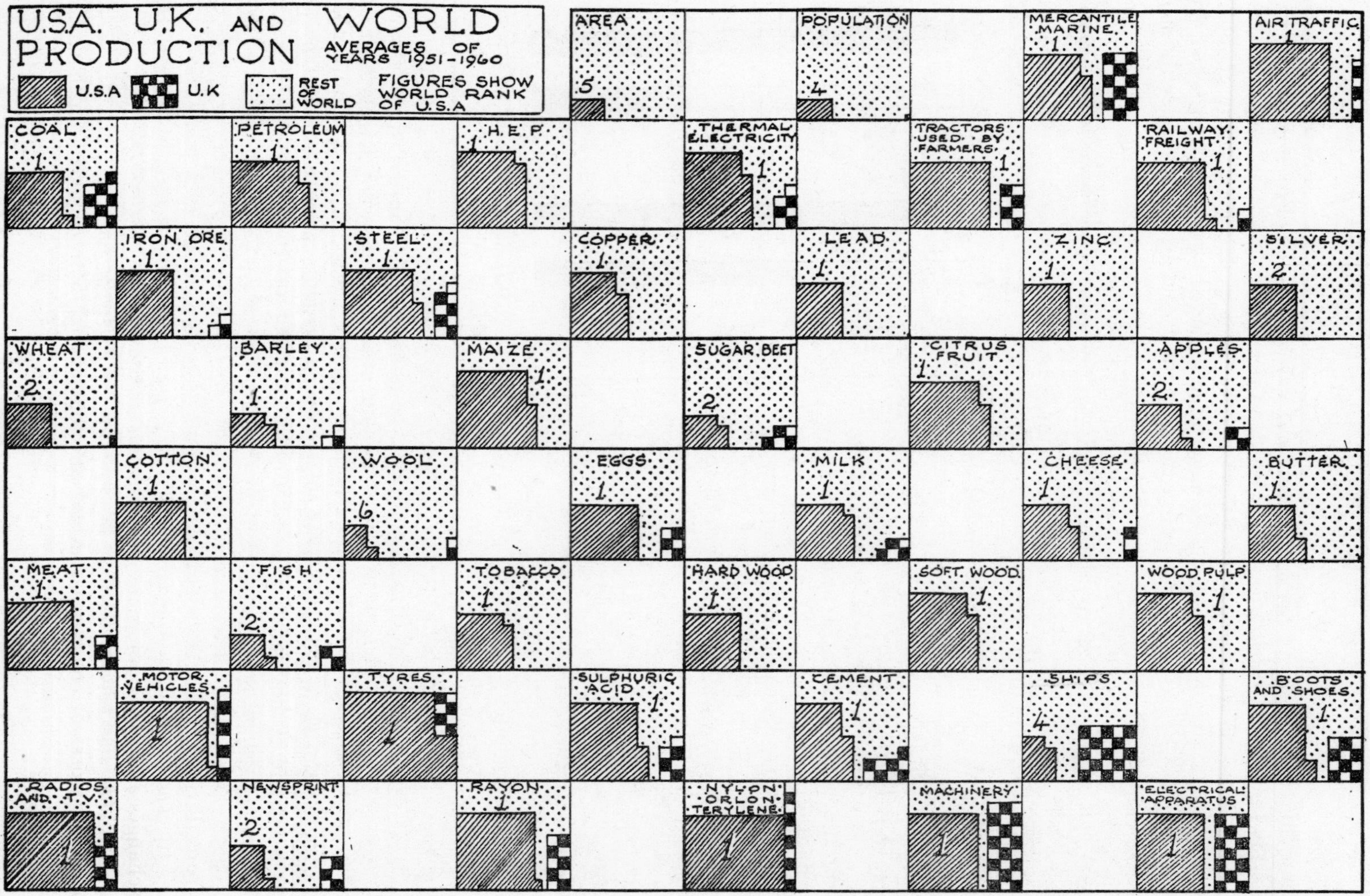

U.S.A. U.K. AND WORLD PRODUCTION
AVERAGES OF YEARS 1951-1960

FIGURES SHOW WORLD RANK OF U.S.A

U.S.A.   U.K   REST OF WORLD

AIR TRAFFIC. 1	SILVER. 2	BUTTER. 1		BOOTS AND SHOES. 1	
RAILWAY FREIGHT 1	APPLES. 2	WOOD PULP 1			ELECTRICAL APPARATUS 1
MERCANTILE MARINE. 1	ZINC. 1	CHEESE. 1		SHIPS. 4	
TRACTORS USED BY FARMERS 1	CITRUS FRUIT. 1	SOFT WOOD 1			MACHINERY 1
POPULATION 4	LEAD. 1	MILK 1		CEMENT. 1	
THERMAL ELECTRICITY 1	SUGAR BEET 2	HARD WOOD 1			NYLON ORLON TERYLENE 1
AREA 5	COPPER. 1	EGGS. 1		SULPHURIC ACID 1	
H.E.P. 1	MAIZE 1	TOBACCO 1			RAYON. 1
STEEL 1	WOOL 6	TYRES. 1			
PETROLEUM 1	BARLEY. 1	FISH 2			NEWSPRINT 2
IRON ORE. 1	COTTON 1	MOTOR VEHICLES. 1			
COAL 1	WHEAT 2	MEAT 1			RADIOS AND T.V. 1

242

PART IX : BRITAIN AFTER THE SECOND WORLD WAR

BRITAIN emerged victorious from the Second World War, a victor which had gained nothing but prestige and had lost its wealth and power. The U.S.S.R. and U.S.A. now dominated the world scene ; when in 1948 an ' iron curtain ' fell across Europe, cutting off Russia and her satellites in Eastern Europe from Western influence and trade, America alone remained pre-eminent in the free world's economy (see Diagram 62). The resources of a group of small islands—minerals or food supplies—could not compare with the vast output of America. Britain's greatness in the nineteenth century had been based, far more than that of any other country, upon her international trade, her international banking business, and her foreign investments. The dominance of Britain, which sprang from her pioneering activities in the sixteenth century, ended with the passing of the colonial era. Two costly World Wars accentuated rather than caused her difficulties.

BRITAIN'S IMMEDIATE POST-WAR DIFFICULTIES

The lend-lease agreements ended when hostilities ceased, but Britain was still obliged to borrow extensively from America. Until their own factories could turn out sufficient goods all the countries of the world turned to the U.S.A. America treated her allies and enemies generously. She wiped out the lend-lease debt of 20,350,000,000 dollars, and offered a credit of 3,750,000,000 dollars at 2 per cent.[1] Unfortunately the terms of the loan restricted Britain's right to make bilateral tariff arrangements with other countries, and forced her from 1947 to make sterling convertible to the dollar for current earnings. All the countries of the world were impoverished : U.S.A. alone could provide the goods they wanted, but dollars to pay for them were scarce, and America's high tariff wall did not encourage imports. Country after country turned their sterling earnings into dollars ; Britain was placed in an impossible position. Restrictions on convertibility had to be reimposed after one month.

F.A.O., I.M.F., I.B., I.T.O.

These difficulties had not been entirely unforeseen. While hostilities still continued plans had been made in an attempt to avoid food and currency troubles which might follow the end of the War. In 1943 a Conference at Hot Springs, Virginia, proposed a *Food and Agriculture Organization (F.A.O.)* (headquarters from 1952 at Rome) ; it aimed to ensure an adequate food supply for an ever-increasing world population. At Bretton Woods during the summer of 1944 two financial organizations were planned.

(i) *The International Monetary Fund (I.M.F.)*, to maintain the stability of the foreign exchanges and to free international payments from exchange restrictions.

(ii) *The International Bank for Reconstruction and Development (I.B.)*, to lend money for major works of reconstruction and development in those countries which required

[1] Canada also gave a loan of 1,250,000,000 dollars on the same terms.

help (in much the same way as Britain had invested in underdeveloped countries during the nineteenth century)—*e.g.*, for hydro-electric schemes in Chile and Brazil.

The *International Trade Organization* (*I.T.O.*), promoted by the U.S.A. at Havana in 1945 and intended to deal with restrictions on free trade, found little support among the countries of the world.

MAP 65

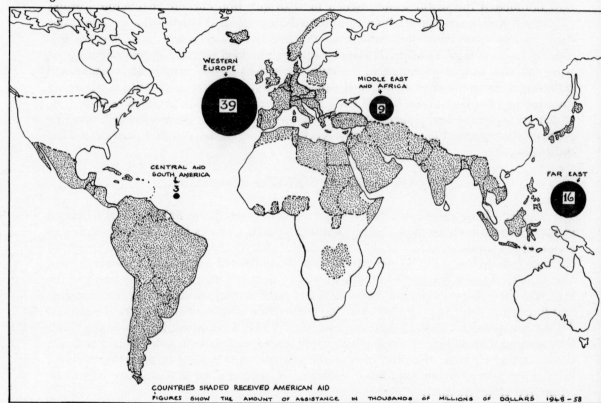

COUNTRIES SHADED RECEIVED AMERICAN AID
FIGURES SHOW THE AMOUNT OF ASSISTANCE IN THOUSANDS OF MILLIONS OF DOLLARS 1948–58

THE MARSHALL AID COUNTRIES

THE MARSHALL PLAN (O.E.E.C.)

It was clear by 1947 that the American hope that these international organizations would ensure trade recovery throughout the impoverished world was doomed to disappointment. It became increasingly evident that neither Britain nor any European country could export enough goods to pay for all the American products they wished to buy. Anxious to support the nations of the non-Communist world, General Marshall, the Secretary to the U.S.A. Treasury, announced an imaginative Aid Plan—offering gifts of goods and money not only to her friends, but also to former enemy countries (see Map 65). Marshall Aid was planned to end in 1952. The sixteen countries which accepted the offer formed an Organization for European Economic Co-operation

(O.E.E.C.) to determine the most pressing needs and apportion the American funds. Countries which received Marshall Aid were encouraged to trade with each other and thus to save their meagre stocks of dollars (a form of discrimination against U.S.A. trade). Between 1948 and 1952 a stupendous total of £4,278,000,000 was given away by America. In addition 700,000,000 dollars were made available for military aid— Mutual Defence Assistance.

E.P.U., G.A.T.T.

Marshall Aid had enabled Europe to cope with the dollar shortage; it also encouraged co-operation between the European countries, which culminated in the formation of a European Payments Union (E.P.U.), which simplified the means of settling international debts among its members. Meanwhile negotiations for the reduction of tariffs among more than twenty countries had culminated in a General Agreement on Tariffs and Trade (G.A.T.T.), substantially reducing rates of duty and lowering preferences.

DIAGRAM 63

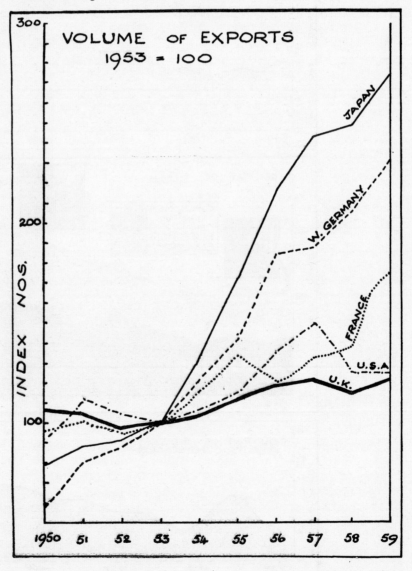

VOLUME OF EXPORTS 1953 = 100

DIAGRAM 64

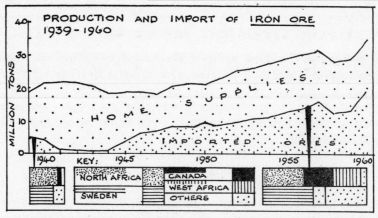

PRODUCTION AND IMPORT OF IRON ORE
1939 - 1960

HOME SUPPLIES

IMPORTED ORES

KEY:
NORTH AFRICA | CANADA
WEST AFRICA
SWEDEN | OTHERS

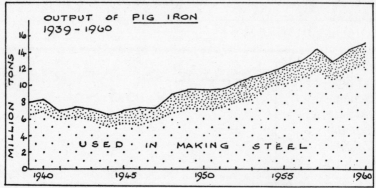

OUTPUT OF PIG IRON
1939 - 1960

USED IN MAKING STEEL

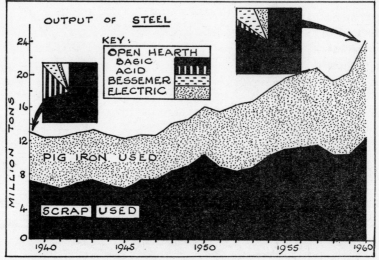

OUTPUT OF STEEL

KEY:
OPEN HEARTH
BASIC
ACID
BESSEMER
ELECTRIC

PIG IRON USED

SCRAP USED

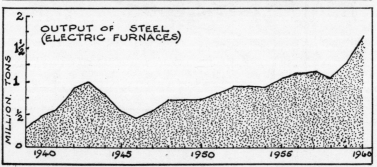

OUTPUT OF STEEL
(ELECTRIC FURNACES)

49. BRITISH INDUSTRY AFTER THE WAR

For fifteen years after the War most British industries prospered; the output of manufactured goods was nearly doubled. There was full employment for the workers, and manufacturers had little difficulty in selling their products, yet Britain lagged behind her competitors. Inflation was rife and continuous, and often her exports were insufficient to maintain a favourable balance of payments.

It became imperative to find new ways of ensuring that the best use was made of Britain's resources of men and materials. In 1962 the Conservative Government set up a National Economic Development Council (popularly known as 'Neddy'). Incomes were rising faster than production, and a National Incomes Commission ('Nicky') was formed to try to promote a balance between the two. It was cold-shouldered by the trade unions, who feared that their power to demand better conditions might be limited.

In October 1964 the newly formed Labour Government gave priority to economic problems, removing the responsibility for planning the national economy from the Treasury to a new Ministry of Economic Affairs, and at the same time setting up a Ministry of Technology.

Coal and Industrial Power

Though the output from the mines increased after the War there was little available for export, as home consumption had also increased; at times coal had to be imported. Most of the small, older mines were run at a loss and many were closed, especially in Scotland, South Wales, South Lancashire, and Durham. The large new collieries in South Yorkshire and the North Midlands using coal-cutting and conveying machinery were profitable, and the average output per man for the whole country rose steadily.

The demand for coal by industrial and household consumers decreased as gas, oil, and electricity replaced coal in the open fires and steam boilers of home, office, and factory. The consumption of coal by the Gas and Electricity Boards rose sharply. Many schemes to produce electric current by water-power were inaugurated by the North of Scotland Hydro-Electric Board (established 1943), and by 1960 thirty stations were working in the North of Scotland. A new super-grid, working on a high voltage, became necessary in 1955 to transmit electric power more effectively all over the country. Generating stations using oil and nuclear fuel were also planned; electricity from the first nuclear reactor was switched into the National Grid in 1956.

Iron and Steel and Shipbuilding

The iron and steel industry flourished after 1945. New plant was built—*e.g.*, to produce seamless steel tubes and continuous steel strip used in the motor-car and tinplate industries. Diagram 64 shows the increases and changes in production.

Immediately after the end of the War British shipyards were busy, launching about half the world's new tonnage. The shipbuilders did not modernize either their yards or their methods, and the workpeople continued to demand old craft distinctions. By 1960 Japan was launching a fifth and Germany an eighth of the new tonnage from up-to-date, newly built shipyards. Britain's proportion steadily declined.

Textiles

After the post-War boom the cotton industry slumped again; the number of workers continued to fall. In 1959 there were fewer than 200,000 (cp. 1912: 622,000). The Government was not prepared to prohibit the import of cotton goods from Hong Kong or India. A further scheme to scrap surplus machinery was necessary in 1959. Meanwhile the use of artificial fibres increased. Rayon was now challenged by new synthetic textile fibres of great strength—*e.g.*, nylon, ' Terylene,' and ' Courtelle.'

Other Industries

Immense progress was made in the motor-car, aircraft, and chemical industries. There were new developments in pharmaceuticals, pesticides, and radio isotopes. Hybrid industries emerged such as chemical textiles, petro-chemicals (including detergents and some paints and plastics), chemical engineering, and electronic engineering (including radios, radar, computers, T.V. equipment). The boundaries between industries had become less clear-cut—man-made fibres such as ' Terylene ' were more correctly part of the chemical than of the textile industry.

Many of the new products were consumer goods and often luxuries, light industries contrasting with the older heavy staple industries. The factories in which they were produced were built in the great centres of population where the goods could be sold, and not in the older industrial areas on the coalfields. They were operated by oil and electricity. The tendency was for industry to move south, especially to the suburbs of London and Birmingham and to new satellite towns. A striking feature of the consumer goods industries is their use of mass-production methods, standardization of products, and new management techniques.

50. BRITISH AGRICULTURE AFTER THE WAR

WHEN the War was over farmers were still encouraged to grow bigger crops, because the more food produced at home the less needed to be imported. The scarcity of wheat was so world-wide that bread was temporarily rationed in 1946 for the first time. Foreign currency to pay for imports was also scarce, and was needed for food and raw materials which could not be produced at home.

The Agriculture Act 1947 was an attempt to realize a stable and efficient agricultural system capable of increasing the amount of home-grown food. Stability was achieved by assuring the farmer a market for his products and guaranteed prices which were agreed at annual price reviews. This involved protection against foreign imports and the continuation of the payment of subsidies.

The prosperous farmer became more efficient, using his increased working capital to improve and extend his farm buildings, to buy new tractors and new tractor-drawn implements, and to maintain his land and stock in the best condition. This he did by putting in new drains where necessary, and applying lime and fertilizers. He cleansed his crops by using selective weed-killers, killed off noxious insects and animals by using pesticides, converted much permanent pasture into long leys which gave better herbage for animal fodder, and introduced many new and often revolutionary techniques—*e.g.*, electric milking-machines, artificial insemination of cattle, egg production by keeping poultry in batteries and deep litter, and similar mass-producing techniques in rearing broiler chickens and cattle. These technical changes resulted in increased yields of all farm products and moreover economized labour (see Diagram 47). Horse-drawn plough teams almost disappeared from British farms: the farm worker needed to be a motor mechanic. The facilities for agricultural research and specialized education for intending farmers were expanded.

The high and increasing cost of support to the farmer (approaching £350,000,000 in 1963) led to a demand for fewer and lower subsidies, and the transfer of the cost from the taxpayer to the consumer (by charging him higher prices for his food as is the practice in the Common Market countries).

DIAGRAM 65

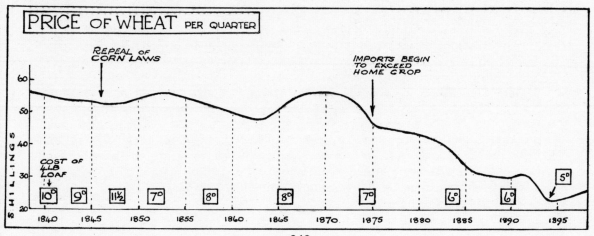

DIAGRAM 66

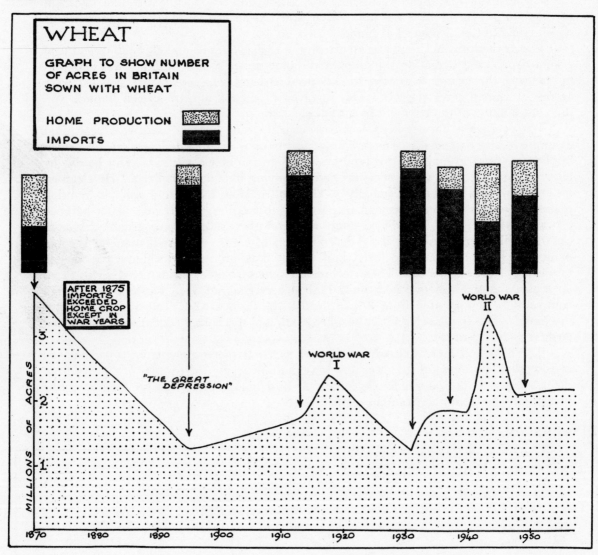

WHEAT

GRAPH TO SHOW NUMBER
OF ACRES IN BRITAIN
SOWN WITH WHEAT

HOME PRODUCTION
IMPORTS

AFTER 1875
IMPORTS
EXCEEDED
HOME CROP
EXCEPT IN
WAR YEARS

"THE GREAT
DEPRESSION"

WORLD WAR
I

WORLD WAR
II

MILLIONS OF ACRES

3.

2.

1.

1870 1880 1890 1900 1910 1920 1930 1940 1950

DIAGRAM 67

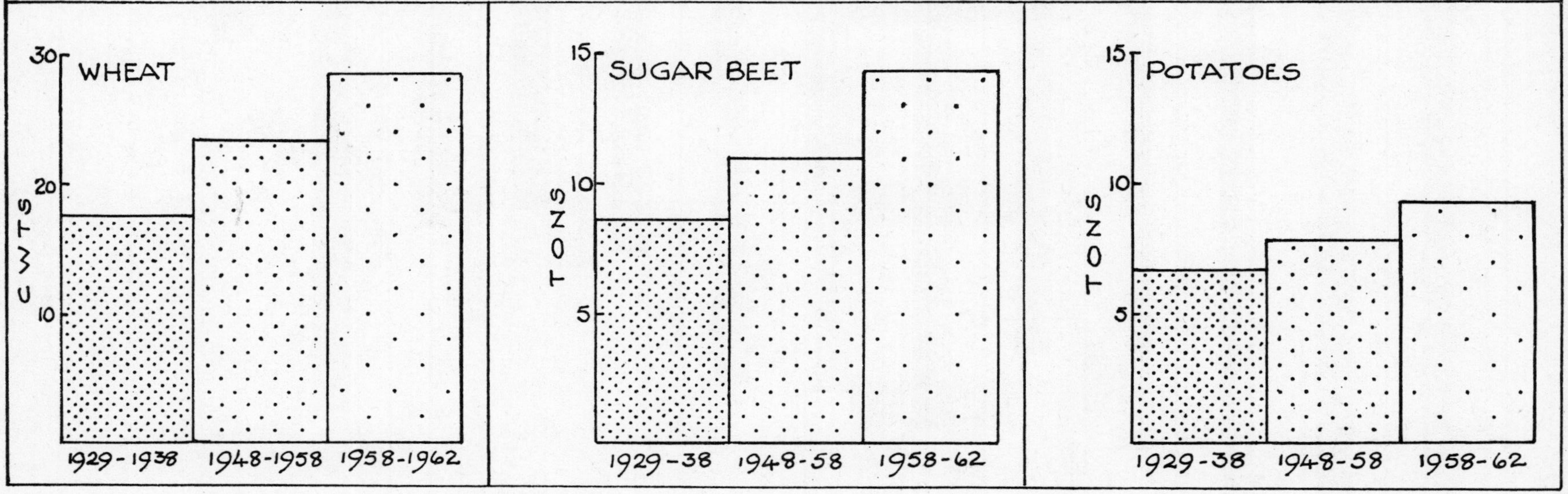

CROP YIELDS PER ACRE : HOME FOOD PRODUCTION WAS 83% ABOVE THE PRE-WAR LEVEL IN 1962.

DIAGRAM 68

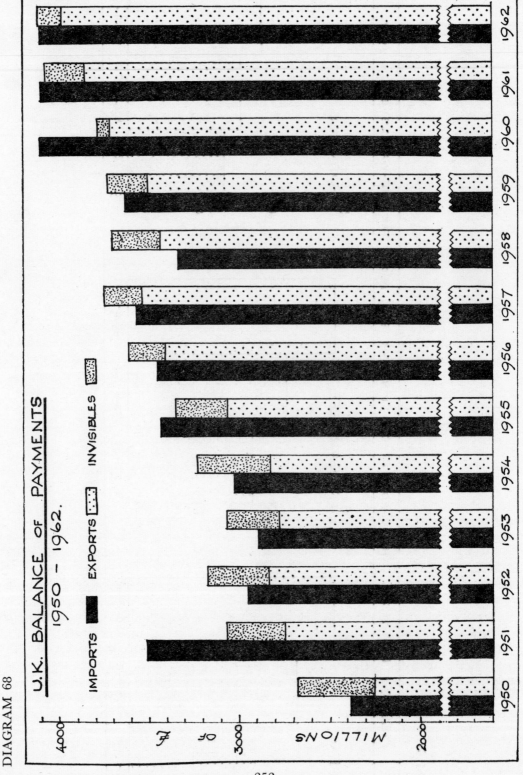

U.K. BALANCE of PAYMENTS
1950 - 1962.

IMPORTS ▪ EXPORTS ⬝⬝ INVISIBLES ⬝⬝

4000

£ of £

3000

MILLIONS

2000

1950 1951 1952 1953 1954 1955 1956 1957 1958 1959 1960 1961 1962

51. BRITISH TRADE AFTER THE WAR

In 1945 Britain's great problem was how she could extend her foreign trade so as to maintain, and if possible improve, the standard of living of her people.

Both imports and exports grew, though the commodities of trade and the countries traded with changed. Diagram 69 shows that the imports of food and of raw materials (except petroleum, used more and more as the number of road motors increased) declined relatively: this was because (a) Britain grew more of her own food, and (b) the type of exports which increased (motor-cars) depended less on imported raw materials than the type which declined (cotton cloth). Diagram 68 shows a steady increase was achieved in the total exports. Coal and cotton exports continued to decline, but the products of the metal, engineering, and chemical industries greatly expanded. Examples are motor vehicles, aircraft, machine tools, electrical and electronic equipment, diesel locomotives, combine harvesters, fork-lift trucks, plastics, nylons, cellulose, synthetic detergents, and sulphonamides. Many of these new industrial products, the result of recent scientific research, represented the export value of skilled labour rather than of primary raw material.

Despite Britain's achievement the volume of exports was insufficient to maintain a healthy balance of trade. Neither were her earnings from shipping and insurance services and foreign investments (invisible income) which supplement her trading profits large enough to compensate for the deficiency: Britain was not exporting enough. Many firms, sheltered behind a tariff wall, found it more profitable to sell their goods at home where they were in strong demand rather than abroad where they had to face keen competition. A large proportion of the exports went to backward Commonwealth countries, markets which were likely to be lost when these rapidly developing countries built their own factories. The proportion of sales to countries of Western Europe and the U.S.A. increased, but greater effort was required to capture these prosperous markets.

The difficulties which persisted in Britain's balance of payments are partly attributable to continuing inflation. From 1945 to 1960 prices rose by some 4 per cent. or 5 per cent. each year (the greatest rise in peace-time for a century); national production rose only by about 3 per cent. each year and production per man by only $2\frac{1}{4}$ per cent., while money incomes (wages, salaries, and profits) on the average increased by $7\frac{1}{2}$ per cent. each year. The Government urged higher production for the export markets without sufficient success; it checked the home demand by raising the bank rate, thus making hire-purchase borrowing more expensive. When trade flagged and unemployment threatened, however, the policy was reversed; borrowing was made easier by a reduction in the bank rate. See Diagram 71.

During the four years prior to 1962 world industrial production increased by nearly 30 per cent., that of the United Kingdom by about 15 per cent. In the same period world trade in manufactures increased by about 35 per cent., that of the United Kingdom by about 15 per cent.

253

DIAGRAM 69

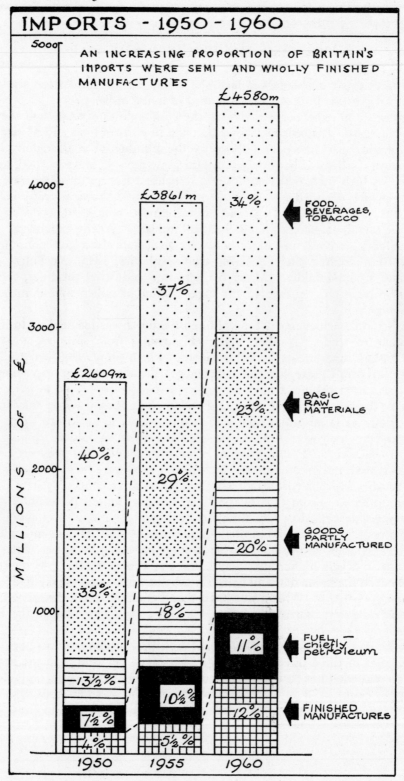

IMPORTS - 1950 - 1960

AN INCREASING PROPORTION OF BRITAIN'S IMPORTS WERE SEMI AND WHOLLY FINISHED MANUFACTURES

£4580m

£3861m

£2609m

5000

4000

3000

2000

1000

MILLIONS OF £

34% — FOOD, BEVERAGES, TOBACCO

37%

40%

23% — BASIC RAW MATERIALS

29%

35%

20% — GOODS PARTLY MANUFACTURED

18%

13½%

11% — FUEL — chiefly petroleum

10½%

7½%

12% — FINISHED MANUFACTURES

5½%

4%

1950   1955   1960

DIAGRAM 70

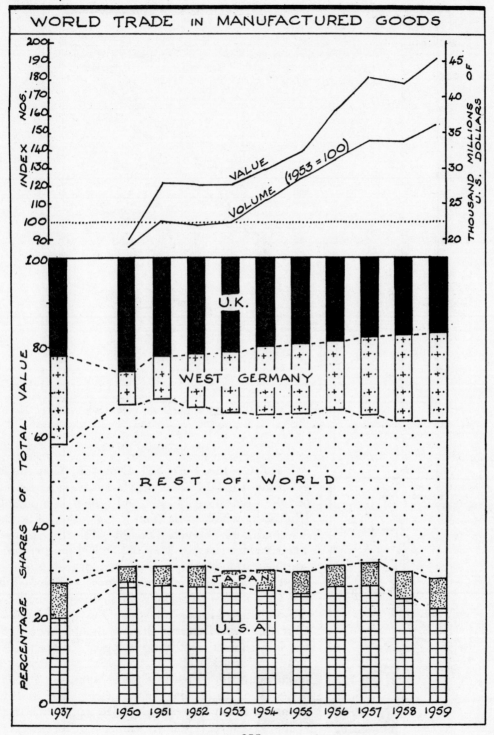

WORLD TRADE IN MANUFACTURED GOODS

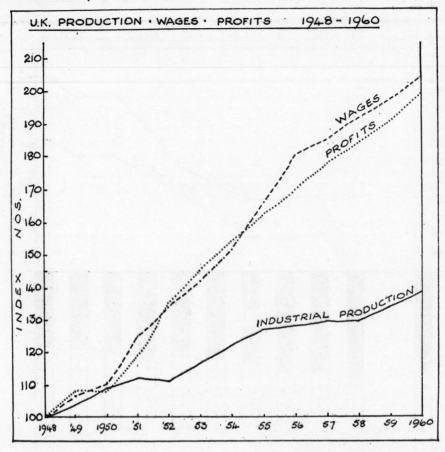

INLAND TRANSPORT

FROM 1945 to 1960 road transport became more and more important, and the railways suffered a loss of both passenger and freight traffic. New high-speed motorways were built (the first, M1, from London to Birmingham was opened in 1959) and by-passes to relieve town centres. The engineers of these modern roads designed splendid new bridges across river estuaries—*e.g.*, the Tamar (1961), the Medway (1963), the Forth (1964), and the Severn. Traffic problems in the large cities, especially in London, proved difficult to solve, despite the establishment of one-way streets, parking-meters, and pedestrian crossings.

Large sums of money were spent in an attempt to modernize the British railway system after it had become State-owned (see p. 220). Many suburban and a few main lines—*e.g.*, London–Manchester and –Liverpool, were electrified, and diesel traction replaced some steam locomotives. Unprofitable branch lines were gradually eliminated: the use of motor delivery vans enabled the railways to close many local goods yards.

In an attempt to reduce the heavy annual losses, in 1960, Dr Beeching was appointed Chairman of the Railways Board. His programme of reorganization and modernization, designed to make British Railways pay their way, involved drastic closures of lines; some of his proposals, however, were not acceptable, especially among isolated rural communities in remote areas—*e.g.*, the Scottish Highlands.

SEA AND AIR TRANSPORT

The technical advances in aviation achieved during the Second World War (gyroscopic compasses, radar) resulted in safer and speedier air travel. Whittle's idea of the jet-propelled engine (1937) was first introduced into an aeroplane in 1941, and raised the speed of aircraft to over 1000 miles an hour, while the Germans developed unmanned rockets which used liquid oxygen and alcohol as fuel. By 1962 the speed record had reached over 4000 miles per hour, and a rocket aircraft piloted by an American had reached a height of 47 miles. The first piloted space flights were successfully made by Russian spaceships and American space capsules in 1961. Further spectacular orbits of the earth were later accomplished by Russia and U.S.A. Air travel grew largely at the expense of sea transport, especially across the Atlantic. The nationalized British European Airways Corporation introduced many inland air services which competed with British Railways.

POSTS, TELEGRAPHS, WIRELESS COMMUNICATION

As we have seen on p. 170, the B.B.C. had begun to transmit pictures without wires in 1936. A rival Independent Television service was inaugurated in 1954, financed by the revenue received from advertising programmes. The Pilkington Report (1962) envisaged the introduction of a higher (625 lines) standard of definition (introduced 1964) and the beginning of colour television.

CONTROLS

THE termination of hostilities did not end the war-time system of Government control of manpower, prices, and the allocation of vital food and raw materials in short supply. Aiming to keep consumer prices low and husbanding currency, the Government continued many restrictions. Not until 1954 was the last remnant of war-time food-rationing abandoned. The prices of bread, milk, and potatoes had to be controlled because of the method of paying subsidies to the farmers who produced them. Control over the rents of larger houses was abolished in 1957, and certain restrictions on the sale and leasing of smaller houses were lifted at the same time. Bulk-buying by the State was reduced after 1949, and by 1957 was largely confined to materials of strategic importance. Until 1959 new capital issues continued to require the consent of a Capital Issues Committee. There were restrictions on the purchase of foreign currency.

NATIONALIZATION

An election immediately after the War carried a Labour Government into power pledged to implement a socialist policy. During the period 1945 to 1949 many public institutions and key industries were brought under public ownership by Act of Parliament : 1946, the Bank of England, the coal mines, civil aviation, and wireless communications ; 1947, the docks and waterways, the electricity supply stations, the railways, and a large section of road transport ; 1948, the gas works ; 1949, the main part of the steel industry. These enterprises were run by different types of public corporations under the general control of a Minister of State, who appointed as members of the main boards persons with special qualifications for running the industries. The main purpose of nationalization was to give an efficient public service, though the businesses were expected over the years to cover expenses, including interest on the money paid to purchase them from the previous owners.

The Conservative Government in 1952 restored the main part of road haulage to private enterprise, and in 1953 began the gradual denationalization of the steel industry.

CONTROL OF MONOPOLIES

The growth of large-scale organizations in agriculture, industry, and trade led inevitably to restrictive practices and the exploitation of monopoly power. A Commission was set up in 1948 to investigate industries which the Board of Trade suspected might be guilty of monopoly practice. An Act of 1956 set up a Restrictive Practices Court which had the duty of considering all restrictive trading agreements. In general restrictive agreements as to price and conditions of sale are presumed to be against the public interest and are void (Retail Prices Act 1964).

THE WELFARE STATE

The social reforms begun by the Liberal Government 1906–14 and extended between the two Wars (see p. 235) were greatly expanded at the end of the Second World War. The recognition of a Government's responsibility for its needy people was growing in most countries after the War; Britain's social services, though an example to the world, did not give security to *all* classes of society. The maintenance of a high and stable level of employment adopting the methods advocated by J. M. Keynes to achieve this end was accepted as the Government's official policy in the White Paper on Employment policy issued in 1944.

The Beveridge Report, also in 1944, recommended the main channels of further and comprehensive development of national insurance. It was implemented by the National Insurance and Family Allowances Acts of 1945, and these have been amended and added to by other later legislation.

Family Allowances. Originally 5 shillings weekly for every child after the first.

Weekly insurance contributions became payable by everybody in the country to cover benefits payable during absence from work through sickness, industrial injury, and unemployment. Maternity and death grants were also paid. The contributions also covered pensions to widows and to women at 60 and

DIAGRAM 72

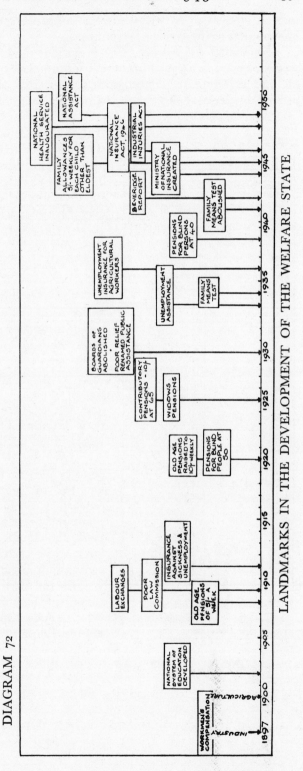

LANDMARKS IN THE DEVELOPMENT OF THE WELFARE STATE

men at 65 years. As with previous insurance schemes (see p. 236), the employers also contributed to the weekly premiums.

National Health Service. The provisions made in 1911 for medical care (see p. 149) were extended in 1948 to become a comprehensive National Health Service, available to all, and including free dental, optical, and medical treatment by the general practitioners as well as specialist services in the hospitals.

National Assistance. The Poor Law reforms of 1929 were extended in 1948 by the National Assistance Act, which authorized assistance to those who had not paid contributions to any national insurance fund, and to those whose benefits from national insurance were insufficient to meet their needs. By 1965 the total annual cost of these social services had risen to over £2,000,000,000.

DIAGRAM 73

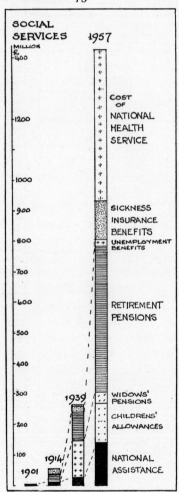

HOUSING: TOWN AND COUNTRY PLANNING

The destruction of houses during the War, the desire of young people to have houses of their own, and the necessity for slum-clearance combined to create an acute housing problem on a national scale. Luxury building was forbidden. Authority to buy land and subsidies were given to local authorities to build low-rented houses. Owing to a grave shortage of bricks and timber even the local authorities were limited in their building programmes, and private building was very limited until after 1952.

The evil of unregulated urban sprawls into the countryside—a feature of the inter-War years—was avoided by planning. A series of Acts from 1945 onward gave local authorities power to refuse their planning permission to any building which violated their development scheme. Green belts round the large cities, national parks, and new satellite towns were also inaugurated.

By 1964 five million new homes had been built, but there still remained a large unsatisfied demand, and the price of houses and building land rose sharply, especially around London and in South-east England.

54. TRADE UNIONISM SINCE THE WAR

THE unions had worked well with the Government during the War, and one of the first acts of the Labour Government when it came to power in 1945 was to repeal the Trade Disputes and Trade Union Act of 1927 (see p. 233). The number of members in 1946 had reached 8,700,000, a total which grew, with some fluctuations, to 9,900,000 in 1963 (less than half the working population of about 24,000,000).

Between 1946 and 1963 the number of unions had declined by amalgamations from 753 to 596. Of these 318 had fewer than 1000 members, while the eight largest unions had more than 250,000 members.

With the development of new and modern techniques of manufacture in many industries, the old divisions between craftsmen became blurred, and there were many disputes about the demarcation of jobs, frequently leading to bitter inter-union quarrels. Strikes occurred which were not caused by disagreement between management and workers. The T.U.C. Disputes Committee worked to reduce the number of these quarrels, while strikes were less likely where the unions had combined or federated—e.g., the Confederation of Shipbuilding and Engineering Unions.

National agreements negotiated between the headquarters staff of the unions and national employers' associations became the usual form of collective bargaining. But the wage rates negotiated at national level were often lower than the earnings taken home by the individual worker because of additions locally negotiated. Most collective agreements were made voluntarily, but under the Wages Councils Act of 1945 the Government was empowered to initiate bargaining between employers and unions and to enforce the terms of employment agreed upon. The State further assisted the growth of collective bargaining by the Terms and Conditions of Employments Act 1959, under which the Industrial Court (see p. 233) can compel an employer to adhere to an agreement voluntarily made between employers and unions. To-day the majority of wage-earners are covered by some form of voluntary collective agreement or statutory wage regulation.

The war-time legislation of 1940 making strikes illegal prevailed until 1951, and between 1946 and 1952 there were no official national strikes of any importance. The legislation was not invoked against the small and localized strikes which took place. In the 1950's, however, a number of national stoppages occurred—e.g., in engineering and shipbuilding (1957 and 1962) and in printing (1959). The number of days of work lost each year through strikes increased considerably after 1955, reaching 6,000,000 days in 1962. (Britain's record, however, compares favourably with most other countries—e.g., U.S.A.) Many more days are lost by accidents and illness than by strikes.

One disturbing feature of the period was the growth of ' unofficial strikes.' The effective power of the trade unions was challenged by shop stewards on the factory floor. In large factories shop stewards of several unions formed committees for mutual support. These committees sometimes initiated strikes in spite of their own union's instructions, and complicated the problem of settling disputes with the management.

By 1951 the bulk of the population of England and Wales lived not only in towns, but in particular industrial regions, for as some towns expanded they linked up with their neighbours, and thus formed continuous urban areas. These urban regions are known as conurbations. Listed in the Census of Population are six ' official ' conurbations: they are shown on Map 67. In 1961 these six regions in an area of less than three million acres housed over 18,000,000 of the total population of 46,000,000 living in the 37,000,000 acres of England and Wales: over a third of the people lived in less than one-twelfth of the area.

MAP 67

CONURBATIONS (1951)

Since the First World War the outer parts of the conurbations have grown faster than the centres: few vacant spaces remained to be filled in, and the movement of population was from the city centres to the suburbs, an urban sprawl which necessitated a provision of ' green belts ' in which building was forbidden. As we have seen on p. 194, the urban population grew at the expense of the surrounding countryside. The population of the conurbations also grew because of migration from the smaller towns; they also receive most of the immigrants from abroad. The 1961 census revealed that one in ten of the population of the County of London was born outside Britain. The number of West Indians and Pakistanis attracted by high wages and the opportunity of full employment has sharply increased. There was a 352,000 excess of immigrants over emigrants 1951–61. The Commonwealth Immigrants Act 1962 gave the Government power to restrict their number.

By the Distribution of Industry Act 1945 the Government attempted to check the southward drift of the population from the northern coalfields, but with little success. Further attempts were made by the Distribution of Industry Act 1958, and the Local Employment Act 1960.

MAP 68

NEW TOWNS

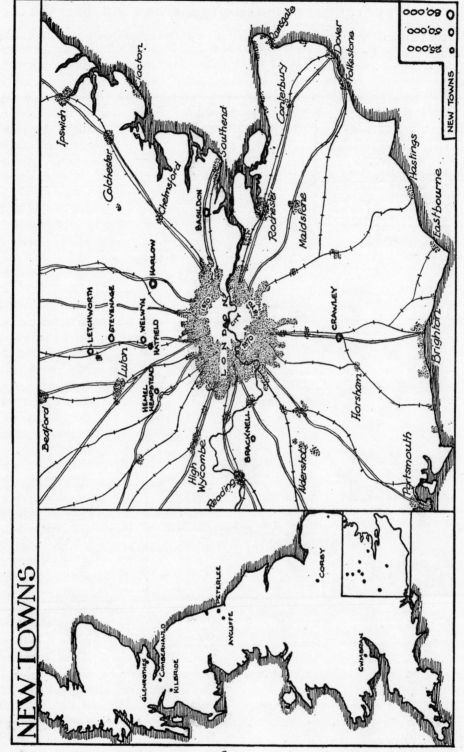

As Map 69 shows, the areas in which population grew most rapidly were in the Midlands and South-east of England.

MAP 69

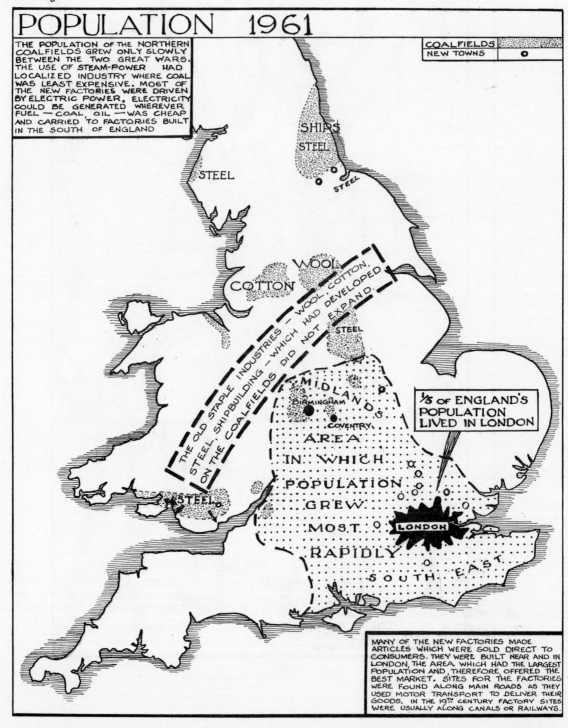

POPULATION 1961

THE POPULATION OF THE NORTHERN COALFIELDS GREW ONLY SLOWLY BETWEEN THE TWO GREAT WARS. THE USE OF STEAM-POWER HAD LOCALIZED INDUSTRY WHERE COAL WAS LEAST EXPENSIVE. MOST OF THE NEW FACTORIES WERE DRIVEN BY ELECTRIC POWER. ELECTRICITY COULD BE GENERATED WHEREVER FUEL — COAL, OIL — WAS CHEAP AND CARRIED TO FACTORIES BUILT IN THE SOUTH OF ENGLAND

COALFIELDS
NEW TOWNS   o

STEEL

SHIPS
STEEL
STEEL

WOOL
COTTON

STEEL

THE OLD STAPLE INDUSTRIES — WOOL, COTTON, STEEL, SHIPBUILDING — WHICH HAD DEVELOPED ON THE COALFIELDS DID NOT EXPAND

MIDLANDS
BIRMINGHAM
COVENTRY

⅓ of ENGLAND'S POPULATION LIVED IN LONDON

AREA IN WHICH POPULATION GREW MOST RAPIDLY

STEEL

LONDON

SOUTH EAST

MANY OF THE NEW FACTORIES MADE ARTICLES WHICH WERE SOLD DIRECT TO CONSUMERS. THEY WERE BUILT NEAR AND IN LONDON, THE AREA WHICH HAD THE LARGEST POPULATION AND, THEREFORE, OFFERED THE BEST MARKET. SITES FOR THE FACTORIES WERE FOUND ALONG MAIN ROADS AS THEY USED MOTOR TRANSPORT TO DELIVER THEIR GOODS. IN THE 19TH CENTURY FACTORY SITES WERE USUALLY ALONG CANALS OR RAILWAYS.

INDEX

Persons

ALCOCK AND BROWN, 223
Alfred, King, 17, 19
Allan, W., 145
Applegarth, R., 146
Arch, J., 148, 163
Arkwright, R., 86, 87
Attwood, T., 144

Baird, W., 170
Bakewell, R., 109, 160
Bedford, Duke of, 109
Beeching, Dr R., 257
Bell, A. G., 170
Bell, T., 87
Bentham, J., 126, 137
Berthollet, C., 87
Bessemer, H., 165, 167, 168, 209
Bevin, E., 237
Blériot, L., 223
Boulton, M., 93
Bramah, J., 169
Bridgewater, Duke of, 84, 97
Bright, J., 133
Brindley, J., 97, 99
Brunel, I., 154, 157
Burns, J., 148

Cabot, J. AND S., 54, 56
Cartier, J., 56
Cartwright, E., 87
Cartwright, Major, 126
Chadwick, E., 126, 137, 140
Chamberlain, J., 184
Chancellor, R., 56, 57
Chardonnet, Count H. de, 165
Charlemagne, 17
Charles II, 67, 82, 178
Cobbett, W., 126
Cobden, R., 133
Coke, T., of Holkham, 109
Columbus, C., 55
Cook, Captain, 123
Cort, H., 91
Cortez, H., 54, 55
Crompton, S., 87

Daimler, G., 210
Darby, A., 84, 89
Davy, Sir H., 168
Dunlop, J., 210

Edward the Elder, 19
Edward III, 43, 45
Egbert of Wessex, 17

Elizabeth I, 45, 57, 64, 177
Elkington, J., 109

Fielden, J., 139, 144
Ford, H., 210
Frost, J., 145
Fulton, R., 157

George III, 109
Gilbert, H., 69
Gilchrist, P., 165, 168
Gladstone, W. E., 131, 179
Godwin, W., 126

Hardie, K., 148
Hargreaves, J., 86
Henry VII, 56
Henry VIII, 61
Henry of Portugal, Prince, 55
Highs, T., 87
Homfray, S., 91
Horrocks, J., 87
Hudson, G., 155
Huguenots, 79
Hume, J., 141
Huntsman, B., 91
Huskisson, W., 131, 134

Jenner, Sir Edward, 117

Kay, J. AND R., 86
Kennedy (*see* M'Connell), 120
Ket, R., 62
Keynes, J., 225, 259
King, Dr, 144

Lawes, Sir John, 160
Lee, W., 79
Lenoir, J., 210
Lollards, 49, 50
Lovett, W., 144, 145
Lowndes, W., 82

McAdam, J. L., 100–106
M'Connell and Kennedy, 120
Malthus, T., 122, 125
Mann, T., 148
Marconi, G., 170
Marshall, General, 244
Martin, P. E., 165, 167, 209
Marx, K., 127, 148
Maudslay, H., 169
Merchant Adventurers, 45, 58
Merchant Staplers, 43, 45
Metcalf, J., 100, 102, 103

Morris, W., 210
Morse, S., 170
Murdoch, W., 93
Myddleton, H., 117

Neilson, J., 91, 165, 168
Newcomen, T., 93

Oastler, R., 138, 144
O'Connor, F., 144, 145
Oglethorpe, J., 67
Osborne, W., 149
Otto, N., 210
Owen, R., 127, 138, 141, 143, 148

Paine, T., 126
Palmer, J., 102
Panhard, R., 210
Paterson, W., 82
Paul, L., 86
Peel, Sir Robert (the elder), 138
Peel, Sir Robert (the younger), 131, 139, 179
Penn, W., 69
Perkin, W., 212
Pilgrim Fathers, 67
Pitt, W., 110, 130, 131, 178–181
Place, F., 126, 141
Polo, Marco, 36

Raleigh, Sir Walter, 67
Ransome, R., 160
Ricardo, D., 125, 126
Roberts, R., 87, 169
Robinson, F., 131
Roebuck, J., 90, 91, 93

Sadler, M., 138, 139
Savery, Captain T., 93
Schuman, R., 256
Shaftesbury, Lord, 127, 139
Siemens, Sir William, 165, 167, 209
Sinclair, Sir John, 105
Smith, A., 125, 126, 131, 215
Smith, J., 160
Stephens, J., 144
Stephenson, G., 151, 154
Stump, W., 73
Sturge, J., 145
Symington, W., 157

Telford, T., 102, 103
Tennant, C., 87
Thomas, S., 165

265

Statutes, Place-Names, and Industries